TALES OF

PSYCHOLOGY

SHORT STORIES TO MAKE YOU WISE

TALES OF PSYCHOLOGY

SHORT STORIES TO MAKE YOU WISE

ALMA HALBERT BOND, PH.D.

PARAGON HOUSE

St. Paul, Minnesota

First Edition, 2002

Published in the United States by
Paragon House
2700 University Avenue West
St. Paul, MN 55114

Library of Congress Cataloging-in-Publishing data

Tales of psychology : short stories to make you wise / [edited by] Alma Halbert Bond. — 1st ed.
     p. cm.
Includes bibliographical references.
ISBN 1-55778-806-5 (cloth)
    1. Psychological fiction, American. 2. Psychological fiction, English. I. Bond, Alma Halbert.

PS648.P75 T35 2002
813'.0108353—dc21

                              2001044804

10 9 8 7 6 5 4 3 2 1

For current information about all releases from Paragon House,
visit the web site at http://www.paragonhouse.com

This book is dedicated to Dr. Margaret Ray,
friend, advisor, and mentor for over 40 years.

COPYRIGHT ACKNOWLEDGMENTS

CONTENTS

ACKNOWLEDGMENTS

When I was a young student analyst, I dreamed that I was surrounded by a circle of great analysts; Freud, Jung, Adler, and others famous at the time. The men were all taller than me. They picked me up until I was as tall as they, and I became taller than I might have been. Ever since then, the study of psychoanalysis has made me "taller than I might have been." Thus, I am grateful to my analytic forefathers and foremothers whose influence permeates every aspect of my life, including my understanding of each of the stories in this book.

INTRODUCTION

Tales of Psychology consists of short stories that I have collected over a lifetime. The stories are selected for their insight into human nature and their merit as fine works of literature. Each story is followed by a discussion of the psychological principles revealed in it, as I see them.

Reading this book will be a unique opportunity for lay readers and professional psychologists and writers alike to deepen their knowledge of human psychology. The book is recommended for students of human nature enrolled in psychological programs as well as the self-taught. *Tales of Psychology* began as a text for a course I am teaching online for WriterSchool.com on the Psychology of Writing, which demonstrated to me that artists can learn the psychological understructure of their characters from the insight of an experienced psychologist. Similarly, I believe lay people can absorb the teachings of these master writers in a captivating, painless manner. It is entirely possible that in some cases, reading a particular story can change the life of a reader, reveal the depths of his or her own psyche or that of a loved one, demonstrate what is pathological and requires medical assistance, or reassure the individual of what is normal behavior. No one who reads these stories in depth will ever be the same again. Regardless of the book's side benefits, it will be a delightful reading experience for everyone.

The book covers a wide variety of human beings of all ages, degrees of emotional health, social class, and nationalities. In so diverse a group of personalities, everyone can find his or her own life situation. The authors range from Pulitzer Prize winners to the relatively obscure. But whatever the degree of fame or experience, in each case the writer has seen deeply into the human soul.

Sometimes a story like *Paul's Case*, by Willa Cather, will set off a profound psychological resonance and remain a permanent fixture of our emotional memories. Others, like Conrad Aiken's *Silent Snow, Secret Snow*, are stored in the back of our minds, and for no reason that is immediately discernable, pop out at unexpected moments. Yet another type, like Henry James's *The Middle Years*, can lead us through difficult stages of development, so that we can say, "Ah, yes, I know those feelings! If s/he could get through them, perhaps I can, too." *Tales of Psychology* is a book that includes all three kinds. It is made up of tales which rip aside the veil of convention and disclose a hidden truth.

Tales of Psychology is a very personal collection of short stories that have changed my life. Readers used to speak of losing themselves in a book or story; nowadays it is more common to hear them speak of wanting to find themselves in literature. While I have lost myself in many of these stories, they also have helped me find myself. With some, such as *The Test*, by Angelica Gibbs, I knew as I was reading them that my life would never again be the same. Others like *A Distant Episode*, come back to haunt me after certain frightening life experiences. In many cases these stories have left as deep a mark as the early words of one's parents or first lover. They provide a psychological education and a fresh point of view to young and old, professionals and laymen, the naive and the world-weary.

There were two major criteria for including a story in the book: First, that it be well written, in many cases a literary *tour de force*. *Silent Snow, Secret Snow* is an exquisite example of the juncture of psychology and literature. Secondly, the story must reveal a profound psychological truth or give vivid insight into behavior that indelibly brands it into the mind of the reader, such as in Paul Bowles' *A Distant Episode*. I have tried to select stories that cover a wide range of human experience, including love, marriage, life and death, grief, mourning, catastrophe, sadomasochism, friendship, childhood, adolescence, mid-life crisis, aging, inner conflict, character types, mechanisms of defense, split-off personality, race relations, alcoholism, mental retardation, and even one story about a happy childhood. Given a choice between two stories of equal value that illustrate a similar psychological issue, I selected the one about or written by a member of a minority group. The stories are all in the English language, as it would take another lifetime and many volumes to cover the insightful works written in other languages, in countries of Northern Europe, France, Italy, Russia, Latin America, and the Third World. The period covered is from the early twentieth century to the present day. This volume consists purely of my own selections, as determined by personal taste and insights gained in over thirty-five years of private practice as a psychoanalyst. My choices, needless to say, were hampered by questions of space (many fine stories had to be excluded because they simply were too long to fit into the book) and the ever present difficulties of obtaining copyrights.

My lifetime favorite is *Paul's Case*, which casts light on the possible folly of taking one's own life. I have used the story many times with suicidal patients, and believe it contributed to the saving of lives. Another of my favorites since my college days is the above mentioned *Silent Snow, Secret Snow*, which in unsurpassed beauty of language leads us deep into the recesses of a disturbed boy's mind. *The Test*, by Angelica Gibbs, woke me up to the realities of the racial discrimination in the United States as no academic text could have done. At this point in my life, I am particularly fond of Woody Allen's *My Apology*, with its refreshing candor on his feelings about death and dying. I searched for answers among the pundits for many years, and found only Woody's philosophy on that score helpful. Oddly enough, his "deadly" serious humor appears to be the best way to approach the terror the thought of death inspires in us all.

A number of stories deal with defense mechanisms of the ego, and will guide the reader into intricate workings of the mind. A *Complicated Nature*, by William Trevor, illuminates one man's characteristic method of dealing with feelings, and its effect on his life and those of others around him. A *Distant Episode*, the story which has haunted me since my freshman year in college, is an appalling portrayal of a man who uses an obsessional defense to deal with unimaginable horror. The story shows how it was essential to his survival, and illuminated the deluge of feeling which flooded his psyche when the defense exploded. I don't believe anyone who reads this story will ever forget it. Carson McCullers' *Madame Zilensky and the King of Finland* poignantly demonstrates the way in which a chronic liar lights up her dull, work-infested life, and how the assault on an indispensable defense can lead to a breakdown and depression. In *Truth and Consequences*, Brendan Gill demonstrates how one person's honesty can help another to break through a false self based on the needs of another.

A number of stories deal with life changes. Anne Tyler's *Teenage Wasteland* and *Roses, Rhododendron*, by Alice Adams explore vastly different aspects of adolescence. Henry James's *The Middle Years* looked into a man's mid-life crisis decades before the term came into use. Sherwood Anderson, one of the first generation of writers to be profoundly influenced by Sigmund Freud, gives an accurate picture in *The Other Woman* of the manner in which many men in pre-Freudian times dealt with their oedipal fears and desires.

The stories reflect many kinds of conflict. *The Right Thing* describes a person caught in a conflict between instincts and conscience. Morley Callaghan's *A Cap for Steve* depicts the pain of an adolescent boy who yearns for a loving father, and how he changes, too, when his father is able to grow. *How to Win* fills the reader with sympathy as it portrays the pain endured by a loving mother whose child suffers from the inability to control his aggression. *In the Region of Ice*, Joyce Carol Oates vividly paints the dilemma of a highly repressed nun whose instincts are awakened by a psychotic student. In *The Death of Justina*, the unsurpassable John Cheever aptly depicts the desperate battle of a man to conquer his alcoholism, and the steps that lead to its defeat. *A Small, Good Thing*, by the great Raymond Carver, is a poignant study of the extreme personality changes that can be brought about by the mourning process.

On a different level, *Verona: A Young Woman Speaks* is a rare description of a happy childhood. Harold Brodkey portrays the sensual bliss experienced at life's beginnings, when the milk keeps flowing, one's parents are loving, when all is well and hope is never-ending.

John Cheever wrote in one of his short stories that "Fiction is art and art is the triumph over chaos (no less)." *Tales of Psychology* has already helped its writers to "triumph over chaos." It will help readers to do the same.

1

A SMALL, GOOD THING

RAYMOND CARVER

Saturday afternoon she drove to the bakery in the shopping center. After looking through a loose-leaf binder with photographs of cakes taped onto the pages, she ordered chocolate, the child's favorite. The cake she chose was decorated with a space ship and launching pad under a sprinkling of white stars, and a planet made of red frosting at the other end. His name, SCOTTY, would be in green letters beneath the planet. The baker, who was an older man with a thick neck, listened without saying anything when she told him the child would be eight years old next Monday. The baker wore a white apron that looked like a smock. Straps cut under his arms, went around in back and then to the front again, where they secured under his heavy waist. He wiped his hands on his apron as he listened to her. He kept his eyes down on the photographs and let her talk. He let her take her time. He'd just come to work and he'd be there all night, baking, and he was in no real hurry.

She gave the baker her name, Ann Weiss, and her telephone number. The cake would be ready on Monday morning, just out of the oven, in plenty of time for the child's party that afternoon. The baker was not jolly. There were no pleasantries between them, just the minimum exchange of words, the necessary information. He made her feel uncomfortable, and she didn't like that. While he was bent over the counter with the pencil in his hand, she studied his coarse features and wondered if he'd ever done anything else with his life besides be a baker. She was a mother and thirty-three years old, and it seemed to her that everyone, especially someone the baker's age—a man old enough to be her father—must have children who'd gone through this special time of cakes and birthday parties. There must be that between them, she thought. But he was abrupt with her—not rude, just abrupt. She gave up trying to make friends with him. She looked into the back of the bakery and could see a long, heavy wooden table with aluminum pie pans stacked at one end; and beside the table a metal container filled with empty racks. There was an enormous oven. A radio was playing country-Western music.

The baker finished printing the information on the special order card and closed up the binder. He looked at her and said, "Monday morning." She thanked him and drove home.

On Monday morning, the birthday boy was walking to school with another boy. They were passing a bag of potato chips back and forth and the birthday boy was trying to find out what his friend intended to give him for his birthday that afternoon. Without looking, the birthday boy stepped off the curb at an intersection and was immediately knocked down by a car. He fell on his side with his head in the gutter and his legs out in the road. His eyes were closed, but his legs moved back and forth as if he were trying to climb over something. His friend dropped the potato chips and started to cry. The car had gone a hundred feet or so and stopped in the middle of the road. The man in the driver's seat looked back over his shoulder. He waited until the boy got unsteadily to his feet. The boy wobbled a little. He looked dazed but okay. The driver put the car into gear and drove away.

The birthday boy didn't cry, but he didn't have anything to say about anything either. He wouldn't answer when his friend asked him what it felt like to be hit by a car. He walked home, and his friend went on to school. But after the birthday boy was inside his house, and telling his mother about it—she sitting beside him on the sofa, holding his hands in her lap, saying, "Scotty, honey, are you sure you feel all right, baby?" thinking she would call the doctor anyway—he suddenly lay back on the sofa, closed his eyes, and went limp. When she couldn't wake him up, she hurried to the telephone and called her husband at work. Howard told her to remain calm, remain calm, and then he called an ambulance for the child and left for the hospital himself.

Of course, the birthday party was canceled. The child was in the hospital with a mild concussion and suffering from shock. There'd been vomiting, and his lungs had taken in fluid which needed pumping out that afternoon. Now he simply seemed to be in a very deep sleep—but no coma, Dr. Francis had emphasized, no coma, when he saw the alarm in the parents' eyes. At eleven o'clock that night, when the boy seemed to be resting comfortably enough after the many X-rays and the lab work, and it was just a matter of his waking up and coming around, Howard left the hospital. He and Ann had been at the hospital with the child since afternoon, and he was going home for a short while to bathe and change clothes. "I'll be back in an hour," he said. She nodded. "It's fine," she said. "I'll be right here." He kissed her on the forehead and they touched hands. She sat in the chair beside the bed and looked at the child. She was waiting for him to wake up and be all right. Then she could begin to relax.

Howard drove home from the hospital. He took the wet, dark streets very fast, then caught himself and slowed down. Until now, his life had gone smoothly and to his satisfaction—college, marriage, another year of college for the advanced degree in business, a junior partnership in an investment firm. Fatherhood. He was happy, and, so far, lucky—he knew that. His parents were still living, his brothers and his sister were established, his friends from college had gone out to take their places in the world. So far, he had kept away from any real harm, from those forces he knew existed and that could cripple or bring down a man if the luck went bad, if things suddenly turned. He pulled into the driveway and parked. His left leg began to tremble. He sat in the car for a minute and tried to deal with the present situation in a rational manner. Scotty had been hit by a car and was in the hospital, but he was going to be all right. Howard closed his eyes and ran his hand over his face. He got out of the car and went up to the front door. The dog was barking inside the house. The telephone rang and rang while he unlocked the door and fumbled for the light switch. He shouldn't have left the hospital, he shouldn't have. "Goddamn it!" he said. He picked up the receiver and said, "I just walked in the door!"

"There's a cake here that wasn't picked up," the voice on other end of the line said.

"What are you saying?" Howard asked.

"A cake," the voice said. "A sixteen-dollar cake."

Howard held the receiver against his ear, trying to understand. "I don't know anything about a cake," he said. "Jesus, what are you talking about?"

"Don't hand me that," the voice said.

Howard hung up the telephone. He went into the kitchen and poured himself some whiskey. He called the hospital. But the child's condition remained the same; he was still sleeping and nothing had changed there. While water poured into the tub, Howard lathered his face and shaved. He'd just stretched out in the tub and closed his eyes when the telephone rang again. He hauled himself out, grabbed a towel, and hurried through the house, saying, "Stupid, stupid," for having left the hospital. But when he picked up the receiver and shouted, "Hello!" there was no sound at the other end of the line. Then the caller hung up.

He arrived back at the hospital a little after midnight. Ann still sat in the chair beside the bed. She looked up at Howard, and then she looked back at the child. The child's eyes stayed closed, the head was still wrapped in bandages. His breathing was quiet and regular. From an apparatus over the bed hung a bottle of glucose with a tube running from the bottle to the boy's arm.

"How is he?" Howard said. "What's all this?" waving at the glucose and the tube.

"Dr. Francis's orders," she said. "He needs nourishment. He needs to keep up his strength. Why doesn't he wake up, Howard? I don't understand, if he's all right."

Howard put his hand against the back of her head. He ran his fingers through her hair. "He's going to be all right. He'll wake up in a little while. Dr. Francis knows what's what."

After a time, he said, "Maybe you should go home and get some rest. I'll stay here. Just don't put up with this creep who keeps calling. Hang up right away."

"Who's calling?" she asked.

"I don't know who, just somebody with nothing better to do than call up people. You go on now."

She shook her head. "No," she said. "I'm fine."

"Really," he said. "Go home for a while, and then come back and tell me in the morning. It'll be all right. What did Dr. Francis say? He said Scotty's going to be all right. We don't have to worry. He's just sleeping now, that's all."

A nurse pushed the door open. She nodded at them as she went to the bedside. She took the left arm out from under the covers and put her fingers on the wrist, found the pulse, then consulted her watch. In a little while, she put the arm back under the covers and moved to the foot of the bed, where she wrote something on a clipboard attached to the bed.

"How is he?" Ann said. Howard's hand was a weight on her shoulder. She was aware of the pressure from his fingers.

"He's stable," the nurse said. Then she said, "Doctor will be in again shortly. Doctor's back in the hospital. He's making rounds right now."

"I was saying maybe she'd want to go home and get a little rest," Howard said. "After the doctor comes."

"She could do that," the nurse said. "I think you should both feel free to do that, if you wish." The nurse was a big Scandinavian woman with blond hair. There was a trace of an accent in her speech.

"We'll see what the doctor says," Ann said. "I want to talk to the doctor. I don't think he should keep sleeping like this. I don't think that's a good sign." She brought her hand up to her eyes and let her head come forward a little. Howard's grip tightened on her shoulder, and then his hand moved up to her neck, where his fingers began to knead the muscles there.

"Dr. Francis will be here in a few minutes," the nurse said. Then she left the room.

Howard gazed at his son for a time, the small chest quietly rising and falling under the covers. For the first time since the terrible minutes after Ann's telephone call to him at his office, he felt a genuine fear starting in his limbs. He began shaking his head. Scotty was fine, but instead of sleeping at home in his own bed, he was in a hospital bed with bandages around his head and a tube in his arm. But this help was what he needed right now.

Dr. Francis came in and shook hands with Howard, though they'd just seen each other a few hours before. Ann got up from the chair. "Doctor?"

"Ann," he said and nodded. "Let's just see first how he's doing," the doctor said. He moved to the side of the bed and took the boy's pulse. He peeled back one eyelid and then the other. Then the doctor turned back the covers and listened to the boy's heart and lungs with his stethoscope. He pressed his fingers here and there on the abdomen. When he was finished, he went to the end of the bed and studied the chart. He noted the time, scribbled something on the chart, and then looked at Howard and Ann.

"Doctor, how is he?" Howard said. "What's the matter with him exactly?"

"Why doesn't he wake up?" Ann asked.

The doctor was a handsome, big-shouldered man with a tanned face. He wore a three-piece suit, a striped tie, and ivory cufflinks. His gray hair was combed along the sides of his head, and he looked

as if he had just come from a concert. "He's all right," the doctor
said. "Nothing to shout about, he could be better, I think. But he's
all right. Still, I wish he'd wake up. He should wake up pretty soon."
The doctor looked at the boy again. "We'll know some more in a
couple of hours, after the results of a few more tests are in. But he's
all right, believe me, except for the hairline fracture of the skull.
He does have that."

"Oh, no," Ann said.

"And a bit of a concussion, as I said before. Of course, you
know he's in shock," the doctor said. "Sometimes you see this in
shock cases. This sleeping."

"But he is out of any real danger?" Howard said. "You said
before he's not in a coma. You wouldn't call this a coma, then—
would you, doctor?" Howard waited. He looked at the doctor.

"No, I don't want to call it a coma," the doctor said and glanced
over at the boy once more. "He's just in a very deep sleep. It's a
restorative measure the body is taking on its own. He's out of any
real danger, I'd say that for certain, yes. But we'll know more when
he wakes up and the other tests are in," the doctor said.

"It's a coma," Ann said. "Of sorts."

"It's not a coma yet, not exactly," the doctor said. "I wouldn't
want to call it a coma. Not yet, anyway. He's suffered shock. In
shock cases, this kind of reaction is common enough; it's a tempo-
rary reaction to bodily trauma. Coma. Well, coma is a deep, prolonged unconsciousness, something that could go on for days, or
weeks even. Scotty's not in that area, not as far as we can tell. I'm
certain his condition will show improvement by morning. I'm bet-
ting that it will. We'll know more when he wakes up, which
shouldn't be long now. But by all means feel free to leave the hospital for a while if you want. This is not easy, I know."

The doctor gazed at the boy again, watching him, and then he
turned to Ann and said, "You try not to worry, little mother. Believe me, we're doing all that can be done. It's just a question of a
little more time now." He nodded at her, shook hands with Howard
again, and then he left the room.

Ann put her hand over the child's forehead. "At least he doesn't have a fever," she said. Then she said, "My God, he feels so cold, though. Howard? Is he supposed to feel like this? Feel his head."

Howard touched the child's temples. His own breathing had slowed. "I think he's supposed to feel this way right now," he said. "He's in shock, remember? That's what the doctor said. The doctor was just in here. He would have said something if Scotty wasn't okay."

Ann stood there for a while longer, working her lip with her teeth. Then she moved over to her chair and sat down. Howard sat in the chair next to her chair. They looked at each other. He wanted to say something else and reassure her, but he was afraid, too. He took her hand and put it in his lap, and this made him feel better, her hand being there. They sat like that for a while, watching the boy and not talking. From time to time, he squeezed her hand. Finally, she took her hand away.

"I've been praying," she said.

He nodded.

She said, "I almost thought I'd forgotten how, but it came back to me. All I had to do was close my eyes and say, 'Please God, help us—help Scotty,' and then the rest was easy. The words were right there. Maybe if you prayed, too," she said to him.

"I've already prayed," he said. "I prayed this afternoon—yesterday afternoon, I mean—after you called, while I was driving to the hospital. I've been praying," he said.

"That's good," she said. For the first time, she felt they were together in it, this trouble. She realized with a start that until now, it had only been happening to her and to Scotty. She hadn't let Howard into it, though he was there and needed all along. She felt glad to be his wife.

The same nurse came in and took the boy's pulse again and checked the flow from the bottle hanging above the bed.

In an hour, another doctor came in. He said his name was Parsons, from Radiology. He had a bushy mustache. He was wearing loafers, a Western shirt, and a pair of jeans.

"We're going to take him downstairs for more pictures," he told them. "We need to do some more pictures, and we want to do a scan."

"What's that?" Ann said. "A scan?" She stood between this new doctor and the bed. "I thought you'd already taken all your X-rays."

"I'm afraid we need some more," he said. "Nothing to be alarmed about. We just need some more pictures, and we want to do a brain scan on him."

"My God," Ann said.

"It's a perfectly normal procedure in cases like this," this new doctor said. "We just need to find out for sure why he isn't back awake yet. It's normal medical procedure, and nothing to be alarmed about. We'll be taking him down in a few minutes," this doctor said.

In a little while two orderlies came into the room with a gurney. They were black-haired, dark-complexioned men in white uniforms, and they said a few words to each other in a foreign tongue as they unhooked the boy from the tube and moved him from his bed to the gurney. Then they wheeled him from the room. Howard and Ann got on the same elevator. Ann gazed at the child. She closed her eyes as the elevator began its descent. The orderlies stood at either end of the gurney without saying anything, though once one of the men made a comment to the other in their own language, and the other man nodded slowly in response.

Later that morning, just as the sun was beginning to lighten the windows in the waiting room outside the X-ray department, they brought the boy out and moved him back up to his room. Howard and Ann rode up on the elevator with him once more, and once more they took up their places beside the bed.

They waited all day, but still the boy did not wake up. Occasionally, one of them would leave the room to go downstairs to the cafeteria to drink coffee and then, as if suddenly remembering and feeling guilty, get up from the table and hurry back to the room. Dr. Francis came again that afternoon and examined the boy once more and then left after telling them he was coming along and could wake up at any minute now. Nurses, different nurses from the night before, came in from time to time. Then a young woman from the lab knocked and entered the room. She wore white slacks and a white blouse and carried a little tray of things which she put on the stand beside the bed. Without a word to them, she took blood from the boy's arm. Howard closed his eyes as the woman found the right place on the boy's arm and pushed the needle in.

"I don't understand this," Ann said to the woman.

"Doctor's orders," the young woman said. "I do what I'm told. They say draw that one, I draw. What's wrong with him, anyway?" she said. "He's a sweetie."

"He was hit by a car," Howard said. "A hit-and-run."

The young woman shook her head and looked again at the boy. Then she took her tray and left the room.

"Why won't he wake up?" Ann said. "Howard? I want some answers from these people."

Howard didn't say anything. He sat down again in the chair and crossed one leg over the other. He rubbed his face. He looked at his son and then he settled back in the chair, closed his eyes, and went to sleep.

Ann walked to the window and looked out at the parking lot. It was night, and the cars were driving into and out of the parking lot with their lights on. She stood at the window with her hands gripping the sill, and knew in her heart that they were into something now, something hard. She was afraid, and her teeth began to chatter until she tightened her jaws. She saw a big car stop in front of the hospital and someone, a woman in a long coat, get into the car. She wished she were that woman and somebody, anybody, was driving her away from here to somewhere else, a place where she would find Scotty waiting for her when she stepped out of the car, ready to say *Mom* and let her gather him in her arms.

In a little while, Howard woke up. He looked at the boy again.

Then he got up from the chair, stretched, and went over to stand beside her at the window. They both stared out at the parking lot. They didn't say anything. But they seemed to feel each other's insides now, as though the worry had made them transparent in a perfectly natural way. The door opened and Dr. Francis came in. He was wearing a different suit and tie this time. His gray hair was combed along the sides of his head, and he looked as if he had just shaved. He went straight to the bed and examined the boy. "He ought to have come around by now. There's just no good reason for this," he said. "But I can tell you we're all convinced he's out of any danger. We'll just feel better when he wakes up. There's no reason, absolutely none, why he shouldn't come around. Very soon. Oh, he'll have himself a dilly of a headache when he does, you can count on that. But all of his signs are fine. They're as normal as can be."

"It is a coma, then? Ann said.

The doctor rubbed his smooth cheek. "We'll call it that for the time being, until he wakes up. But you must be worn out. This is hard. I know it is hard. Feel free to go out for a bite," he said. "It would do you good. I'll put a nurse in here while you're gone if you'll feel better about going. Go and have yourselves something to eat."

"I couldn't eat anything," Ann said.

"Do what you need to do, of course," the doctor said. "Anyway I wanted to tell you that all the signs are good, the tests are negative, nothing showed up at all, and just as soon as he wakes up he'll be over the hill."

"Thank you, doctor," Howard said. He shook hands with the doctor again. The doctor patted Howard's shoulder and went out.

"I suppose one of us should go home and check on things," Howard said. "Slug needs to be fed, for one thing."

"Call one of the neighbors," Ann said. "Call the Morgans. Anyone will feed a dog if you ask them to."

"All right," Howard said. After a while, he said, "Honey, why don't *you* do it? Why don't you go home and check on things, and then come back? It'll do you good. I'll be right here with him. Seriously," he said. "We need to keep our strength up on this. We'll want to be here for a while even after he wakes up."

"Why don't *you* go?" she said. "Feed Slug. Feed yourself." "I already went," he said. "I was gone for exactly an hour and fifteen minutes. You go home for an hour and freshen up. Then come back."

She tried to think about it, but she was too tired. She closed her eyes and tried to think about it again. After a time, she said, "Maybe I *will* go home for a few minutes. Maybe if I'm not just sitting right here watching him every second, he'll wake up and be all right. You know? Maybe he'll wake up if I'm not here. I'll go home and take a bath and put on clean clothes. I'll feed Slug. Then I'll come back."

"I'll be right here," he said. "I'll keep an eye on things here." His eyes were bloodshot and small, as if he'd been drinking for a long time. His clothes were rumpled. His beard had come out again. She touched his face, and then she took her hand back. She understood he wanted to be by himself for a while, not have to talk or share his worry for a time. She picked her purse up from the nightstand, and he helped her into her coat.

"I won't be gone long," she said.

"Just sit and rest for a little when you get home," he said. "Eat something. Take a bath. After you get out of the bath, just sit for a while and rest. It'll do you a world of good, you'll see. Then come back," he said. "Let's try not to worry. You heard what Dr. Francis said."

She stood in her coat for a minute trying to recall the doctor's exact words, looking for any nuances, any hint of something behind his words other than what he had said. She tried to remember if his expression had changed any when he bent over to examine the child. She remembered the way his features had composed themselves as he rolled back the child's eyelids and then listened to his breathing.

She went to the door where she turned and looked back. She

looked at the child, and then she looked at the father. Howard
nodded. She stepped out of the room and pulled the door closed
behind her.

She went past the nurses' station and down to the end of the
corridor, looking for the elevator. At the end of the corridor, she
turned to her right and entered a little waiting room where a Negro family sat in wicker chairs. There was a middle-aged man in a
khaki shirt and pants, a baseball cap pushed back on his head. A
large woman wearing a housedress and slippers was slumped in
one of the chairs. A teenaged girl in jeans, hair done in dozens of
little braids, lay stretched out in one of the chairs, smoking a cigarette, her legs crossed at the ankles. The family swung their eyes to
Ann as she entered the room. The little table was littered with
hamburger wrappers and Styrofoam cups.

"Franklin," the large woman said as she roused herself. "Is it
about Franklin?" Her eyes widened. "Tell me now, lady," the
woman said. "Is it about Franklin?" She was trying to rise from her
chair, but the man had closed his hand over her arm.

"Here, here," he said. "Evelyn."

"I'm sorry," Ann said. "I'm looking for the elevator. My son is
in the hospital, and now I can't find the elevator."

"Elevator is down that way, turn left," the man said as he aimed
a finger.

The girl drew on her cigarette and stared at Ann. Her eyes
were narrowed to slits, and her broad lips parted slowly as she let
the smoke escape. The Negro woman let her head fall on her shoulder and looked away from Ann, no longer interested.

"My son was hit by a car," Ann said to the man. She seemed to
need to explain herself. "He has a concussion and a little skull
fracture, but he's going to be all right. He's in shock now, but it
might be some kind of coma, too. That's what really worries us,
the coma part. I'm going out for a little while, but my husband is
with him. Maybe he'll wake up while I'm gone."

"That's too bad," the man said and shifted in the chair. He
shook his head. He looked down at the table, and then he looked

back at Ann. She was still standing there. He said, "Our Franklin, he's on the operating table. Somebody cut him. Tried to kill him. There was a fight where he was at. At this party. They say he was just standing and watching. Not bothering nobody. But that doesn't mean nothing these days. Now he's on the operating table. We're just hoping and praying, that's all we can do now." He gazed at her steadily.

Ann looked at the girl again, who was still watching her, and at the older woman, who kept her head down, but whose eyes were not closed. Ann saw the lips moving silently, making words. She had an urge to ask what those words were. She wanted to talk more with these people who were in the same kind of waiting she was in. She was afraid, and they were afraid. They had that in common. She would have liked to have said something else about the accident, told them more about Scotty, that it had happened on the day of his birthday, Monday, and that he was still unconscious. Yet she didn't know how to begin. She stood looking at them without saying anything more.

She went down the corridor the man had indicated and found the elevator. She waited a minute in front of the closed doors, still wondering if she was doing the right thing. Then she put out her finger and touched the button.

She pulled into the driveway and cut the engine. She closed her eyes and leaned her head against the wheel for a minute. She listened to the ticking sounds the engine made as it began to cool. Then she got out of the car. She could hear the dog barking inside the house. She went to the front door, which was unlocked. She went inside and turned on lights and put on a kettle of water for tea. She opened some dog food and fed Slug on the back porch. The dog ate in hungry little smacks. It kept running into the kitchen to see that she was going to stay. As she sat down on the sofa with her tea, the telephone rang.

"Yes," she said as she answered. "Hello!"

"Mrs. Weiss," a man's voice said. It was five o'clock in the morn-

ing and she thought she could hear machinery or equipment of
some kind in the background.

"Yes, yes! What is it?" she said. "This is Mrs. Weiss. This is she.
What is it, please?" She listened to whatever it was in the background. "Is it Scotty, for Christ's sake?"

"Scotty," the man's voice said. "It's about Scotty, yes. It has to
do with Scotty, that problem. Have you forgotten about Scotty?"
the man said. Then he hung up.

She dialed the hospital's number and asked for the third floor.
She demanded information about her son from the nurse who
answered the telephone. Then she asked to speak to her husband.
It was, she said, an emergency.

She waited, turning the telephone cord in her fingers. She
closed her eyes and felt sick at her stomach. She would have to
make herself eat. Slug came in from the back porch and lay down
near her feet. He wagged his tail. She pulled at his ear while he
licked her fingers. Howard was on the line.

"Somebody just called here," she said. "He said it was about
Scotty," she cried.

"Scotty's fine," Howard told her. "I mean, he's still sleeping.
There's been no change. The nurse has been in twice since you've
been gone. A nurse or else a doctor. He's all right."

"This man called. He said it was about Scotty," she told him.

"Honey, you rest for a little while, you need the rest. It must be
that same caller I had. Just forget it. Come back down here after
you've rested. Then we'll have breakfast or something."

"Breakfast," she said. "I don't want any breakfast."

"You know what I mean," he said. "Juice, something. I don't
know. I don't know anything, Ann. Jesus, I'm not hungry either.
Ann, it's hard to talk now. I'm standing here at the desk. Dr. Francis
is coming again at eight o'clock this morning. He's going to have
something to tell us then, something more definite. That's what
one of the nurses said. She didn't know any more than that. Ann?
Honey, maybe we'll know something more then. At eight o'clock.
Come back here before eight. Meanwhile, I'm right here and

Scotty's all right. He's still the same," he added.

"I was drinking a cup of tea," she said, "when the telephone rang. They said it was about Scotty. There was a noise in the background. Was there a noise in the background on that call you had, Howard?"

"I don't remember," he said. "Maybe the driver of the car, maybe he's a psychopath and found out about Scotty somehow. But I'm here with him. Just rest like you were going to do. Take a bath and come back by seven or so, and we'll talk to the doctor together when he gets here. It's going to be all right, honey. I'm here, and there are doctors and nurses around. They say his condition is stable."

"I'm scared to death," she said.

She ran water, undressed, and got into the tub. She washed and dried quickly, not taking the time to wash her hair. She put on clean underwear, wool slacks, and a sweater. She went into the living room, where the dog looked up at her and let its tail thump once against the floor. It was just starting to get light outside when she went out to the car.

She drove into the parking lot of the hospital and found a space close to the front door. She felt she was in some obscure way responsible for what had happened to the child. She let her thoughts move to the Negro family. She remembered the name Franklin and the table that was covered with hamburger papers, and the teenaged girl staring at her as she drew on her cigarette. "Don't have children," she told the girl's image as she entered the front door of the hospital. "For God's sake, don't."

She took the elevator up to the third floor with two nurses who were just going on duty. It was Wednesday morning, a few minutes before seven. There was a page for a Dr. Madison as the elevator doors slid open on the third floor. She got off behind the nurses, who turned in the other direction and continued the conversation she had interrupted when she'd gotten into the elevator. She walked down the corridor to the little alcove where the Negro family had been waiting. They were gone now, but the chairs were scattered in such a way that it looked as if people had just jumped up from them the minute before. The tabletop was cluttered with the same cups and papers, the ashtray was filled with cigarette butts.

She stopped at the nurses' station. A nurse was standing behind the counter, brushing her hair and yawning.

"There was a Negro boy in surgery last night," Ann said. "Franklin was his name. His family was in the waiting room. I'd like to inquire about his condition."

A nurse who was sitting at a desk behind the counter looked up from a chart in front of her. The telephone buzzed and she picked up the receiver, but she kept her eyes on Ann.

"He passed away," said the nurse at the counter. The nurse held the hairbrush and kept looking at her. "Are you a friend of the family or what?"

"I met the family last night," Ann said. "My own son is in the hospital. I guess he's in shock. We don't know for sure what's wrong. I just wondered about Franklin, that's all. Thank you." She moved down the corridor. Elevator doors the same color as the walls slid open and a gaunt, bald man in white pants and white canvas shoes pulled a heavy cart off the elevator. She hadn't noticed these doors last night. The man wheeled the cart out into the corridor and stopped in front of the room nearest the elevator and consulted a clipboard. Then he reached down and slid a tray out of the cart. He rapped lightly on the door and entered the room. She could smell the unpleasant odors of warm food as she passed the cart. She hurried on without looking at any of the nurses and pushed open the door to the child's room

Howard was standing at the window with his hands behind his back. He turned around as she came in.

"How is he?" she said. She went over to the bed. She dropped her purse on the floor beside the nightstand. It seemed to her she had been gone a long time. She touched the child's face. "Howard?"

"Dr. Francis was here a little while ago," Howard said. She looked at him closely and thought his shoulders were bunched a little.

"I thought he wasn't coming until eight o'clock this morning," she said quickly.

"There was another doctor with him. A neurologist."

"A neurologist," she said.

Howard nodded. His shoulders were bunching, she could see that.

"What'd they say, Howard? For Christ's sake, what'd they say? What is it?"

"They said they're going to take him down and run more tests on him, Ann. They think they're going to operate, honey. Honey, they *are* going to operate. They can't figure out why he won't wake up. It's more than just shock or concussion, they know that much now. It's in his skull, the fracture, it has something, something to do with that, they think. So they're going to operate. I tried to call you, but I guess you'd already left the house."

"Oh, God," she said. "Oh, please, Howard, please," she said, taking his arms.

"Look!" Howard said. "Scotty! Look, Ann! He turned her toward the bed.

The boy had opened his eyes, then closed them. He opened them again now. The eyes stared straight ahead for a minute, then moved slowly in his head until they rested on Howard and Ann, then traveled away again.

"Scotty," his mother said, moving to the bed.

"Hey, Scott," his father said. "Hey, son."

They leaned over the bed. Howard took the child's hand in his hands and began to pat and squeeze the hand. Ann bent over the boy and kissed his forehead again and again. She put her hands of either side of his face. "Scotty, honey, it's Mommy and Daddy," she said. "Scotty?"

The boy looked at them, but without any sign of recognition. Then his mouth opened, his eyes scrunched closed, and he had no more air in his lungs. His face seemed to relax and soften then. His lips parted as his last breath was puffed through his throat and exhaled gently through the clenched teeth.

The doctors called it a hidden occlusion and said it was a one-in-a-million circumstance.

Dr. Francis was shaken. "I can't tell you how badly I feel. I'm so very sorry. I can't tell you," he said as he led them into the doctors' lounge. There was a doctor sitting in a chair with his leg hooked over the back of another chair, watching an early-morning TV show. He was wearing a green delivery-room outfit, loose green pants and green blouse, and a green cap that covered his hair. He looked at Howard and Ann and then looked at Dr. Francis. He got to his feet and turned off the set and went out of the room. Dr. Francis guided Ann to the sofa, sat down beside her, and began to talk in a low, consoling voice. At one point, he leaned over and embraced her. She could feel his chest rising and falling evenly against her shoulder. She kept her eyes open and let him hold her. Howard went into the bathroom, but he left the door open. After a violent fit of weeping, he ran water and washed his face. Then he came out and sat down at the little table that held a telephone. He looked at the telephone as though deciding what to do first. He made some calls. After a time, Dr. Francis used the telephone.

"Is there anything else I can do for you at the moment?" he asked them.

Howard shook his head. Ann stared at Dr. Francis as if unable to comprehend his words.

The doctor walked them to the hospital's front door. People were entering and leaving the hospital. It was eleven o'clock in the morning. Ann was aware of how slowly, almost reluctantly, she moved her feet. It seemed to her that Dr. Francis was making them leave when she felt they should stay, when it would be more the right thing to do to stay. She gazed out into the parking lot and then turned around and looked back at the front of the hospital. She began shaking her head. "No, no," she said. "I can't leave him here, no." She heard herself say that and thought how unfair it was that the only words that came out were the sort of words used on

TV shows where people were stunned by violent or sudden deaths. She wanted her words to be her own. "No," she said, and for some reason the memory of the Negro woman's head lolling on the woman's shoulder came to her. "No," she said again.

"I'll be talking to you later in the day," the doctor was saying to Howard. "There are still some things that have to be done, things that have to be cleared up to our satisfaction. Some things that need explaining."

"An autopsy," Howard said.

Dr. Francis nodded.

"I understand," Howard said. Then he said, "Oh. Jesus. No, I don't understand, doctor. I can't, I can't. I just can't."

Dr. Francis put his arm around Howard's shoulders. "I'm sorry. God, how I'm sorry." He let go of Howard's shoulders and held out his hand. Howard looked at the hand, and then he took it. Dr. Francis put his arms around Ann once more. He seemed full of some goodness she didn't understand. She let her head rest on his shoulder, but her eyes stayed open. She kept looking at the hospital. As they drove out of the parking lot, she looked back at the hospital.

At home, she sat on the sofa with her hands in her coat pockets. Howard closed the door to the child's room. He got the coffee-maker going and then he found an empty box. He had thought to pick up some of the child's things that were scattered around the living room. But instead he sat down beside her on the sofa, pushed the box to one side, and leaned forward, arms between his knees. He began to weep. She pulled his head over into her lap and patted his shoulder. "He's gone," she said. She kept patting his shoulder. Over his sobs, she could hear the coffee-maker hissing in the kitchen. "There, there," she said tenderly. "Howard, he's gone. He's gone and now we'll have to get used to that. To being alone."

In a little while, Howard got up and began moving aimlessly around the room with the box, not putting anything into it, but collecting some things together on the floor at one end of the sofa.

She continued to sit with her hands in her coat pockets. Howard put the box down and brought coffee into the living room. Later, Ann made calls to relatives. After each call had been placed and the party had answered, Ann would blurt out a few words and cry for a minute. Then she would quietly explain, in a measured voice, what had happened and tell them about arrangements. Howard took the box out to the garage, where he saw the child's bicycle. He dropped the box and sat down on the pavement beside the bicycle. He took hold of the bicycle awkwardly so that it leaned against his chest. He held it, the rubber pedal sticking into his chest. He gave the wheel a turn.

Ann hung up the telephone after talking to her sister. She was looking up another number when the telephone rang. She picked it up on the first ring.

"Hello," she said, and she heard something in the background, a humming noise. "Hello!" she said. "For God's sake," she said, "Who is this? What is it you want?"

"Your Scotty, I got him ready for you," the man's voice said. "Did you forget him?"

"You evil bastard!" she shouted into the receiver. "How can you do this, you evil son of a bitch?"

"Scotty," the man said. "Have you forgotten about Scotty?" Then he hung up on her.

Howard heard the shouting and came in to find her with her head on her arms over the table, weeping. He picked up the receiver and listened to the dial tone.

Much later, just before midnight, after they had dealt with many things, the telephone rang again.

"You answer it," she said. "Howard, it's him, I know." They were sitting at the kitchen table with coffee in front of them. Howard had a small glass of whiskey beside his cup. He answered on the third ring.

"Hello," he said. "Who is this? Hello! Hello! The line went dead. "He hung up," Howard said. "Whoever it was."

"It was him," she said. "That bastard. I'd like to kill him," she said. "I'd like to shoot him and watch him kick," she said.

"Ann, my God," he said.

"Could you hear anything"" she said. "In the background? A noise, machinery, something humming?"

"Nothing, really. Nothing like that," he said. "There wasn't much time. I think there was some radio music. Yes, there was a radio going, that's all I could tell. I don't know what in God's name is going on," he said.

She shook her head. "If I could, could get my hands on him." It came to her then. She knew who it was. Scotty, the cake, the telephone number. She pushed the chair away fro the table and got up. "Drive me down to the shopping center," she said. "Howard."

"What are you saying?"

"The shopping center. I know who it is. It's the baker, the son-of-a-bitching baker, Howard. That's who has the number and keeps calling us. To harass us about the cake. The baker, that bastard."

They drove to the shopping center. The sky was clear and stars were out. It was cold, and they ran the heater in the car. They parked in front of the bakery. All of the shops and stores were closed, but there were cars at the far end of the lot in front of the movie theater. The bakery windows were dark, but when they looked through the glass they could see a light in the back room and, now and then, a big man in an apron moving in and out of the white, even light. Through the glass, she could see the display cases and some little tables with chairs. She tried the door. She rapped on the glass. But if the baker heard them, he gave no sign. He didn't look in their direction.

Someone unlocked the door and opened it. The baker stood in the light and peered out at them. "I'm closed for business," he said. "What do you want at this hour? It's midnight. Are you drunk or something?"

She stepped into the light that fell through the open door. He blinked his heavy eyelids as he recognized her. "It's you," he said.

"It's me," she said. "Scotty's mother. This is Scotty's father. We'd like to come in."

The baker said, "I'm busy now. I have work to do."

She had stepped inside the doorway anyway. Howard came in behind her. The baker moved back. "It smells like a bakery in here. Doesn't it smell like a bakery in here, Howard?"

"What do you want?" the baker said. "Maybe you want your cake? That's it, you decided you want your cake. You ordered a cake, didn't you?"

"You're pretty smart for a baker," she said. "Howard, this is the man who's been calling us." She clenched her fists. She stared at him fiercely. There was a deep burning inside her, an anger that made her feel larger than herself, larger than either of these men.

"Just a minute," the baker said. "You want to pick up your three-day-old-cake? That it? I don't want to argue with you, lady. There it sits over there, getting stale. I'll give it to you for half of what I quoted you. No. You want it? You can have it. It's no good to me, no good to anyone now. It cost me time and money to make that cake. If you want it, okay, if you don't, that's okay, too. I have to get back to work." He looked at them and rolled his tongue behind his teeth.

"More cakes," she said. She knew she was in control of it, of what was increasing in her. She was calm.

"Lady, I work sixteen hours a day in this place to earn a living," the baker said. He wiped his hands on his apron. "I work day and night in here, trying to make ends meet." A look crossed Ann's face that made the baker move back and say, "No trouble now." He reached to the counter and picked up a rolling pin with his right hand and began to tap it against the palm of his other hand. "You want to take the cake or not? I have to get back to work. Bakers work at night," he said again. His eyes were small, mean-looking, she thought, nearly lost in the bristly flesh around his cheeks. His neck was thick with fat.

"I know bakers work at night," Ann said. "They make phone

calls at night, too. You bastard," she said.

The baker continued to tap the rolling pin against his hand. He glanced at Howard. "Careful, careful," he said to Howard.

"My son's dead," she said with a cold, even finality. "He was hit by a car Monday morning. We've been waiting with him until he died. But, of course, you couldn't be expected to know that, could you? Bakers can't know everything—can they, Mr. Baker? But he's dead. He's dead, you bastard!" Just as suddenly as it had welled in her, the anger dwindled, gave way to something else, a dizzy feeling of nausea. She leaned against the wooden table that was sprinkled with flour, put her hands over her face, and began to cry, her shoulders rocking back and forth. "It isn't fair," she said. "It isn't fair."

Howard put his hand at the small of her back and looked at the baker. "Shame on you," Howard said to him. "Shame."

The baker put the rolling pin back on the counter. He undid his apron and threw it on the counter. He looked at them, and then he shook his head slowly. He pulled a chair out from under the card table that held papers and receipts, an adding machine, and a telephone directory. "Please sit down," he said. "Let me get you a chair," he said to Howard. "Sit down now, please." The baker went into the front of the shop and returned with two little wrought-iron chairs. "Please sit down, you people."

Ann wiped her eyes and looked at the baker. "I wanted to kill you," she said. "I wanted you dead."

The baker had cleared a space for them at the table. He shoved the adding machine to one side, along with the stacks of notepaper and receipts. He pushed the telephone directory onto the floor, where it landed with a thud. Howard and Ann sat down and pulled their chairs up to the table. The baker sat down, too.

"Let me say how sorry I am," the baker said, putting his elbows on the table. "God alone knows how sorry I am. Listen to me. I'm just a baker, I don't claim to be anything else. Maybe once, maybe years ago, I was a different kind of human being. I've forgotten, I don't know for sure. But I'm not any longer, if I ever was. Now I'm just a baker. That don't excuse my doing what I did, I know. But I'm deeply sorry, I'm sorry for your son, and sorry for my part in this," the baker said. "I don't have any children myself, so I can only imagine what you must be feeling. All I can say to you now is that I'm sorry. Forgive me, if you can," the baker said. "I'm not an evil man, I don't think. Not evil, like you said on the phone. You got to understand what it comes down to is I don't know how to act anymore, it would seem. Please," the man said, "Let me ask you if you can find it in your hearts to forgive me."

It was warm inside the bakery. Howard stood up from the table and took off his coat. He helped Ann from her coat. The baker looked at them for a minute and then nodded and got up from the table. He went to the oven and turned off some switches. He found cups and poured coffee from an electric coffee-maker. He put a carton of cream on the table, and a bowl of sugar.

"You probably need to eat something," the baker said. "I hope you'll eat some of my hot rolls. You have to eat and keep going. Eating is a small, good thing in a time like this," he said.

He served them warm cinnamon rolls just out of the oven, the icing still runny. He put butter on the table with them. He waited. He waited until they each took a roll from the platter and began to eat. "It's good to eat something," he said, watching them. "There's more. Eat up. Eat all you want. There's all the rolls in the world in here."

They ate rolls and drank coffee. Ann was suddenly hungry, and the rolls were warm and sweet. She ate three of them, which pleased the baker. Then he began to talk. They listened carefully. Although they were tired and in anguish, they listened to what the baker had to say. They nodded when the baker began to speak of loneliness, and of the sense of doubt and limitation that had come to him in his middle years. He told them what it was like to be childless all these years. To repeat the days with the ovens end- lessly full and endlessly empty. The party food, the celebrations he'd worked over. Icing knuckle-deep. The tiny wedding couples stuck into cakes. Hundreds of them, no, thousands by now. Birthdays. Just imagine all those candles burning. He had a necessary trade. He was a baker. He was glad he wasn't a florist. It was better to be feeding people. This was a better smell anytime than flowers.

"Smell this," the baker said, breaking open a dark loaf. "It's a heavy bread, but rich." They smelled it, then he had them taste it. It had the taste of molasses and coarse grains. They listened to him. They ate what they could. They swallowed the dark bread. It was like daylight under the fluorescent trays of light. They talked on into the early morning, the high, pale cast of light in the windows, and they did not think of leaving.

A *Small, Good Thing* by Raymond Carver is a story about the growth that can occur in people after a tragedy, when evil and pettiness disappear under the great onslaught of death. People who feel their grief deeply often experience personality shifts that last the rest of their lives. Ann and Howard Weiss's eight-year-old son, Scotty, is struck by a car and dies a few days later. Ann realizes for the first time that she and her husband were in it together, that before that she had felt it had only been happening to her and to Scotty, that she hadn't let Howard in. This is a tremendous insight, as the relationship between mother and son must have excluded the father from the beginning. Had Scotty lived, his life would have taken a different developmental path from that moment on. Another sign of Ann's growth comes in the hospital waiting room, when she talks with a black family with a desperately injured son, and realizes how much they have in common.

Mrs. Weiss had ordered a birthday cake for Scotty's birthday. When they fail to pick up the cake, the baker harasses them with threatening phone calls. They storm into his bakery and Ann expresses a rage that is new to her. Feeling calm and, for the first time, in control of her anger, she feels "larger than herself, larger than these men."

Knowing only that his phone calls are vile and evil, she curses out the baker. Then she tells him that Scotty is dead. The baker, who of course had not known of the child's death before his phone calls, is in shock. He slowly takes off his apron and brings in two chairs for them. He expresses his sorrow at the loss of their son, as well as for his ruthless actions. He tells them he has to work sixteen hours a day to make a meager living. He says he is not an evil man, but simply doesn't know how to act. He speaks of his loneliness, how it feels to be childless all those years, and that he is glad to be feeding people. Then the baker asks their forgiveness for his cruelty. They listen carefully to what he has to say. When he sees that they have heard him, he brings warm rolls and coffee, and tells them to eat, that "eating is a small, good thing in a time like this." They eat and drink and sit talking in the bakery all night long. All three are able to forgive the others' pettiness, as they uncover the human denominator in each of them. The "small, good thing," a symbol of their growth and development, turns out not to be so small, after all.

The ending of the story made me break down and sob.

2

A CAP FOR STEVE

MORLEY CALLAGHAN

Dave Diamond, a poor man, a carpenter's assistant, was a small, wiry, quick-tempered individual who had learned how to make every dollar count in his home. His wife, Anna, had been sick a lot, and his twelve-year-old son, Steve, had to be kept in school. Steve, a big-eyed, shy kid, ought to have known the value of money as well as Dave did. It had been ground into him.

But the boy was crazy about baseball, and after school, when he could have been working as a delivery boy or selling papers, he played ball with the kids. His failure to appreciate that the family needed a few extra dollars disgusted Dave. Around the house he wouldn't let Steve talk about baseball, and he scowled when he saw him hurrying off with his glove after dinner.

When the Phillies came to town to play an exhibition game with the home team and Steve pleaded to be taken to the ball park, Dave, of course, was outraged. Steve knew they couldn't afford it. But he had got his mother on his side. Finally Dave made a bargain with them. He said that if Steve came home after school and worked hard helping to make some kitchen shelves he would take him that night to the ball park.

Steve worked hard, but Dave was still resentful. They had to coax him to put on his good suit. When they started out Steve held aloof, feeling guilty, and they walked down the street like strangers; then Dave glanced at Steve's face and, half-ashamed, took his arm more cheerfully.

As the game went on, Dave had to listen to Steve's recitation of the batting average of every Philly that stepped up to the plate; the time the boy must have wasted learning these averages began to appall him. He showed it so plainly that Steve felt guilty again and was silent. After the game Dave let Steve drag him onto the field to keep him company while he tried to get some autographs from the Philly players, who were being hemmed in by gangs of kids blocking his way to the club-house. But Steve, who was shy, let the other kids block him off from the players. Steve would push his way in, get blocked out, and come back to stand mournfully beside Dave. And Dave grew impatient. He was wasting valuable time. He wanted to get home; Steve knew it and was worried.

Then the big, blond Philly outfielder, Eddie Condon, who had been held up by a gang of kids tugging at his arm and thrusting their score cards at him, broke loose and made a run for the club-house. He was jostled, and his blue cap with the red peak, tilted far back on his head, fell off. It fell at Steve's feet, and Steve stooped quickly and grabbed it. "Okay, son," the outfielder called, turning back. But Steve, holding the hat in both hands, only stared at him.

"Give him his cap, Steve," Dave said, smiling apologetically at the big outfielder who towered over them. But Steve drew the hat closer to his chest. In an awed trance he looked up at big Eddie Condon. It was an embarrassing moment. All the other kids were watching. Some shouted, "Give him his cap."

"My cap, son," Eddie Condon said, his hand out.

"Hey, Steve," Dave said, and he gave him a shake. But he had to jerk the cap out of Steve's hands.

"Here you are," he said.

The outfielder, noticing Steve's white, worshiping face and

pleading eyes, grinned and then shrugged. "Aw, let him keep it,"
he said.

"No, Mr. Condon, you don't need to do that," Steve protested.

"It's happened before. Forget it," Eddie Condon said, and he
trotted away to the club-house.

Dave handed the cap to Steve; envious kids circled around
them and Steve said, "He said I could keep it, Dad. You heard
him, didn't you?"

"Yeah, I heard him," Dave admitted. The wonder in Steve's
face made him smile. He took the boy by the arm and they hurried off the field.

On the way home Dave couldn't get him to talk about the
game; he couldn't get him to take his eyes off the cap. Steve could
hardly believe in his own happiness. "See," he said suddenly, and
he showed Dave that Eddie Condon's name was printed on the
sweatband. Then he went on dreaming. Finally he put the cap on
his head and turned to Dave with a slow, proud smile. The cap
was way too big for him; it fell down over his ears. "Never mind,"
Dave said. "You can get your mother to take a tuck in the back."

When they got home Dave was tired and his wife didn't understand the cap's importance, and they couldn't get Steve to go
to bed. He swaggered around wearing the cap and looking in the
mirror every ten minutes. He took the cap to bed with him.

Dave and his wife had a cup of coffee in the kitchen, and Dave
told her again how they had got the cap. They agreed that their
boy must have an attractive quality that showed in his face, and
that Eddie Condon must have been drawn to him—why else would
he have singled Steve out from all the kids?

But Dave got tired of the fuss Steve made over that cap and of
the way he wore it from the time he got up in the morning until
the time he went to bed. Some kid was always coming in, wanting
to try on the cap. It was childish, Dave said, for Steve to go around
assuming that the cap made him important in the neighborhood,
and to keep telling them how he had become a leader in the park
a few blocks away where he played ball in the evenings. And Dave

wouldn't stand for Steve's keeping the cap on while he was eating. He was always scolding his wife for accepting Steve's explanation that he'd forgotten he had it on. Just the same, it was remarkable what a little thing like a ball cap could do for a kid, Dave admitted to his wife as he smiled to himself.

One night Steve was late coming home from the park. Dave didn't realize how late it was until he put down his newspaper and watched his wife at the window. Her restlessness got on his nerves. "See what comes from encouraging the boy to hang around with those park loafers," he said. "I don't encourage him," she protested. "You do," he insisted irritably, for he was really worried now. A gang hung around the park until midnight. It was a bad park. It was true that on one side there was a good district with fine, expensive houses, but the kids from that neighborhood left the park to the kids from the poorer homes. When his wife went out and walked down to the corner it was his turn to wait and worry and watch at the open window. Each waiting moment tortured him. At last he heard his wife's voice and Steve's voice, and he relaxed and sighed; then he remembered his duty and rushed angrily to meet them.

"I'll fix you, Steve, once and for all," he said. "I'll show you you can't start coming into the house at midnight."

"Hold your horses, Dave," his wife said. "Can't you see the state he's in?" Steve looked utterly exhausted and beaten.

"What's the matter?" Dave asked quickly.

"I lost my cap," Steve whispered; he walked past his father and threw himself on the couch in the living-room and lay with his face hidden.

"Now, don't scold him, Dave," his wife said.

"Scold him. Who's scolding him?" Dave asked indignantly. "It's his cap, not mine. If it's not worth his life to hold on to it, why should I scold him?" But he was implying resentfully that he alone recognized the cap's value.

"So you are scolding him," his wife said. "It's his cap, not yours. What happened, Steve?"

Steve told them he had been playing ball and he found that

when he ran the bases the cap fell off; it was still too big despite the tuck his mother had taken in the band. So the next time he came to bat he tucked the cap in his hip pocket. Someone had lifted it, he was sure.

"And he didn't even know whether it was still in his pocket," Dave said sarcastically.

"I wasn't careless, Dad," Steve said. For the last three hours he had been wandering around to the homes of the kids who had been in the park at the time; he wanted to go on, but he was too tired. Dave knew the boy was apologizing to him, but he didn't know why it made him angry.

"If he didn't hang on to it, it's not worth worrying about now," he said, and he sounded offended.

After that night they knew that Steve didn't go to the park to play ball; he went to look for the cap. It irritated Dave to see him sit around listlessly, or walk in circles, trying to force his memory to find a particular incident which would suddenly recall to him the moment when the cap had been taken. It was no attitude for a growing, healthy boy to take, Dave complained. He told Steve firmly once and for all that he didn't want to hear anything more about the cap.

One night, two weeks later, Dave was walking home with Steve from the shoemaker's. It was a hot night. When they passed an ice-cream parlour Steve slowed down. "I guess I couldn't have a soda, could I?" Steve said. "Nothing doing," Dave said firmly. "Come on now," he added as Steve hung back, looking in the window.

"Dad, look!" Steve cried suddenly, pointing at the window. "My cap! There's my cap! He's coming out!"

A well-dressed boy was leaving the ice-cream parlor; he had on a blue ball cap with a red peak, just like Steve's cap. "Hey, you!" Steve cried, and he rushed at the boy, his small face fierce and his eyes wild. Before the boy could back away Steve had snatched the cap from his head. "That's my cap!" he shouted.

"What's this?" the bigger boy said. "Hey, give me my cap or I'll give you a poke on the nose."

Dave was surprised that his own shy boy did not back away. He watched him clutch the cap on his left hand, half-crying with excitement as he put his head down and drew back his right fist: he was willing to fight. And Dave was proud of him.

"Wait now," Dave said. "Take it easy, son," he said to the other boy, who refused to back away.

"My boy says it's his cap," Dave said.

"Well, he's crazy. It's my cap."

"I was with him when he got this cap," Steve said. "When the Phillies played here. It's a Philly cap."

"Eddie Condon gave it to me," Steve said. "And you stole it from me, you jerk."

"Don't call me a jerk, you little squirt. I never saw you before in my life."

"Look," Steve said, pointing to the printing on the cap's sweatband. "It's Eddie Condon's cap. See? See, Dad?"

"Yeah. You're right, son. Ever see this boy before, Steve?"

"No," Steve said reluctantly.

The other boy realized he might lose the cap. "I bought it from a guy," he said. "I paid him. My father knows I paid hm." He said he got the cap at the ball park. He groped for some magically impressive words and suddenly found them. "You'll have to speak to my father," he said.

"Sure, I'll speak to your father," Dave said. "What's your name? Where do you live?"

"My name is Hudson. I live about ten minutes away on the other side of the park." The boy appraised Dave, who wasn't any bigger than he was and who wore a faded blue windbreaker and no tie. "My father is a lawyer," he said boldly. "He wouldn't let me keep the cap if he didn't think I should."

"Is that a fact?" Dave asked belligerently. "Well, we'll see. Come on. Let's go." And he got between the two boys and they walked along the street. They didn't talk to each other. Dave knew the Hudson boy was waiting to get to the protection of his home, and Steve knew it, too, and he looked up apprehensively at Dave. And

Dave, reaching for his hand, squeezed it encouragingly and strode along, cocky and belligerent, knowing that Steve relied on him.

The Hudson boy lived in that row of fine apartment houses on the other side of the park. At the entrance to one of these houses Dave tried not to hang back and show he was impressed, because he could feel Steve hanging back. When they got into the small elevator Dave didn't know why he took off his hat. In the carpeted hall on the fourth floor the Hudson boy said, "Just a minute," and entered his own apartment. Dave and Steve were left alone in the corridor, knowing that the other boy was preparing his father for the encounter. Steve looked anxiously at his father, and Dave said, "Don't worry, son," and he added resolutely, "No one's putting anything over on us."

A tall balding man in a brown velvet smoking jacket suddenly opened the door. Dave had never seen a man wearing one of those jackets, although he had seen them in department-store windows. "Good evening," he said, making a depreciatory gesture at the cap Steve still clutched tightly in his left hand. "My boy didn't get your name. My name is Hudson."

"Mine's Diamond."

"Come on in," Mr. Hudson said, putting out his hand and laughing good-naturedly. He led Dave and Steve into his living-room. "What's this about that cap?" he asked. "The way kids can get excited about a cap. Well, it's understandable, isn't it?"

"So it is," Dave said, moving closer to Steve, who was awed by the broadloom rug and the fine furniture. He wanted to show Steve he was at ease himself, and he wished Mr. Hudson wouldn't be so polite. That meant Dave had to be polite and affable, too, and it was hard to manage when he was standing in the middle of the floor in his windbreaker.

"Sit down, Mr. Diamond," Mr. Hudson said. Dave took Steve's arm and sat him down beside him on the chesterfield. The Hudson boy watched his father. And Dave looked at Steve and saw that he wouldn't face Mr. Hudson or the other boy; he kept looking up at Dave, putting all his faith in him.

"Well, Mr. Diamond, from what I gathered from my boy, you're able to prove this cap belonged to your boy."

"That's a fact," Dave said.

"Mr. Diamond, you'll have to believe my boy bought that cap from some kid in good faith."

"I don't doubt it," Dave said. "But no kid can sell anything that doesn't belong to him. You know that's a fact, Mr. Hudson."

"Yes, that's a fact," Mr. Hudson agreed. "But that cap means a lot to my boy, Mr. Diamond."

"It means a lot to my boy, too, Mr. Hudson."

"Sure it does. But supposing we called in a policeman. You know what he'd say? He'd ask you if you were willing to pay my boy what he paid for the cap. That's usually the way it works out," Mr. Hudson said, friendly and smiling, as he eyed Dave shrewdly.

"But that's not right. It's not justice," Dave protested. "Not when it's my boy's cap."

"I know it isn't right. But that's what they do."

"All right. What did you say your boy paid for the cap?" Dave said reluctantly.

"Two dollars."

"Two dollars!" Dave repeated. Mr. Hudson's smile was still kindly, but his eyes were shrewd, and Dave knew the lawyer was counting on his not having the two dollars. Mr. Hudson thought he had Dave sized up; he looked at him and decided he was broke. Dave's pride was hurt, and he turned to Steve. What he saw in Steve's face was more powerful than the hurt to his pride: it was the memory of how difficult it had been to get an extra nickel, the talk he heard about the cost of food, the worry in his mother's face as she tried to make ends meet, and the bewildered embarrassment that he was here in a rich man's home, forcing his father to confess that he couldn't afford to spend two dollars. Then Dave grew angry and reckless. "I'll give you the two dollars," he said.

Steve looked at the Hudson boy and grinned brightly. The Hudson boy watched his father."I suppose that's fair enough," Mr. Hudson said. "A cap like this can be worth a lot to a kid. You know how it is. Your boy might want to sell—I mean be satisfied. Would he take five dollars for it?

"Five dollars? Dave repeated. "Is it worth five dollars, Steve?" he asked uncertainly.

Steve shook his head and looked frightened.

"No, thanks, Mr. Hudson," Dave said firmly.

"I'll tell you what I'll do," Mr. Hudson said. "I'll give you ten dollars. The cap has a sentimental value for my boy, a Philly cap, a big-leaguer's cap. It's only worth about a buck and a half, really," he added. But Dave shook his head again. Mr. Hudson frowned. He looked at his own boy with indulgent concern, but now he was embarrassed. "I'll tell you what I'll do," he said. "This cap—well, it's worth as much as a day at the circus to my boy. Your boy should be recompensed. I want to be fair. Here's twenty dollars," and he held out two ten-dollar bills to Dave. That much money for a cap, Dave thought, and his eyes brightened. But he knew what the cap had meant to Steve; to deprive him of it now that it was within his reach would be unbearable. All the things he needed in his life gathered around him; his wife was there, saying he couldn't afford to reject the offer, he had no right to do it; and he turned to Steve to see if Steve thought it wonderful that the cap could bring them twenty dollars.

"What do you say, Steve?" he asked uneasily.

"I don't know," Steve said. He was in a trance. When Dave smiled, Steve smiled too, and Dave believed that Steve was as impressed as he was, only more bewildered, and maybe even more aware that they could not possibly turn away that much money for a ball cap.

"Well, here you are," Mr. Hudson said, and he put the two bills in Steve's hand. "It's a lot of money. But I guess you had a right to expect as much."

With a dazed, fixed smile Steve handed the money slowly to his father, and his face was white.

Laughing jovially, Mr. Hudson led them to the door. His own boy followed a few paces behind.

In the elevator Dave took the bills out of his pocket. "See, Stevie," he whispered eagerly. "That windbreaker you wanted? And ten dollars for your bank! Won't Mother be surprised?"

"Yeah," Steve whispered, the little smile still on his face. But Dave had to turn away quickly so their eyes wouldn't meet, for he saw that it was a scared smile.

Outside, Dave said "Here, you carry the money home, Steve. You show it to your mother."

"No, you keep it," Steve said, and then there was nothing to say. They walked in silence.

"It's a lot of money," Dave said finally. When Steve didn't answer him, he added angrily, "I turned to you, Steve. I asked you, didn't I?"

"That man knew how much his boy wanted that cap," Steve said.

"Sure. But he recognized how much it was worth to us."

"No, you let him take it away from us," Steve blurted.

"That's unfair," Dave said. "Don't dare say that to me."

"I don't want to be like you," Steve muttered, and he darted across the road and walked along on the other side of the street.

"It's unfair," Dave said angrily, only now he didn't mean that Steve was unfair, and he didn't know quite why. He had been trapped, not just by Mr. Hudson, but by his own life. Across the road Steve was hurrying along with his head down, wanting to be alone. They walked most of the way home on opposite sides of the street, until Dave could stand it no longer. "Steve," he called, crossing the street. "It was very unfair. I mean, for you to say..." but Steve started to run. Dave walked as fast as he could and Steve was getting beyond him, and he felt enraged and suddenly he yelled, "Steve!" and he started to chase his son. He wanted to get hold of Steve and pound him, and he didn't know why. He gained on him, he gaped for breath and he almost got him by the shoulder. Turning, Steve saw his father's face in the street light and was terrified; he circled away, got to the house, and rushed in, yelling, "Mother!"

"Son, son!" she cried, rushing from the kitchen. As soon as she threw her arms around Steve, shielding him, Dave's anger left him and he felt stupid. He walked past them into the kitchen.

"What happened?" she asked anxiously. "Have you both gone crazy?" What did you do, Steve?"

"Nothing," he said sullenly.

"What did your father do?"

"We found the boy with my ball cap, and he let the boy's father take it from us."

"No, no," Dave protested. "Nobody pushed us around. The man didn't put anything over us." He felt tired and his face was burning. He told what had happened; then he slowly took the two ten-dollar bills out of his wallet and tossed them on the table and looked up guiltily at his wife.

It hurt him that she didn't pick up the money, and that she didn't rebuke him. "It's a lot of money, son," she said slowly. "Your father was only trying to do what he knew was right, and it'll work out, and you'll understand." She was soothing Steve, but Dave knew she felt that she needed to be gentle with him, too, and he was ashamed.

When she went with Steve to his bedroom, Dave sat by himself. His son had contempt for him, he thought. His son, for the first time, had seen how easy it was for another man to handle him, and he had judged him and had wanted to walk alone on the other side of the street. He looked at the money and he hated the sight of it.

His wife returned to the kitchen, made a cup of tea, talked soothingly, and said it was incredible that he had forced the Hudson man to pay him twenty dollars for the cap, but all Dave could think of was Steve was scared of me.

Finally, he got up and went into Steve's room. The room was in darkness, but he could see the outline of Steve's body on the bed, and he sat down beside him and whispered, "Look, son, it was a mistake. I know why. People like us—in circumstances where money can scare us. No, no," he said, feeling ashamed and shak-

ing his head apologetically; he was taking the wrong way of show-
ing the boy they were together; he was covering up his own failure. For the failure had been his, and it had come out of being so
separated from his son that he had been blind to what was beyond
the price in a boy's life. He longed now to show Steve he could be
with him from day to day. His hand went out hesitantly to Steve's
shoulder. "Steve, look," he said eagerly. "The trouble was I didn't
realize how much I enjoyed it that night at the ball park. If I had
watched you playing for your own team—the kids around here say
you could be a great pitcher. We could take that money and buy a
new pitcher's glove for you, and a catcher's mitt. Steve, Steve, are
you listening? I could catch you, work with you in the lane. Maybe
I could be your coach...watch you become a great pitcher." In the
half-darkness he could see the boy's pale face turn to him.

Steve, who had never heard his father talk like this, was shy
and wondering. All he knew was that his father, for the first time,
wanted to be with him in his hopes and adventures. He said, "I
guess you do know how important that cap was." His hand went
out to his father's arm. "With that man the cap was—well it was
just something he could buy, eh, Dad?" Dave gripped his son's
hand hard. The wonderful generosity of childhood—the price a
boy was willing to pay to be able to count on his father's admiration and approval—made him feel humble, then strangely exalted.

A *Cap For Steve* by Morley Callaghan is a story about a boy's deep
longing for a father he can look up to and emulate. Steve's craving
is expressed symbolically and obsessively in a baseball hat formerly
owned by Eddie Condon, a famous baseball player with the Phillies.

Steve had contempt for his father, Dave, a poor carpenter's
assistant who "had learned how to make every dollar count," and
who thought Steve's time at the baseball field was wasted, and that

he should earn money by selling newspapers instead. Because he lacked a father who loved and understood him and who could serve as a model of how to be a strong and loving man, Steve had a poor image of himself, and was looked down upon by the other boys.

When the Phillies came to town, Steve and his obliging mother badgered the reluctant Dave into taking the child to the game. When they started out, Dave noticed that "they walked down the street like strangers." In the first indication that he is capable of change, he took the boy's arm. At the game Steve found his idol in the big, blond outfielder, Eddie Condon. When Condon dropped his blue cap with the red peak, Steve, who had gone down to the field to try to get some autographs, quickly stooped down and picked up the cap. When the big-leaguer noticed Steve's white, worshiping face and pleading eyes, he generously allowed the boy to keep the cap. Steve then carried it around with him all day long, and even slept with it at night. His prized possession increased his confidence and self-esteem, and he soon became a leader in the nearby park where the boys played ball.

Unfortunately, Steve lost his cap, and dejectedly spent two weeks looking for it. In a scene which dramatically delineates the relationship between Steve and his father, the two were walking home from the shoemaker's and passed an ice-cream parlor. Steve asked for a soda, and his father said, "Nothing doing."

Steve looked in the window and got excited to see his cap on a boy who was eating ice cream in the store. The ice cream is symbolic of the indulged child who, in contrast to Steve, is nurtured and loved. Steve and his father confronted the boy, who said he had bought the cap and refused to return it. He said they should all go to see his father, a lawyer, who would tell them what to do. Here again is a hint that a father should know the answers, and not be ineffectual like Dave.

The boy's father offered Steve money for the cap, but he turned it down. The offer got larger and larger, until finally it reached twenty dollars, a huge sum for a poor working man and his family.

Dave could no longer resist the offer, and asked Steve if it would be all right to accept the money. Steve half-heartedly agreed, but then was disconsolate. Feeling that his father had betrayed him, Steve even refused to walk down the street with him. He said, "*I don't want to be like you.*"

Dave gradually understood that his son's obsessional need for the cap covered a deep yearning for a strong and understanding father. He came into Steve's bedroom, placed his hand on his son's shoulder for the first time, and said he would coach him and help him to become a great pitcher. Steve realized that his father wanted to be with him in his hopes and fears, and said, "I guess you do know how important that cap was." His hand reached out to touch his father's arm.

There is no doubt that Dave's remarkable growth will bring about a change in Steve's personality and his life. We can predict from his rapid self-improvement after he was given the cap by Condon that Steve's new relationship with his father will enable the boy to pick up his development and go on to become an effective, self-assured young man.

3

MADAME ZILENSKY AND THE KING OF FINLAND

CARSON McCULLERS

To Mr. Brook, the head of the music department at Ryder College, was due all the credit for getting Madame Zilensky on the faculty. The college considered itself fortunate; her reputation was impressive, both as a composer and as a pedagogue. Mr. Brook, who took on himself the responsibility of finding a house for the head of the music department at Ryder College, was due all the credit for getting Madame Zilensky a comfortable place with a garden, which was convenient to the college and next to the apartment house where he himself lived.

No one in Westbridge had known Madame Zilensky before she came. Mr. Brook had seen her pictures in musical journals, and once he had written to her about the authenticity of a certain Buxtehude manuscript. Also, when it was being settled that she was to join the faculty, they had exchanged a few cables and letters on practical affairs. She wrote in a clear, square hand, and the only thing out of the ordinary was the fact that they contained an occasional reference to objects and persons altogether unknown to Mr. Brook, such as "the yellow car in Lisbon" or "poor Heinrich." These lapses Mr. Brook put down to the confusion of getting herself and her family out of Europe.

Mr. Brook was a somewhat pastel person; years of Mozart minuets, of explanations about diminished sevenths and minor triads, had given him a watchful vocational patience. For the most part, he kept to himself. Years before, when the music department had decided to gang together and spend the summer in Salzburg, Mr. Brook sneaked out of the arrangement at the last moment and took a solitary trip to Peru. He had a few eccentricities himself and was tolerant of the peculiarities of others; indeed, he rather relished the ridiculous. Often, when confronted with some grave and incongruous situation, he would feel a little inside tickle, which stiffened his long, mild face and sharpened the light in his gray eyes.

Mr. Brook met Madame Zilensky at the Westbridge station a week before the beginning of the fall semester. He recognized her instantly. She was a tall, straight woman with a pale and haggard face. Her eyes were deeply shadowed and she wore her dark, ragged hair pushed back from her forehead. She had large, delicate hands, which were very grubby. About her person as a whole there was something noble and abstract that made Mr. Brook draw back for a moment and stand nervously undoing his cuff links. In spite of her clothes—a long, black skirt and a broken-down old leather jacket—she made an impression of vague elegance. With Madame Zilensky were three children, boys, between the ages of ten and six, all blond, blank-eyed, and beautiful. There was one other person, an old woman who turned out later to be the Finnish servant.

This was the group he found at the station. The only luggage they had with them was two immense boxes of manuscripts, the rest of the paraphernalia having been forgotten in the station at Springfield when they changed trains. That is the sort of thing that can happen to anyone. When Mr. Brook got them all into a taxi, he thought the worst difficulties were over, but Madame Zilensky suddenly tried to scramble over his knees and get out of the door.

"My God! She said. I left my—how do you say?—my tick-tick-tick—"

"Your watch?" asked Mr. brook.

"Oh no!" she said vehemently. "You know, my tick-tick-tick," and she waved her forefinger from side to side, pendulum fashion.

"Tick-tick," said Mr. Brook, putting his hands to his forehead and closing his eyes. "Could you possibly mean a metronome?"

"Yes! Yes! I think I must have lost it there where we changed trains."

Mr. Brook managed to quiet her. He even said, with a kind of dazed gallantry, that he would get her another one the next day. But at the time he was bound to admit to himself that there was something curious about this panic over a metronome when there was all the rest of the lost luggage to consider.

The Zilensky menage moved into the house next door, and on the surface everything was all right. The boys were quiet children. Their names were Sigmund, Boris, and Sammy. They were always together and they followed each other around Indian file, Sigmund usually the first. Among themselves they spoke a desperate-sounding family Esperanto made up of Russian, French, Finnish, German, and English; when other people were around, they were strangely silent. It was not any one thing that the Zilenskys did or said that made Mr. Brook uneasy. There were just little incidents. For example, something about the Zilensky children subconsciously bothered him when they were in a house, and finally he realized that what troubled him was the fact that the Zilensky boys never walked on a rug; they skirted it single file on the bare floor, and if a room was carpeted, they stood in the doorway and did not go inside. Another thing was this: weeks passed and Madame Zilensky seemed to make no effort to get settled or to furnish the house with anything more than a table and some beds. The front door was left open day and night, and soon the house began to take on a queer, bleak look like that of a place abandoned for years.

The college had every reason to be satisfied with Madame Zilensky. She taught with a fierce insistence. She could become deeply indignant if some Mary Owens or Bernadine Smith would not clean up her Scarlatti trills. She got hold of four pianos for her college studio and set four dazed students to playing Bach fugues together. The racket that came from her end of the department was extraordinary, but Madame Zilensky did not seem to have a nerve in her, and if pure will and effort can get over a musical idea, then Ryder College could not have done better. At night Madame Zilensky worked on her twelfth symphony. She seemed never to sleep; no matter what time of night Mr. Brook happened to look out of his sitting-room window, the light in her studio was always on. No, it was not because of any professional consideration that Mr. Brook became so dubious.

It was in late October when he felt for the first time that something was unmistakably wrong. He had lunched with Madame Zilensky and had enjoyed himself, as she had given him a very detailed account of an African safari she had made in 1928. Later in the afternoon she stopped in at his office and stood rather abstractly in the doorway.

Mr. Brook looked up from his desk and asked, "Is there anything you want?"

"No, thank you," said Madame Zilensky. She had a low, beautiful sombre voice. "I was only just wondering. You recall the metronome. Do you think perhaps that I might have left it with that French?"

"Who?" asked Mr. Brook.

"Why, that French I was married to," she answered.

"Frenchman," Mr. Brook said mildly. He tried to imagine the husband of Madame Zilensky, but his mind refused. He muttered half to himself, "The father of the children."

"But no," said Madame Zilensky with decision. "The father of Sammy."

Mr. Brook had a swift prescience. His deepest instincts warned him to say nothing further. Still, his respect for order, his conscience, demanded that he ask, "And the father of the other two?"

Madame Zilensky put her hand to the back of her head and ruffled up her short, cropped hair. Her face was dreamy, and for several moments she did not answer. Then she said gently, "Boris is of a Pole who played the piccolo."

"And Sigmund?" he asked. Mr. Brook looked over his orderly desk, with the stack of corrected papers, the three sharpened pencils, the ivory-elephant paperweight. When he glanced up at Madame Zilensky, she was obviously thinking hard. She gazed around at the corners of the room, her brows lowered and her jaw moving from side to side. At last she said, "We were discussing he father of Sigmund?"

"Why, no," said Mr. Brook. "There is no need to do that."

Madame Zilensky answered in a voice both dignified and final. "He was a fellow countryman."

Mr. Brook really did not care one way or the other. He had no prejudices; people could marry seventeen times and have Chinese children so far as he was concerned. But there was something about this conversation with Madame Zilensky that bothered him. Suddenly, he understood. The children didn't look at all like Madame Zilensky, but they looked exactly like each other, and as they all had different fathers, Mr. Brook thought the resemblance astonishing.

But Madame Zilensky had finished with the subject. She zipped up her leather jacket and turned away.

"That is exactly where I left it," she said, with a quick nod. "*Chez* that French."

Affairs in the music department were running smoothly. Mr. Brook did not have any serious embarrassments to deal with, such as the harp teacher last year who had finally eloped with a garage mechanic. There was only this nagging apprehension about Madame Zilensky. He could not make out what was wrong in his relations with her or why his feelings were so mixed. To begin with, she was a great globe-trotter, and her conversations were incongruously seasoned with references to far-fetched places. She would go along for days without opening her mouth, prowling through the corridor with her hands in the pockets of her jacket and her face locked in meditation. Then suddenly she would buttonhole Mr. Brook and launch out on a long, volatile monologue, her eyes reckless and bright and her voice warm with eagerness. She would talk about anything or nothing at all. Yet, without exception, there was something queer, in a slanted sort of way, about every episode she ever mentioned. If she spoke of taking Sammy to the barbershop, the impression she created was just as foreign as if she were telling of an afternoon in Baghdad. Mr. Brook could not make it out.

The truth came to him very suddenly, and the truth made everything perfectly clear, or at least clarified the situation. Mr. Brook had come home early and lighted a fire in the little grate in his sitting room. He felt comfortable and at peace that evening. He sat before the fire in his stocking feet, with a volume of William Blake on the table by his side, and he had poured himself a half-glass of apricot brandy. At ten o'clock he was drowsing cosily before the fire, his mind full of cloudy phrases of Mahler and floating half-thoughts. Then all at once, out of this delicate stupor, four words came to his mind: "The King of Finland." The words seemed familiar, but for the first moment he could not place them. Then all at once he tracked them down. He had been walking across the campus that afternoon when Madame Zilensky stopped him and began some preposterous rigamarole, to which he had only half listened; he was thinking about the stack of canons turned in by his counterpoint class. Now the words, the inflections of her voice, came back to him with insidious exactitude. Madame Zilensky had started off with the following remark: "One day, when I was standing in front of a *patisserie*, the King of Finland came by in a sled."

Mr. Brook jerked himself up straight in his chair and put down his glass of brandy. The woman was a pathological liar. Almost every word she uttered outside of class was an untruth. If she worked all night, she would go out of her way to tell you she spent the evening at the cinema. If she ate lunch at the Old Tavern, she would be sure to mention that she had lunched with her children at home. The woman was simply a pathological liar, and that accounted for everything.

Mr. Brook cracked his knuckles and got up from his chair. His first reaction was one of exasperation. That day after day Madame Zilensky would have the gall to sit there in his office and deluge him with her outrageous falsehoods! Mr. Brook was intensely provoked. He walked up and down the room, then he went into his kitchenette and made himself a sardine sandwich.

An hour later, as he sat before the fire, his irritation had changed into a scholarly and thoughtful wonder. What he must do, he told himself, was to regard the whole situation impersonally and look on Madame Zilensky as a doctor looks on a sick patient. Her lies were of the guileless sort. She did not dissimulate with any intention to deceive, and the untruths she told were never used to any possible advantage. That was the maddening thing; there was simply no motive behind it all.

Mr. Brook finished off the rest of the brandy. And slowly, when it was almost midnight, a further understanding came to him. The reason for the lies of Madame Zilensky was painful and plain. All her life long Madame Zilensky had worked—at the piano, teaching, and writing those beautiful and immense twelve symphonies. Day and night she had drudged and struggled and thrown her soul into her work, and there was not much of her left over for anything else. Being human, she suffered from this lack and did what she could to make up for it. If she passed the evening bent over a table in the library and later declared that she had spent that time playing cards, it was as though she had managed to do both those things. Through the lies, she lived vicariously. The lies doubled the little of her existence that was left over from work and augmented the little rag end of her personal life.

Mr. Brook looked into the fire, and the face of Madame

Zilensky was in his mind—a severe face, with dark, weary eyes and delicately disciplined mouth. He was conscious of a warmth in his chest, and a feeling of pity, protectiveness, and dreadful understanding. For a while he was in a state of lovely confusion.

Later on he brushed his teeth and got into his pajamas. He must be practical. What did this clear up? That French, the Pole with the piccolo, Baghdad? And the children, Sigmund, Boris, and Sammy—who were they? Were they really her children after all, or had she simply rounded them up from somewhere? Mr. Brook polished his spectacles and put them on the table by his bed. He must come to an immediate understanding with her. Otherwise, there would exist in the department a situation which could become most problematical. It was two o'clock. He glanced out of his window and saw that the light in Madame Zilensky's workroom was still on. Mr. Brook got into bed, made terrible faces in the dark, and tried to plan what he would say next day.

Mr. Brook was in his office by eight o'clock. He sat hunched up behind his desk, ready to trap Madame Zilensky as she passed down the corridor. He did not have to wait long, and as soon as he heard her footsteps he called out her name.

Madame Zilensky stood in the doorway. She looked vague and jaded. "How are you? I had such a fine night's rest," she said.

"Pray be seated, if you please," said Mr. Brook. "I would like a word with you."

Madame Zilensky put aside her portfolio and leaned back wearily in the armchair across from him. "Yes?" she asked.

"Yesterday you spoke to me as I was walking across the campus," he said slowly. "And if I am not mistaken, I believe you said something about a pastry shop and the King of Finland. Is that correct?"

Madame Zilensky turned her head to one side and stared retrospectively at a corner of the window sill.

"Something about a pastry shop," he repeated.

Her tired face brightened. "But of course," she said eagerly. "I told you about the time I was standing in front of this shop and the King of Finland—"

"Madame Zilensky!" Mr. Brook cried. "There *is* no King of Finland."

Madame Zilensky looked absolutely blank. Then, after an instant, she started off again. "I was standing in front of Bjarne's *patisserie* when I turned away from the cakes and suddenly saw the King of Finland—"

"Madame Zilensky, I just told you that there is no King of Finland."

"In Helsingfors," she started off again desperately, and again he let her get as far as the King, and then no further.

"Finland is a democracy," he said. "You could not possibly have seen the King of Finland. Therefore, what you have just said is an untruth. A pure untruth."

Never afterward could Mr. Brook forget the face of Madame Zilensky at that moment. In her eyes there was astonishment, dismay, and a sort of cornered horror. She had the look of one who watches his whole interior world split open and disintegrate.

"It is a pity," said Mr. Brook with real sympathy. She raised her chin and said coldly, "I am a Finn."

"That I do not question," answered Mr. Brook. On second thought, he did question it a little.

"I was born in Finland and I am a Finnish citizen."

"That may very well be," said Mr. Brook in a rising voice.

"In the war," she continued passionately, "I rode a motorcycle and was a messenger."

"Your patriotism does not enter into it."

"Just because I am getting out the first papers—"

"Madame Zilensky!" said Mr. Brook. His hands grasped the edge of the desk. "That is only an irrelevant issue. The point is that you maintained and testified that you saw—that you saw—" But he could not finish. Her face stopped him. She was deadly pale and there were shadows around her mouth. Her eyes were wide open, doomed, and proud. And Mr. Brook felt suddenly like a murderer. A great commotion of feelings—understanding, remorse, and unreasonable love—made him cover his face with his hands.

He could not speak until this agitation in his insides quieted down, and then he said very faintly, "Yes. Of course. The King of Finland. And was he nice?"

An hour later, Mr. Brook sat looking out of the widow of his office. The trees along the quiet Westbridge street were almost bare, and the gray buildings of the college had a calm, sad look. As he idly took in the familiar scene, he noticed the Drakes' old Airedale waddling along down the street. It was a thing he had watched a hundred times before, so what was it that struck him as strange? Then he realized with a kind of cold surprise that the old dog was running along backward. Mr. Brook watched the Airedale until he was out of sight, then resumed his work on the canons which had been turned in by the class in counterpoint.

Madame Zelinsky and the King of Finland, by Carson McCullers, is the story of a defense mechanism of the ego and the function it sometimes serve. Despite the fact that Madame Zilensky was a brilliant, prolific composer, musician, and college professor at Ryder College, she was a pathological liar. Her lies, such as that when she was standing outside a *patisserie*, the King of Finland came by on a sled, were harmless enough. Nevertheless, they greatly disturbed Mr. Brook, the head of the music department. When pondering about the situation, he suddenly remembered that Finland is a democracy and has no king. At first he was greatly exasperated, and then came to an understanding of her pathology. The woman, he realized, was a workaholic, who worked day and night on her teaching and the twelve beautiful symphonies she had composed. She had no time for any other life. If she worked all night and then said she had spent the time playing cards, Mr. Brook thought, "it was as though she had managed to do both those things.

Through the lies, she lived vicariously." Despite his understanding, however, he decided he would have to confront her, to avoid
a problematic situation.

"Finland is a democracy," he said to her. "You could not have
possibly seen the King of Finland." Madame Zilensky responded
with "a sort of cornered horror. She had the look of one who watches
her whole interior world split open and disintegrate." He had succeeded in demolishing Madam Zilensky's major defense, her
means of making an empty life bearable, the motor that kept her
going, the structure that kept her from falling apart. Then Mr.
Brooks realized that her lying, though compulsive, was quite harmless, and felt like a murderer. He reneged and said faintly, "Yes.
The King of Finland. And was he nice?"

The ending of the story has an O. Henry twist. Mr. Brooks,
out of a barely acknowledged love for Madame Zilensky, takes
over her defense and in similar manner distorts reality. He has
"caught" her symptom in order to join her in her world.

This story should be required reading for every embryo psychotherapist, as an example of the harm that can be done by breaking down the defenses of a patient who is not ready to face the
truth.

4

TRUTH AND CONSEQUENCES

BRENDON GILL

S he had straight blond hair and a red mouth, and she was
lame. Every day she played golf and went swimming in the
center of a crowd of boys. Charles, sitting with his mother
on the hotel porch, watched her and nodded while his mother
repeated, "Isn't it extraordinary, a girl like that? I wonder what in
the world they see in her." Charles took to walking past the pool
during the morning as the girl and boys lay there side by side,
laughing. He listened carefully to her voice. It was low, unhurried,
forceful. So, he thought, was her language. Every other word
seemed to him to be "damn," "Hell," and worse. She spoke of
God, to whom Charles was preparing to dedicate his life, as if He
were a friend in the next block. "I swear to God," the girl said. "I
must have told you this one, for God's sake." Charles walked out of
the range of jokes that followed. He was eighteen and he was spending this last vacation with his mother before entering a seminary.
In eight more summers he would be a priest. The girl's language
sent sharp lightnings through him. He had never seen or heard
anyone like her before in his life.

One night after dinner, while his mother was upstairs swallow-

---

Truth and Consequences, by Brendon Gill. First appeared in THE NEW
YORKER MAGAZINE, 1941. Reprinted by permission of Holly Gill.

ing a pill, the girl sat down beside him on the hotel porch. Her lips were smiling, her eyes the color of her blue, open blouse. "We ought to know each other," she said. "You ought to join the rest of us at the pool."

"I'm with Mother."

The girl covered his hand with hers. "Well, for God's sake, you're old enough to swim by yourself, aren't you?"

Charles felt that he ought to explain before it was too late, before she said something he could never forget. "I'm going to be a priest," he said.

The girl kept smiling. "A priest? With a turn-around collar and everything?"

He nodded.

"So you can't come swimming with the gang?"

"That has nothing to do with it. I just thought I ought to tell you. I always do tell people."

"You can still come dancing with us if you want to?"

"Certainly."

"Could you take me to a movie if you want to?"

"Yes."

"I never met a boy who was going to be a priest. Could you take me out for a ride tonight if you wanted to?"

He said in relief, "We didn't bring our car."

"Oh, hell. I mean in my car. I mean just for example. I didn't say I'd go with you." She stared at him slowly from head to foot. "It would be funny, with a boy who was going to be a priest."

Fortunately, Charles thought, his mother would be coming downstairs at any moment now. She would make short shrift of the girl. "You oughtn't to keep swearing like that," he said.

He expected her to laugh, but she didn't. She ran her hand up and down the bare brown leg that was shorter than the other. "Like what?" she said.

"Like 'for God's sake.' That's taking the name of the Lord in vain. That's one of the Ten Commandments."

"I'm an awful damn fool," the girl said. "I talk like that to keep people from thinking about my leg. But I didn't know you were going to be a priest."

Charles wanted to get rid of her, but he didn't know how. He stood up and said, "I don't think you ought to worry about things like that. I hadn't even noticed."

She stood up beside him. Her eyes shone in the mountain light. "Oh, damn you, please don't lie to me," she said. "Of course you've noticed. But does it bother you? Does it make you want to stay away from me?"

"No," he said. "Oh, no."

She slipped her hand under his arm. "Thanks for saying that so nice and hard. I haven't asked anybody that in a long time.

Without having willed it, stupidly, Charles found himself walking the length of the porch beside the girl. Her blond hair touched the shoulder of his coat. It was difficult to tell, looking down at her, that she was lame. He bent his head to smell her perfume. "Tell me what you do," he said.

"You mean, bang, just like that, what do I do?"

"Not that you have to tell me."

"But I do. It's just that there aren't any surprises in me. I'm not beautiful or tormented—or not much tormented, I don't do anything. I got out of Walker's and I had a party and now I guess I'll be on the loose like this for a couple of years. Finally somebody may ask me to marry him, and quick like a fish I will. I hope I'll have sense enough for that. And I'll be terribly glad when I've done it. I'll try to be good about satisfying him, the way all those awful books say, and about having good kids for him, and all that."

Charles felt himself stumbling. She had told him everything about herself. She had told him the truth, which he hadn't wanted. They reached the end of the porch and stood facing the valley between the mountains. Two old men were playing croquet in the gathering darkness, the wooden mallets and balls knocking softly together, the white trousers moving like disembodied spirits across the lawn. Charles and the girl could hear, below them in the kitchen, the clatter of dishes being washed and stacked and the high, tired voices of the waitresses.

"Now talk about you," the girl said. "You think you want to be a priest?"

"Why—yes."

"It isn't just a vow your mother made while she was carrying you?"

Charles laughed, and was surprised at how easily he laughed. "Well," he said, "I guess Mother's always wanted me to be a priest, especially after Dad died. We went abroad then, Mother and I. We spent the summer in Rome. We had an audience with the Pope, the old one, a little man with thick glasses and a big ring. We got so we were going to Mass and even Communion every day. When we came back to this country I started in at a Catholic school. I liked it. I graduated this year. I'm going down to the seminary in the fall. I guess I'll like that, too."

"But isn't there more to it than that?" the girl said. "I'm not a Catholic—I'm not anything—but don't you have to have some kind of a call, bells ringing, something like that?"

"You mean a vocation. Yes. Well, I guess I have a vocation all right."

"But what is it? How can you be sure?"

Charles gripped the railing of the porch. He had never been able to answer that question. He remembered kneeling beside his mother's bed, month after month, year after year. "Don't you feel it, darling?" his mother had whispered. "Don't you feel how wonderful it will be? Don't you feel how God wants you?" Charles had told himself finally that he was able to answer that question. The next day his mother, dabbing her eyes, had said, "Here's my boy, Father Duffy. I'm giving him to you." And Father Duffy had said, "Ah, you're an example to Irish mothers everywhere. Are you sure you want to come with us, boy?" "Yes, Father, I do," Charles had said, watching his mother. He had spoken an answer, written an answer, lived an answer, but he had never believed it. He had been waiting to believe it. Now he heard himself saying, for the first time, "No, I can't be sure."

The girl said, "Then you're not going to be a priest. You mustn't be. Why are you so damned afraid to fact the truth?"

Charles saw his mother walking heavily along the porch. He studied her as if she were a stranger. What an enormous old woman she was, and how strong she was, and how she had driven him! He took the girl's hand. It was cool and unmoving. He felt the porch floor trembling under his mother's approach.

⁓⌁⁓

Truth and Consequences, by Brendan Gill, is a deceptively simple little story about the contagiousness of truth. It could easily be called A *Moment of Insight.* Charles, a young man of 18, is planning to enter a seminary in order to become a priest. He is on vacation with his mother, with whom he spent all his time. On one occasion when his mother was upstairs taking a pill, Charles was approached by a young lady whom he had noticed with a group of boys at the pool. When she invited him to join them, he said, "I'm with Mother." She confronted him with the truth, "Well, for God's sake, you're old enough to swim by yourself, aren't you?" She continued the honest tone of their conversation, as she told him the sad, unenviable facts of her own life.

Then she asked him why he wanted to be a priest and if he was sure. Charles experienced a flood of memories in which his mother had convinced him that he wanted to be a priest. Then for the first time he was able to admit to himself that he wasn't so sure.

"Then you are not going to be a priest. You mustn't be. Why are you so damned afraid to face the truth?"asked this authentic young woman who was able to face the reality of her own lameness and the probability of a dreary future. Her absolute candor gave Charles the courage to experience his own feelings, much as it happens in a good psychotherapy session. As a result, he was able to take a giant step out of his symbiotic relationship with his mother toward a future in which he could become his own man.

5

ROSES, RHODODENDRON

ALICE ADAMS

One dark and rainy Boston spring of many years ago, I spent all my after-school and evening hours in the living room of our antique-crammed Cedar Street flat, writing down what the Ouija board said to my mother. My father, a spoiled and rowdy Irishman, a sometime engineer, had run off to new Orleans with a girl, and my mother hoped to learn from the board if he would come back. Then, one night in May, during a crashing black thunderstorm (my mother was both afraid and much in awe of such storms), the board told her to move down South, to North Carolina, taking me and all the antiques she had been collecting for years, and to open a store in a small town down there. That is what we did, and shortly thereafter, for the first time in my life, I fell violently and permanently in love: with a house, with a family of three people, and with an area of countryside.

Perhaps too little attention is paid to the necessary preconditions of "falling in love"—I mean the state of mind or place that

---

precedes one's first sight of the loved person (or house or land). In my own case, I remember the dark Boston afternoons as a precondition of love. Later on, for another important time, I recognized boredom in a job. And once the fear of growing old.

In the town that she had chosen, my mother, Margot (she picked out her own name, having been christened Margaret), rented a small house on a pleasant back street. It had a big surrounding screened-in-porch, where she put most of the antiques, and she put a discreet sign out in the front yard: "Margot—Antiques." The store was open only in the afternoons. In the mornings and on Sundays, she drove around the countryside in our ancient and spacious Buick, searching for trophies among the area's country stores and farms and barns. (She is nothing if not enterprising; no one else down there had thought of doing that before.)

Although frequently embarrassed by her aggression—she thought nothing of making offers for furniture that was in use in a family's rooms—I often drove with her during those first few weeks. I was excited by the novelty of the landscape. The red clay banks that led up to the thick pine groves, the swollen brown creeks half hidden by flowering tangled vines. Bare, shaded yards from which rose gaunt, narrow houses. Chickens that scattered, barefoot children who stared at our approach.

"Hello there. I'm Mrs. John Kilgore—Margot Kilgore—and I'm interested in buying old furniture. Family portraits. Silver."

Margot a big brassily bleached blonde in a pretty flowered-silk dress and high-heeled patent sandals. A hoarse and friendly voice. Me a scrawny, pale, curious girl, about ten, in a blue linen dress with smocking across the bodice. (Margot has always had a passionate belief in good clothes, no matter what.)

On other days, Margot would say, "I'm going to look over my so-called books. Why don't you go for a walk or something, Jane?"

And I would walk along the sleepy, leafed-over streets, on the unpaved sidewalks, past houses that to me were as inviting and as interesting as unread books, and I would try to imagine what went on inside. The families. Their lives.

The main street, where the stores were, interested me least. Two-story brick buildings—dry-goods stores, with dentists' and lawyers' offices above. There was also a drugstore, with round marble tables and wire-backed chairs, at which wilting ladies sipped at their Cokes (this was to become a favorite haunt of Margot's). I preferred the civic monuments; a pre-revolutionary Episcopal chapel of yellowish cracked plaster, and several tall white statues to the Civil War dead—all of them quickly overgrown with ivy or Virginia creeper.

These were the early 1940s, and in the next few years the town was to change enormously. Its small textile factories would be given defense contracts (parachute silk); a Navy preflight school would be established at a neighboring university town. But at that moment it was a sleeping village. Untouched.

My walks were not a lonely occupation, but Margot worried that they were, and for some curious reasoning led her to believe that a bicycle would help. (Of course, she turned out to be right.) We went to Sears, and she bought me a big new bike—blue, with balloon tires—on which I began to explore the outskirts of town and countryside.

The house I fell in love with was about a mile out of town, on top of a hill. A small stone bank that was all overgrown with tangled roses led up to its yard, and pink and white roses climbed up a trellis to the roof of the front porch—the roof on which, later, Harriet and I used to sit and exchange our stores of erroneous sexual information. Harriet Farr was the daughter of the house. On one side of the house, there was what looked like a newer wing, with a bay window and a long side porch, below which the lawn sloped down to some flowering shrubs. There was a yellow rosebush, rhododendron, a plum tree, and beyond were woods—pines, and oak and cedar trees. The effect was rich and careless, generous and somewhat mysterious. I was deeply stirred.

As I was observing all this, from my halted bike on the dusty white hilltop, a small plump woman, very erect, came out of the front door and went over to a flower bed below the bay window.

She sat down very stiffly. (Emily, who was Harriet's mother, had some terrible, never diagnosed trouble with her back; she generally wore a brace.) She was older than Margot, with very beautiful white hair that was badly cut in that butchered 1930s way.

From the first, I was fascinated by Emily's obvious dissimilarity to Margot. I think I was also somehow drawn to her contradictions—the shapeless body held up with so much dignity, even while she was sitting in the dirt. The lovely chopped-off hair. (There were even greater contradictions, which I learned of later—she was a Virginia Episcopalian who always voted for Norman Thomas, a feminist who always delayed meals for her tardy husband.)

Emily's hair was one of the first things about the Farr family that I mentioned to Margot after we became friends, Harriet and Emily and I, and I began to spend most of my time in that house.

"I don't think she's ever dyed it," I said, with almost conscious lack of tact.

Of course, Margot was defensive. "I wouldn't dye mine if I thought it would be a decent color on its own."

But by that time Margot's life was also improving. Business was fairly good, and she had finally heard from my father, who began to send sizable checks form New Orleans. He had found work with an oil company. She still asked the Ouija board if she would see him again, but her question was less obsessive.

The second time I rode past that house, there was a girl sitting on the front porch, reading a book. She was about my age. She looked up. The next time I saw her there, we both smiled. And the time after that (a Saturday morning in later June) she got up and slowly came out to the road, to where I had stopped, ostensibly to look at the view—the sweep of fields, the white highway, which wound down to the thick greenery bordering the creek, the fields and trees that rose in dim and distant hills.

"I've got a bike exactly like that," Harriet said indifferently, as though to deny the gesture of having come out to meet me.

For years, perhaps beginning then, I used to seek my antithesis in friends. Inexorably following Margot, I was becoming a big blonde, with some of her same troubles. Harriet was cool and dark, with long, gray eyes. A girl about to be beautiful.

"Do you want to come in? We've got some lemon cake that's pretty good."

Inside, the house was cluttered with odd mixtures of furniture. I glimpsed a living room, where there was a shabby sofa next to a pretty "antique" table. We walked through a dining room that contained a decrepit mahogany table surrounded with delicate fruitwood chairs. (I had a horrifying moment of imagining Margot there, with her accurate eye—making offers in her harsh Yankee voice.) The walls were crowded with portraits and with nineteenth-century oils of bosky landscapes. Books overflowed from rows of shelves along the walls. I would have moved in at once.

We took our lemon cake back to the front porch and ate it there, overlooking that view. I can remember its taste vividly. It was light and tart and sweet, and a beautiful lemon color. With it, we drank cold milk, and then we had seconds and more milk, and we discussed what we liked to read.

We were both at an age to begin reading grown-up books, and there was some minor competition between us to see who had read more of them. Harriet won easily, partly because her mother reviewed books for the local paper, and had brought home [John] Steinbeck, Thomas Wolf, Virginia Woolf, and Elizabeth Bowen. But we also found in common an enthusiasm for certain novels about English children. (Such snobbery!)

"It's the best cake I've ever had!" I told Harriet. I had already adopted something of Margot's emphatic style.

"It's very good," Harriet said judiciously. Then, quite casually, she added, "We could ride our bikes out to Laurel Hill."

We soared dangerously down the winding highway. At the bridge across the creek, we stopped and turned onto a narrow, rutted dirt road that followed the creek through woods as dense and as alien as a jungle would have been—thick pines with low sweeping branches, young leafed-out maples, peeling tall poplars, elms, brambles, green masses of honeysuckle. At times, the road was impassable, and we had to get off our bikes and push them along, over crevices and ruts, through mud or sand. And with all that we kept up our somewhat stilted discussion of literature.

"I love Virginia Woolf!"

"Yes, she's very good. Amazing metaphors."

I thought Harriet was an extraordinary person—more intelligent, more poised, and prettier than any girl of my age I had ever known. I felt that she could become anything at all—a writer, an actress, a foreign correspondent (I went to a lot of movies). And I was not entirely wrong: she eventually became a sometimes-published poet.

We came to a small beach, next to a place where the creek widened and ran over some shallow rapids. On the other side, large gray rocks rose steeply. Among the stones grew isolated, twisted trees, and huge bushes with thick green leaves. The laurel of Laurel Hill. Rhododendron. Harriet and I took off our shoes and waded into the warmish water. The bottom squished under our feet, making us laugh, like the children we were, despite all our literary talk.

Margot was also making friends. Unlike me, she seemed to seek her own likeness, and she found a sort of kinship with a woman named Dolly Murray, a rich widow from Memphis who shared many of Margot's superstitions—fear of thunderstorms, faith in the Ouija board. About ten years older than Margot, Dolly still dyed her hair red; she was a noisy, biased, generous woman. They drank gin and gossiped together, they met for Cokes at the drugstore, and sometimes they drove to a neighboring town to have dinner in a restaurant (in those days, still a daring thing for unescorted ladies to do).

I am sure that the Farrs, outwardly a conventional family, saw me as a neglected child. I was so available for meals and overnight visits. But that is not how I experienced my life—I simply felt free. And an important thing to be said about Margot as a mother is that she never made me feel guilty for doing what I wanted to do.

And of how many mothers can that be said?

There must have been a moment of "meeting" Emily, but I have forgotten it. I remember only her gentle presence, a soft voice, and my own sense of love returned. Beautiful white hair, dark deep eyes, and a wide mouth, whose corners turned and moved to express whatever she felt—amusement, interest, boredom, pain. I have never since seen such a vulnerable mouth.

I amused Emily; I almost always made her smile. She must have seen me as something foreign—a violent, enthusiastic Yankee (I used forbidden words, like "God" and "damn"). Very unlike the decorous young Southern girl that she must have been, that Harriet almost was.

She talked to me a lot; Emily explained to me things about the South that otherwise I would not have picked up. "Virginians feel superior to everyone else, you know," she said in her gentle (Virginian) voice. Some people in my family were quite shocked when I married a man from North Carolina and came down here to live. And a Presbyterian at that! Of course, that's nowhere near as bad as a Baptist, but only Episcopalians really count." This was all said lightly, but I knew that some part of Emily agreed with the rest of her family.

"How about Catholics?" I asked her, mainly to prolong the conversation. Harriet was at the dentist's, and Emily was sitting at her desk answering letters. I was perched on the sofa near her, and we both faced the sweeping green view. But since my father, Johnny Kilgore, was a lapsed Catholic, it was not an entirely frivolous question. Margot was a sort of Christian Scientist (her own sort).

"We hardly know any Catholics," Emily laughed, and then she sighed. "I do sometimes still miss Virginia. You know, when we drive up there I can actually feel the difference as we cross the state line. I've met a few people from South Carolina," she went on, "and I understand that people down there feel the same way Virginians do." (Clearly, she found this unreasonable.)

"West Virginia? Tennessee?"

"They don't seem Southern at all. Neither do Florida and

Texas—not to me."

("Dolly says that Mrs. Farr is a terrible snob," Margot told me, inquiringly.

"In a way," I spoke with a new diffidence that I was trying to acquire from Harriet.

"Oh.")

Once, I told Emily what I had been wanting to say since my first sight of her. I said, "Your hair is so beautiful. Why don't you let it grow?"

She laughed, because she usually laughed at what I said, but at the same time she looked surprised, almost startled. I understood that what I had said was not improper but that she was totally unused to attentions of that sort from anyone, including herself. She didn't think about her hair. In a puzzled way, she said, "Perhaps I will."

Nor did Emily dress like a woman with much regard for herself. She wore practical, seersucker dresses and sensible, low shoes. Because her body had so little shape, no indentations (this must have been at least partly due to the back brace), I was surprised to notice that she had pretty, shapely legs. She wore little or no makeup on her sun-and-weathered face.

And what of Lawrence Farr, the North Carolina Presbyterian for whom Emily had left her people and her state? He was a small, precisely made man, with fine dark features (Harriet looked very much like him). A lawyer, but widely read in literature, especially the English nineteenth century. He had a courtly manner, and sometimes a wicked tongue; melancholy eyes, and an odd, sudden, ratchety laugh. He looked ten years younger than Emily; the actual difference was less than two.

"Well," said Margot, settling into a Queen Anne chair—a new antique—on our porch one stifling hot July morning. "I heard some really interesting gossip about your friends."

Margot had met and admired Harriet, and Harriet liked her, too—Margot made Harriet laugh, and she praised Harriet's fine brown hair. But on some instinct (I am not sure whose) the parents had not met. Very likely, Emily, with her Southern social antennae, had somehow sensed that this meeting would be a mistake.

That morning, Harriet and I were going on a picnic in the woods to the steep rocky side of Laurel Hill, but I forced myself to listen, or half listen, to Margot's story.

"Well, it seems that some years ago Lawrence Farr fell absolutely madly in love with a beautiful young girl—in fact, the orphaned daughter of a friend of his. Terribly romantic. Of course, she loved him, too, but he felt so awful and guilty that they never did anything about it."

I did not like this story much; it made me obscurely uncomfortable, and I think that at some point both Margot and I wondered why she was telling it. Was she pointing out imperfections in my chosen other family? But I asked, in Harriet's indifferent voice, "He never kissed her?"

"Well, maybe. I don't know. But of course everyone in town knew all about it, including Emily Farr. And with her back! Poor woman," Margot added somewhat piously but with real feeling, too.

I forgot the story readily at the time. For one thing, there was something unreal about anyone as old as Lawrence Farr "falling in love." But looking back to Emily's face, Emily looking at Lawrence, I can see that pained watchfulness of a woman who has been hurt, and by a man who could always hurt her again.

In those days, what struck me most about the Farrs was their extreme courtesy to each other—something I had not seen before. Never a harsh word. (Of course I did not know then about couples who cannot afford a single harsh word.)

Possibly because of the element of danger (very slight—the slope was gentle), the roof over the front porch was one of the places Harriet and I liked to sit on warm summer nights when I was invited to stay over. There was a country silence, invaded at intervals by summer country sounds; the strangled croak of tree frogs from down in the glen; the crazy baying of a distant hound. There, in the heavy scent of roses, on the scratchy shingles, Harriet and I talked about sex.

"A girl I know told me that if you do it a lot your hips get very wide."

"My cousin Duncan says it makes boys strong if they do it."

"It hurts women a lot—especially at first. But I knew this girl from Santa Barbara, and she said that out there they say Filipinos can do it without hurting."

"Colored people do it a lot more than whites."

"Of course, they have all those babies. But in Boston so do Catholics!"

We are seized with hysteria. We laugh and laugh, so that Emily hears and calls up to us. "Girls, why haven't you-all gone to bed?" But her voice is warm and amused—she likes having us laughing up there.

And Emily liked my enthusiasm for lemon cake. She teased me about the amounts of it I could eat, and she continued to keep me supplied. She was not herself much of a cook—their maid, a young black girl named Evelyn, did most of the cooking.

Once, but only once, I saw the genteel and opaque surface of that family shattered—saw those three people suddenly in violent opposition to each other, like shards of splintered glass. (But what I have forgotten is the cause—what brought about this terrible explosion?)

The four of us, as so often, were seated at lunch. Emily was at what seemed to be the head of the table. At her right hand was the small silver bell that summoned Evelyn to clear, or to bring a new course. Harriet and I across from each other, Lawrence across from Emily. (There was always a tentativeness about Lawrence's posture. He could have been an honored guest, or a spoiled and favorite child.) We were talking in an easy way. I have a vivid recollection only of words that began to careen and gather momentum, to go out of control. Of voices raised. Then Harriet rushes from the room. Emily's face reddens dangerously, the corners of her mouth twitch downward, and Lawrence, in an exquisitely icy voice, begins to lecture me on the virtues of reading Trollope. I am supposed to help him pretend that nothing has happened, but I can hardly hear what he is saying. I am in shock.

The sudden unleashing of violence, that exposed depth of terrible emotions might have suggested to me that the Farrs were not quite as I had imagined them, not the impeccable family in my mind—but it did not. I was simply and terribly—and selfishly—upset, and hugely relieved when it all seemed to have passed over.

During that summer, the Ouija board spoke only gibberish to Margot, or it answered direct questions with repeated evasions.

"Will I ever see Johnny Kilgore again in this life?"

"Yes no perhaps."

"Honey, that means you've got no further need of the board, not right now. You've got to think everything out with your own heart and instincts," Dolly said.

Margot seemed to take her advice. She resolutely put the board away, and she wrote to Johnny that she wanted a divorce.

I had begun to notice that these days, on these sultry August nights, Margot and Dolly were frequently joined on their small excursions by a man named Larry—a jolly, red-faced man who was in real estate and who reminded me considerably of my father.

I said as much to Margot, and was surprised at her furious reaction. "They could not be more different, they are altogether opposite. Larry is a Southern gentleman. You just don't pay any attention to anyone but those Farrs."

A word about Margot's quite understandable jealousy of the Farrs. Much later in my life, when I was unreasonably upset at the attachment of one of my own daughters to another family (unreasonable because her chosen group were all talented musicians, as she was), a wise friend told me that we all could use more than one set of parents—our relations with the original set are too intense, and need dissipating. But no one, certainly not silly Dolly, was around to comfort Margot with this wisdom.

The summer raced on. ("Not without dust and heat," Lawrence several times remarked, in his private ironic voice.) The roses wilted on the roof and on the banks next to the road. The creek dwindled, and beside it honeysuckle leaves lay limply on the vines. For weeks, there was no rain, and then, one afternoon, there came a dark torrential thunderstorm. Harriet and I sat on the side porch and watched its violent start—the black clouds seeming to rise from the horizon, the cracking, jagged streaks of lightning, the heavy, welcome rain. And, later, the clean smell of leaves and grass and damp earth.

Knowing that Margot would be frightened, I thought of calling her, and then remembered that she would not talk on the phone during storms. And that night she told me, "The phone rang and rang, but I didn't think it was you, somehow."

"No."

"I had the craziest idea that it was Johnny. Be just like him to pick the middle of a storm for a phone call."

"There might not have been a storm in New Orleans."

But it turned out that Margot was right.

"The next day, when I rode up to the Farrs' on my bike, Emily was sitting out in the grass where I had first seen her. I went and squatted beside her there. I thought she looked old and sad, and partly to cheer her I said, "You grow the most beautiful flowers I've ever seen."

She sighed, instead of smiling as she usually did. She said, "I seem to have turned into a gardener. When I was a girl, I imagined that I would grow up to be a writer, a novelist, and that I would have at least four children. Instead, I grow flowers and write book reviews."

I was not interested in children. "You never wrote a novel?"

She smiled unhappily. "No. I think I was afraid that I wouldn't come up to Trollope. I married rather young, you know."

And at that moment Lawrence came out of the house, immaculate in white flannels.

He greeted me, and said to Emily, "My dear, I find that I have some rather late appointments in Hillsboro. You won't wait dinner if I'm a trifle late?"

(Of course she would; she always did.)

"No. Have a good time," she said, and she gave him the anxious look that I had come to recognize as the way she looked at Lawrence.

Soon after that, a lot happened very fast. Margot wrote to Johnny (again) that she wanted a divorce, that she intended to marry Larry. (I wonder if this was ever true.) Johnny telephoned—not once but several times. He told her that she was crazy, that he had a great job with some shipbuilders near San Francisco—a defense contract. He would come to get us, and we would all move out there. Margot agreed. We would make a new life. (Of course, we never knew what happened to the girl.)

I was not as sad about leaving the Farrs and that house, that town, those woods as I was to be later, looking back. I was excited about San Francisco, and I vaguely imagined that someday I would come back and that we would all see each other again. Like parting lovers, Harriet and I promised to write each other every day.

And for quite a while we did write several times a week. I wrote about San Francisco—how beautiful it was: the hills and pastel houses, the sea. How I wished that she could see it.

She wrote about school and friends. She described solitary bike rides to places we had been. She told me what she was reading.

In high school, our correspondence became more generalized. Responding perhaps to the adolescent mores of the early 1940s, we wrote about boys and parties; we even competed in making ourselves sound "popular." The truth (my truth) was that I was sometimes popular, often not. I had, in fact, a stormy adolescence. And at that time I developed what was to be a long-lasting habit. As I reviewed a situation in which I had been ill-advised or impulsive, I would reenact the whole scene in my mind with Harriet in my own role—Harriet, cool and controlled, more intelligent, prettier: even more than I wanted to see her again, I wanted to *be*

Harriet.

Johnny and Margot fought a lot and stayed together, and gradually a sort of comradeship developed between them in our small house on Russian Hill.

I went to Stanford, where I half-heartedly studied history. Harriet was at Radcliffe, studying American literature, writing poetry.

We lost touch with each other.

Margot, however, kept up with her old friend Dolly, by means of Christmas card and Easter notes, and Margot thus heard a remarkable piece of news about Emily Farr. Emily "up and left Lawrence without so much as a by-your-leave," said Dolly, and went to Washington, D.C. to work in the Folger Library. This news made me smile all day. I was so proud of Emily. And I imagined that Lawrence would amuse himself, that they would both be happier apart.

By accident, I married well—that is to say, a man whom I still like and enjoy. Four daughters came at uncalculated intervals, and each is remarkably unlike her sisters. I named one Harriet, although she seems to have my untidy character.

From time to time, over the years, I would see a poem by Harriet Farr, and I always thought it was marvelous, and I meant to write her. But I distrusted my reaction. I had been (I was) so deeply fond of Harriet (Emily, Lawrence, that house and land) and besides, what would I say—"I think your poem is marvelous?" (I have since learned that this is neither an inadequate nor an unwelcome thing to say to writers.) Of course, the true reason for not writing was that there was too much to say. Dolly wrote to Margot that Lawrence was drinking "all over the place." He was not happier without Emily. Harriet, Dolly said, was traveling a lot. She married several times and had no children. Lawrence developed emphysema, and was in such bad shape that Emily quit her job and came back to take care of him—whether because of feelings of guilt or duty or possibly affection, I didn't know. He died, lingeringly and miserably, and Emily, too, died a few years later—at least partly from exhaustion, I would imagine.

Then, at last, I did write Harriet, in care of the magazine in which I had last seen a poem of hers. I wrote a clumsy, gusty letter, much too long, about shared pasts, landscapes, the creek. All that. And as soon as I had mailed it I began mentally rewriting, seeking more elegant pose.

When for a long time I didn't hear from Harriet, I felt worse and worse, cumbersome, misplaced—as too often in life I had felt before. It did not occur to me that an infrequently staffed magazine could be at fault.

Months later, her letter came—from Rome, where she was then living. Alone, I gathered. She said that she was writing it at the moment of receiving mine. It was a long, emotional, and very moving letter, out of character for the Harriet that I remembered (or had invented).

She said, in part, "It was really strange, all that time when Lawrence was dying, and God! So long! And as though 'dying' were all that he was doing—Emily, too, although we didn't know that—all that time the picture that moved me most, in my mind, that moved me to tears, was not of Lawrence and Emily but of you and me. On our bikes at the top of the hill outside our house. Going somewhere. And I first thought that that picture simply symbolized something irretrievable, the lost and irrecoverable past, as Lawrence and Emily would be lost. And I'm sure that was partly it."

"But they were so extremely fond of you—in fact, you are a rare area of agreement. They missed you, and they talked about you for years. It's a wonder that I wasn't jealous, and I think I wasn't, only because I felt included in their affection for you. They liked me best with you.

"Another way to say this would be to say that we were all three a little less crazy and isolated with you around, and God knows, happier."

An amazing letter, I thought. It was enough to make me take a long look at my whole life, and to find some new colors there.

A postscript: I showed Harriet's letter to my husband, and he said, "How odd. She sounds so much like you."

~~∽∾~~

Roses, Rhododendon, by Alice Adams, is a story about a deep friendship between two young adolescent girls, which helped both of
them in the business of growing up. The writer tells how the young
heroine fell in love "with a house, a family of three, and with an
area of countryside." It was a "love affair" which was to leave permanent results on the personalities of both girls. Adams writes,
"Too little is paid to the necessary preconditions of falling in love."
Theodore Reik, a famed psychoanalyst, wrote that being in love is
a little psychosis, that people fall in love to rescue themselves from
a devastating emotional state. His insight is borne out by the youthful protagonist during the dreadful "dark, rainy Boston summer,"
when "her father had run off to New Orleans with a girl" and she
spent most of her time on the Ouija board trying to find out, ostensibly for her mother, if he was going to return.

Adolescence is a time of identity crisis, when young people
need to try out different roles to find the right "fit" for their future
development. To do so satisfactorily requires different models: one's
parents, no matter how good, are not sufficient to answer the need.
This was particularly true for the heroine of the story, who, living
alone with her abandoned mother, desperately hungered for another kind of person and living situation to show her the way. The
moment she came upon the Farrs' house, she knew she had found
what she needed. Harriet's mother Emily was gentle and kind,
and radiated "a sense of love returned," in contrast to Margot, her
own brash mother, a crude business woman insensitive to her
daughter's needs.

Without a respected model, it is very frightening to grow up,
rather like trying to build a house without a blueprint. Seemingly
a girl of impeccable family, Harriet appeared prettier, more intelligent and poised than any girl the protagonist had ever known.

She felt Harriet could become anything she wanted to. A perfect role model, she provided footsteps in which her friend could follow. "As I reviewed a situation in which I had been ill-advised or impulsive," she said, "I would reenact the whole scene in my mind with Harriet in my own role.... Even more than I wanted to see her again, I wanted to *be* Harriet." Because Harriet taught her how to be.

Adolescents need a friend who in many ways are like themselves, as well as one they can emulate. "I've got a bike exactly like that," was Harriet's first remark to her about-to-be new friend. They were also very different in that Harriet was "cool, controlled, more intelligent, prettier." Yet, when the heroine got a letter from Harriet in their adulthood, her husband said, "How odd. She sounds so much like you." Harriet evidently used her friend as a role model, much as her friend used her.

6

A COMPLICATED NATURE

WILLIAM TREVOR

At a party once Attridge overheard a woman saying he gave her the shivers. "Vicious-tongued," this woman, a Mrs. de Paul, had said. "Forked like a serpent's."

It was true, and he admitted it to himself without apology, though "sharp" was how he preferred to describe the quality the woman had referred to. He couldn't help it if his quick eye had a way of rooting out other people's defects and didn't particularly bother to search for virtues.

Sharp about other people, he was sharp about himself as well: Confessing his own defects, he found his virtues tedious. He was kind and generous to the people he chose as his friends, and took it for granted that he should be. He was a tidy man, but took no credit for that since being tidy was part of his nature. He was meticulous about his dress, and he was cultured, being particularly keen on opera—especially the operas of Wagner—and on Velasquez. He had developed his own good taste, and was proud of the job he had made of it.

A man of fifty, with hair that had greyed and spectacles with fine, colourless rims, he was given to slimming, for the weight he had gained in middle age rounded his face and made it pinker than he cared for: vanity was a weakness in him.

Attridge had once been married. In 1952 his parents had died, his father in February and his mother in November. Attridge had been their only child and had always lived with them. Disliking— or so he then considered—the solitude their death left him in, he married in 1953 a girl named Bernice Golder, but this most unfortunate conjunction had lasted only three months. "Nasty dry old thing," his ex-wife had screamed at him on their honeymoon in Siena, and he had enraged her further by pointing out that nasty and dry he might be but old he wasn't. "You were never young," she had replied more calmly than before. "Even as a child you must have been like dust." That wasn't so, he tried to explain: the truth was that he had a complicated nature. But she didn't listen to him.

Attridge lived alone now, existing comfortably on profits from the shares his parents had left him. He occupied a flat in a block, doing all his own cooking and taking pride in the small dinner parties he gave. His flat was just as his good taste wished it to be. The bathroom was tiled with blue Italian tiles, his bedroom severe and male, the hall warmly rust. His sitting room, he privately judged, reflected a part of himself that did not come into the open, a mysterious element that even he knew little about and could only guess at. He'd saved up for the Egyptian rugs, scarlet and black and brown, on the waxed oak boards. He'd bought the first one in 1959 and each year subsequently had contrived to put aside his January and February Anglo-American Telegraph dividends until the floor was covered. He'd bought the last one a year ago.

On the walls of the room there was pale blue hessian, a background for his four tiny Velasquez drawings, and for the Toulouse-Lautrec drawing and the Degas, and the two brown charcoal studies, school of Michelangelo. There was a sofa and a sofa-table, authenticated Sheraton, and a Regency table in marble and gold that he had almost made up his mind to get rid of, and some

Staffordshire figures. There was drama in the decoration and arrangement of the room, a quite flamboyant drama that Attridge felt was related to the latent element in himself, part of his complicated nature.

"I'm hopeless in an emergency," he said in this room one afternoon, speaking with off-putting asperity into his ivory-coloured telephone. A woman called Mrs. Matara, who lived in the flat above his, appeared not to hear him. "Something has gone wrong," you see, she explained in an upset voice, adding that she'd have to come down. She then abruptly replaced the receiver.

It was an afternoon in late November. It was raining, and already—at half-past three—twilight had settled in. From a window of his sittingroom Attridge had been gazing at all this when his telephone rang. He'd been looking at the rain dismally falling and lights going on in other windows and at a man, five stories down, sweeping sodden leaves from the concrete forecourt of the block of flats. When the phone rang he'd thought it might be his friend, old Mrs. Harcourt-Egan. He and Mrs. Harcourt-Egan were to go together to Persepolis in a fortnight's time and there were still some minor arrangements to be made, although the essential booking had naturally been completed long since. It had been a considerable surprise to hear himself addressed by name in a voice he had been quite unable to place. He'd greeted Mrs. Matara once or twice in the lift and that was all: she and her husband had moved into the flats only a year ago.

"I do so apologize," Mrs. Matara said when he opened the door to her. Against his will he welcomed her into the hall and she, knowing the geography of the flat since it was the same as her own, made for the sitting room. "It's really terrible of me," she said, "only I honestly don't know where to turn." She spoke in a hushed and agitated manner, and he sighed as he followed her, resolving to point out when she revealed what her trouble was that Chamberlain, the janitor, was employed to deal with tenants' difficulties. She was just the kind of woman to make a nuisance of herself with a neighbor, you could tell that by looking at her. It irritated him that he hadn't sized her up better when he'd met her in the lift.

She was a woman of about the same age as himself, he guessed, small and thin and black-haired, though the hair, he also guessed, was almost certainly dyed. He wondered if she might be Jewish, which would account for her emotional condition: she had a Jewish look, and the name was presumably foreign. Her husband, whom he had also only met in the lift, had a look about the eyes which Attridge now said to himself might well have been developed in the clothing business. Of Austrian origin, he hazarded, or possibly even Polish. Mrs. Matara had an accent of some kind, although her English appeared otherwise to be perfect. She was not out of the top drawer, but then people of the Jewish race rarely were. His own ex-wife, Jewish also, had most certainly not been.

Mrs. Matara sat on the edge of a chair he had bought for ninety guineas fifteen years ago. It was also certainly Sheraton, a high-back chair with slim arms in inlaid walnut. He'd had it resprung and upholstered and covered in striped pink, four different shades.

"A really ghastly thing," Mrs. Matara said, "a terrible thing has happened in my flat, Mr. Attridge."

She'd fused the whole place. She couldn't turn a tap off. The garbage disposal unit had failed. His ex-wife had made a ridiculous fuss when, because of her own stupidity, she'd broken her electric hair-curling apparatus on their honeymoon. Grotesque she'd looked with the plastic objects in her hair; he's been relieved that they didn't work.

"I can't really mend anything," he said. "Chamberlain is there for that, you know."

She shook her head. She was like a small bird sitting there, a wren or an undersized sparrow. A Jewish sparrow, he said to himself, pleased with this analogy. She had a handkerchief between her fingers, a small piece of material, which she now raised to her face. She touched her eyes with it, one after the other. When she spoke again she said that a man had died in her flat.

"Good heavens!"

"It's terrible!" Mrs. Matara. "Oh, my God!"

He poured a brandy from a Georgian decanter that Mrs. Harcourt-Egan had given him three Christmases ago, after their trip to Sicily. She'd given him a pair, in appreciation of what she called his kindness on that holiday. The gesture had been far too generous; the decanters were family heirlooms, and he'd done so little for her in Sicily apart from reading *Northanger Abbey* aloud when she'd had her stomach upset.

The man, he guessed, was not Mr. Matara. No woman would say that a man had died, meaning her husband. Attridge imagined that a window cleaner had fallen off a step-ladder. Quite clearly, he saw in his mind's eye a step-ladder standing at a window and the body of a man in white overalls huddled on the ground. He even saw Mrs. Matara bending over the body, attempting to establish its condition.

"Drink it all," he said, placing the brandy glass in Mrs. Matara's right hand, hoping as he did so that she wasn't going to drop it.

She didn't drop it. She drank the brandy and then, to Attridge's surprise, held out the glass in a clear request for more.

"Oh, if only you would," she said as she poured it, and he realized that while he'd been pouring the first glass, while his mind had been wandering back to the occasion in Sicily and the gift of the decanters, his guest had made some demand on him.

"You could say he was a friend," Mrs. Matara said.

She went on talking. The man who had died had died of a heart attack. The presence of his body in her flat was an embarrassment. She told a story of a love affair that had begun six years ago. She went into details: she had met the man at a party given by people called Morton, the man had been married, what point was there in hurting a dead man's wife? What point was there in upsetting her own husband, when he need never know? She rose and crossed the room to the brandy decanter. The man, she said, had died in the bed that was her husband's as well as hers.

"I wouldn't have come here—oh, God, I wouldn't have come here if I hadn't been desperate." Her voice was shrill. She was

nearly hysterical. The brandy had brought out two patches of brightness in her cheeks. Her eyes were watering again, but she did not
now touch them with the handkerchief. The water ran, over the
bright patches, trailing mascara and other make-up with it.

"I sat for hours," she cried. "Well, it seemed like hours. I sat
there looking at him. We were both without a stitch, Mr. Attridge."

"Good heavens!"

"I didn't feel anything at all. I didn't love him, you know. All I
felt was, Oh God, what a thing to happen!"

Attridge poured himself some brandy, feeling the need for it.
She reminded him quite strongly of his ex-wife, not just because
of the Jewish thing or the nuisance she was making of herself but
because of the way she had so casually said they'd been without a
stitch. In Siena on their honeymoon his ex-wife had constantly
been flaunting her nakedness, striding about their bedroom. "The
trouble with you," she'd said, "you like your nudes on canvas."

"You could say he was a friend," Mrs. Matara said again. She
wanted him to come with her to her flat. She wanted him to help
her dress the man. In the name of humanity, she was suggesting,
they should falsify the location of death.

He shook his head, outraged, and considerably repelled. The
images in his mind were most unpleasant. There was the naked
male body, dead on a bed. There was Mrs. Matara and himself
pulling the man's clothes on to his body, struggling because *rigor
mortis* was setting in.

"Oh God, what can I do?" cried Mrs. Matara.

"I think you should telephone a doctor, Mrs. Matara."

"Oh, what use is a doctor, for God's sake? The man's dead."

"It's usual—"

"Look, one minute we're having lunch—an omelette, just as
usual, and salad and Pouilly Fuisse—and the next minute the poor
man's dead."

"I thought you said—"

"Oh, you know what I mean. 'Lovely, oh darling, lovely,' he
said, and then he collapsed. Well, I didn't know he'd collapsed. I

mean, I didn't know he was dead. He collapsed just like he always collapses. Post-coital—"

"I'd rather not hear—"

"Oh, for Jesus' sake!" She was shouting. She was on her feet, again approaching the decanter. Her hair had fallen out of the pins that held it and was now disheveled. Her lipstick was blurred, some of it even seared her chin. She looked most unattractive, he considered.

"I cannot help you in this matter, Mrs. Matara," he said as firmly as he could. "I can telephone a doctor—"

"Will you for God's sake stop about a doctor!"

"I cannot assist you with your friend, Mrs. Matara."

"All I want you to do is to help me put his clothes back on. He is too heavy, I can't do it myself—"

"I'm very sorry, Mrs. Matara."

"And slip him down here. The lift is only a few yards—"

"That's quite impossible."

She went close to him, with her glass considerably replenished. She pushed her face at his in a way that he considered predatory. He was aware of the smell of her scent, and of another smell that he couldn't prevent himself from thinking must be the smell of sexual intercourse: he had read of this odour in a book by Ernest Hemingway

"My husband and I are a contentedly married couple," she said, with her lips so near to his that they almost touched. "That man upstairs has a wife who doesn't know a thing, an innocent woman. Don't you understand such things, Mr. Attridge? Don't you see what will happen if the dead body of my lover is discovered in my husband's bed? Can't you visualize the pain it'll cause?"

He moved away. It was a long time since he had felt so angry and yet he was determined to control his anger. The woman knew nothing of civilized behavior or she wouldn't have come bursting into the privacy of a stranger like this, with preposterous and unlawful suggestions. The woman, for all he knew, was unbalanced.

"I'm sorry," he said in what he hoped was an icy voice. "I'm sorry, but for a start I do not see how you and your husband could possibly be a contentedly married couple."

"I'm telling you we are. I'm telling you my lover was content-edly married also. Listen, Mr. Attridge." She approached him again, closing in on him like an animal. "Listen, Mr. Attridge; we met for physical reasons, once a week at lunchtime. For five years, ever since the Mortons' party, we've been meeting once a week, for an omelette and Pouilly Fuisse, and sex. It had nothing to do with our two marriages. But it will now: that woman will see her mar-riage as a failure now. She'll mourn it for the rest of her days, when she should be mourning her husband. I'll be divorced."

"You should have thought of that—"

She hit him with her left hand. She hit him on the face, the palm of her hand stinging the pink, plump flesh.

"Mrs. Matara!"

He had meant to shout her name, but instead his protest came from him in a shrill whisper. Since his honeymoon no one had struck him, and he recalled the fear he's felt when he'd been struck then, in the bedroom in Siena. "I could kill you," his ex-wife had shouted at him. "I'd kill you if you weren't dead already."

"I must ask you to go, Mrs. Matara," he said in the same shrill whisper. He cleared his throat. "At once," he said, in a more suc-cessful voice.

She shook her head. She said he had no right to tell her what she should have thought of. She was upset as few women can ever be upset: in all decency and humanity it wasn't fair to say she should have thought of that. She cried out noisily in his sitting-room and he felt that he was in a nightmare. It had all the horror and absur-dity and violence of a nightmare: the woman standing in front of him with water coming out of her eyes, drinking his brandy and hitting him.

She spoke softly then, not in her violent way. She placed the brandy glass on the marble surface of the Regency table and stood there with her head down. He knew she was still weeping even though he couldn't see her face and couldn't hear any noise coming from her. She whispered that she was sorry.

"Please forgive me, Mr. Attridge. I'm very sorry."

He nodded, implying that he accepted this apology. It was all very nasty, but for the woman it was naturally an upsetting thing to happen. He imagined, when a little time had passed, telling the story to Mrs. Harcourt-Egan and to others, relating how a woman, to all intents and purposes a stranger to him, had telephoned him to say she was in need of assistance and then had come down from her flat with this awful tragedy to relate. He imagined himself describing Mrs. Matara, how at first she'd seemed quite smart and then had become disheveled, how she'd helped herself to his brandy and had suddenly struck him. He imagined Mrs. Hartcourt-Egan and others gasping when he said that. He seemed to see his own slight smile as he went on to say that the woman could not be blamed. He heard himself saying that the end of the matter was that Mrs. Matara just went away.

But in fact Mrs. Matara did not go away. Mrs. Matara continued to stand, weeping quietly.

"I'm sorry, too," he said, feeling that the words, with the finality he'd slipped into them, would cause her to move to the door of the sittingroom.

"If you'd just help me," she said, with her head still bent. "Just to get his clothes on."

He began to reply. He made a noise in his throat.

"I can't manage," she said, "on my own."

She raised her head and looked across the room at him. Her face was blotched all over now, with make-up and tears. Her hair had fallen down a little more, and from where he stood Attridge thought he could see quite large areas of grey beneath the black. A rash of some kind, or it might have been flushing, had appeared on her neck.

"I wouldn't bother you," she said, "if I could manage on my own." She would have telephoned a friend, she said, except there wouldn't be time for a friend to get to the block of flats. "There's very little time, you see," she said.

It was then, while she spoke those words, that Attridge felt the first hint of excitement. It was the same kind of excitement that he experienced just before the final curtain of *Tannhauser*, or whenever, in the Uffizi, he looked upon Credi's Annunciation. Mrs. Matara was a wretched, unattractive creature who had been conducting a typical hole-in-the-corner affair and had received her just rewards. It was hard to feel sorry for her, and yet for some reason it was harder not to. The man who had died had got off scot-free, leaving her to face the music on her own. "You're inhuman," his ex-wife had said in Siena. "You're incapable of love. Or sympathy, or anything else." She'd stood there in her underclothes, taunting him.

"I'll manage," Mrs. Matara said, moving towards the door.

He did not move himself. She'd been so impatient, all the time in Siena. She didn't even want to sit in the square and watch the people. She's been lethargic in the cathedral. All she'd ever wanted was to try again in bed. "You don't like women," she'd said, sitting up with a glass of Brolio in her hand, smoking a cigarette.

He followed Mrs. Matara into the hall, and an image entered his mind of the dead man's wife. He saw her as Mrs. Matara had described her, as an innocent woman who believed herself faithfully loved. He saw her as a woman with fair hair, in a garden, simply dressed. She had borne the children of the man who now lay obscenely dead, she had made a home for him and had entertained his tedious business friends, and now she was destined to suffer. It was a lie to say he didn't like women, it was absurd to say he was incapable of sympathy.

Once more he felt a hint of excitement. It was a confused feeling now, belonging as much in his body as in his mind. In a dim kind of way he seemed again to be telling the story to Mrs. Harcourt-Egan or to someone else. Telling it, his voice was quiet. It spoke of the compassion he had suddenly felt for the small unattractive Jewish woman and for another woman, a total stranger whom he'd never even seen. "A moment of truth," his voice explained to Mrs. Harcourt-Egan and others. "I could not pass these women by."

He knew it was true. The excitement he felt had to do with sympathy, and the compassion that had been engendered in it. His complicated nature worked in that way; there had to be drama, like the drama of a man dead in a bed, and the beauty of being unable to pass the women by, as real as the beauty of the Madonna of the Meadow. With her cigarette and her Brolio, his ex-wife wouldn't have understood that in a million years. In their bedroom in Siena she had expected something ordinary to take place, an act that rats performed.

Never in his entire life had Attridge felt as he felt now. It was the most extraordinary, and for all he knew the most important occasion in his life. As though watching a play, he saw himself assisting the dead, naked man into his clothes. It would be enough to put his clothes on, no need to move the body from one flat to another, enough to move it from the bedroom, "We put it in the lift and left it there," his voice said, still telling the story. "'No need,' I said to her, 'to involve my flat at all.' She agreed; she had no option. The man became a man who'd had a heart attack in a lift, a traveling salesman, God knows who he was."

The story was beautiful. It was extravagant and flamboyant, incredible almost, like all good art. Who really believed in the Madonna of the Meadow, until jolted by the genius of Bellini? *The Magic Flute* was an impossible occasion, until Mozart's music charged you like an electric current.

"Yes. Mr. Attridge?"

He moved towards her, fearing to speak lest his voice emerged from him in the shrill whisper that had possessed it before. He nodded at Mrs. Matara, agreeing in this way to assist her.

Hurrying through the hall and hurrying up the stairs because one flight of stairs was quicker than the lift, he felt the excitement continuing in his body. Actually it would be many months before he could tell Mrs. Harcourt-Egan or anyone else about any of it. It seemed, for the moment at least, to be entirely private.

"What was he?" he asked on the stairs in a whisper.

"Was?"

"Professionally." He was impatient, more urgent now than she. "Salesman or something, was he?

She shook her head. Her friend had been a dealer in antiques, she said.

Another Jew, he thought. But he was pleased because the man could have been on his way to see him, since dealers in antiques did sometimes visit him. Mrs. Matara might have said to the man, at another party given by the Mortons or anywhere else you liked, that Mr. Attridge, a collector of pictures and Staffordshire china, lived in the flat below hers. She could have said to Attridge that she knew a man who might have stuff that would interest him and then the man might have telephoned him, and he'd have said come round one afternoon. And in the lift the man collapsed and died.

She had her latchkey in her hand, about to insert it into the lock of her flat door. Her hand was shaking. Surprising himself, he gripped her arm, preventing it from completing the action with the key. "Will you promise me," he said, "to move away from these flats? As soon as you conveniently can?"

"Of course, of course! How could I stay?"

"I'd find it awkward, meeting you about the place, Mrs. Matara. Is that a bargain?

"Yes, yes."

She turned the key in the lock. They entered a hall that was of the exact proportions of Attridge's but different in other ways. It was a most unpleasant hall, he considered, with bell chimes in it, and two oil paintings that appeared to be the work of some emergent African, one being of Negro children playing on crimson sand, the other of a Negro girl with a baby at her breast.

"Oh, God!" Mrs. Matara cried, turning suddenly, unable to proceed. She pushed herself at him, her sharp head embedding itself in his chest, her hands grasping the jacket of his grey suit.

"Don't worry," he said, dragging his eyes away from the painting of the children on the crimson sand. One of her hands had ceased to grasp his jacket and had fallen into one of his. It was cold and had a fleshless feel.

"We have to do it," he said, and for a second he saw himself again as he would see himself in retrospect: standing with the Jewish woman in her hall, holding her hand to comfort her.

While they still stood there, just as he was about to propel her forward, there was a noise.

"My God," whispered Mrs. Matara.

He knew she was thinking that her husband had returned, and he thought the same himself. Her husband had come back sooner than he usually did. He had found a corpse and was about to find his wife holding hands with a neighbor in the hall.

"Hey!" a voice said.

"Oh no!" cried Mrs. Matara, rushing forward into the room that Attridge knew was her sitting room.

There was the mumble of another voice, and then the sound of Mrs. Matara's tears. It was a man's voice, but the man was not her husband. The atmosphere which came from the scene wasn't right for that.

"There now," the other voice was saying in the sitting room. "There now, there now."

The noise of Mrs. Matara's weeping continued, and the man appeared at the door of the sittingroom. He was fully dressed, a sallow man, tall and black-haired, with a beard. He'd guessed what had happened, he said, as soon as he heard voices in the hall. He'd guessed that Mrs. Matara had gone to get help. In an extremely casual way he said he was really quite all right, just a little groggy due to the silly blackout he'd had. Mrs. Matara was a customer of his, he explained, he was in the antique business. "I just passed out," he said. He smiled at Attridge. He'd had a few silly blackouts recently and despite what his doctor said about there being nothing to worry about he'd have to be more careful. Really embarrassing, it was, plopping out in a client's sitting room.

Mrs. Matara appeared in the sitting room doorway. She leaned against it, as though requiring its support. She giggled through her tears and the man spoke sharply to her, forgetting she was meant to be his client. He warned her against becoming hysterical.

"My god, you'd be hysterical," Mrs. Matara cried, "if you'd been through all that kerfuffle."

"Now, now—"

"For Christ's sake, I thought you were a goner. Didn't I?" she cried, addressing Attridge without looking at him and not waiting for him to reply. "I rushed downstairs to this man here. I was in a frightful state. Wasn't I?"

"Yes."

"We were going to put your clothes on and dump you in his flat."

Attridge shook his head, endeavouring to imply that this was not accurate, that he'd never have agreed to the use of his flat for this purpose. But neither of them was paying any attention to him. The man was looking embarrassed, Mrs. Matara was grim.

"You should damn well have told me if you were having black-outs."

"I'm sorry," the man said. "I'm sorry you were troubled," he said to Attridge. "Please forgive Mrs. Matara."

"Forgive *you*, you mean!" she cried. "Forgive you for being such a damn fool!"

"Do try to pull yourself together, Miriam."

"I tell you, I thought you were dead."

"Well. I'm not. I had a little blackout—"

"Oh, for Christ's sake, stop about your wretched blackout!"

The way she said that reminded Attridge very much of his ex-wife. He'd had a headache once, he remembered, and she'd protested in just the same impatient tone of voice, employing almost the same words. She'd married again, of course—a man called Saunders in ICI.

"At least be civil," the man said to Mrs. Matara.

They were two of the most unpleasant people Attridge had ever come across. It was a pity the man hadn't died. He'd run to fat and was oily, there was a shower of dandruff on his jacket. You could see his stomach was straining his shirt, one of the shirt buttons had actually given way.

"Well, thank you," Mrs. Matara said, approaching Attridge with her right hand held out.

She said it gracelessly, as a duty. The same hand had struck him on the face and later had slipped for comfort into one of his. It was hard and cold when he shook it, with the same fleshless feel as before. "We still have a secret," Mrs. Matara said. She smiled at him in her dutiful way, without displaying interest in him.

The man had opened the halldoor of the flat. He stood by it, smiling also, anxious for Attridge to go.

"This afternoon's a secret," Mrs. Matara murmured, dropping her eyes in a girlish pretense. "All this," she said, indicating her friend. "I'm sorry I hit you."

"Hit him?"

"When we were upset. Downstairs. I hit him." She giggled, apparently unable to help herself.

"Great God!" The man giggled also.

"It doesn't matter," Attridge said.

But it did matter. The secret she spoke of wasn't worth having because it was sordid and nothing else. It was hardly the kind of thing he's wish to tell Mrs. Harcourt-Egan or anyone else.

Yet the other story might even have reached his ex-wife. He imagined her hearing it, and her amazement that a man whom she'd once likened to dust had in the cause of compassion falsified the circumstances of a death. He couldn't imagine the man his ex-wife had married doing such a thing, or Mrs. Matara's husband, or the dandruffy man who now stood by the door of the flat. Such men would have been frightened out of their wits.

"Goodbye," she said.

"Goodbye," the man said, smiling at the door.

Attridge wanted to say something. He wanted to linger for a moment longer and to mention his ex-wife. He wanted to tell them what he had never told another soul, that his ex-wife had done terrible things to him. He disliked all Jewish people, he wanted to say, because of his ex-wife and her lack of understanding. Marriage repelled him because of her. It was she who had made him vicious-tongued. It was she who had embittered him.

He looked from one face to the other. They would not understand and they would not be capable of making an effort, as he had when faced with the woman's predicament. He had always been a little on the cold side, he knew that well. But his ex-wife might have drawn on the other aspects of his nature and dispelled the coldness. Instead of displaying all that impatience, she might have cosseted him and accepted his complications. The love she sought would have come in its own good time, as sympathy and compassion had eventually come that afternoon. Warmth was buried deep in some people, he wanted to say to the two faces in the hall, but he knew that, like his ex-wife, the faces would not understand.

As he went he heard the click of the door behind him and imagined a hushed giggling in the hall. He would be feeling like a prince if the man had really died.

A *Complicated Nature*, by William Trevor, like Anne Tyler's *Teenage Wasteland,* is as insightful as a psychiatric case study. It is a perfect picture of an anal sadistic character structure which is eloquently and accurately described as "Vicious-tongued....Forked like a serpent's." The protagonist Attridge preferred to refer to this quality in himself as "sharp," saying defensively that he "couldn't help it if he had a way of rooting out other people's defects and didn't particularly bother to search for virtues." When his ex-wife screamed at him on their honeymoon that he was "a nasty dry old thing," Attridge answered that he merely had "a complicated nature." Anyway, "It was she who had made him vicious-tongued. It was she who had embittered him."

A character structure such as Attridge's is listed in the Diagnostic and Statistical Manuel of Mental Disorders (3ʳᵈ Edition), American Psychiatric Association, Washington, D.C., 1980, under the category of Compulsive Personality Disorder (pp. 326–328). According to it, such individuals suffer from a restricted ability to express warmth and tender emotions, are unduly conventional, serious, and formal. They are likely to be stingy with emotions and rarely give compliments or gifts. His ex-wife had screamed that he was inhuman and incapable of love or sympathy. Although Attridge congratulated himself for finally developing compassion and sympathy for his troubled neighbor, in truth he agreed to help her largely in order to be able to describe his "warmth and compassion" to Mrs. Harcourt-Egan, his only real friend. His exhibitionistic drive was strong, and he enjoyed looking at his "productions."

Preoccupation with rules and order interfere with the ability of people like Attridge to "grasp the big picture." They insist that others submit to their way of doing things, and are unaware of the feelings this behavior elicits. A man who disliked women, Attridge found sex, along with other bodily functions, distasteful, and apparently was impotent. All his wife had wanted to do on their honeymoon was "to try *again* in bed." He was critical of his neighbor's sexual behavior and completely unable to empathize with her dreadful dilemma. "You should have thought of that," he told her, as she mourned the death of both her marriage and her lover who had been struck down while they were having sex.

According to the psychoanalytic theory of psychosexual stages, Attridge was fixated at the anal sadistic level of development. Such people have never recovered from faulty toilet training in which, typically, they were forced to give up their anal "treasures" before they were ready. His ex-wife had likened him to dust, a brilliant comment on an anal character. As a result of early traumatic experiences with toilet training, people like Attridge tenaciously hold on to their feelings and possessions all their lives. Many collectors suffer from this type of pathology. True to form, Attridge was a collector of antiques, which he felt compelled to hoard even when he no longer wanted them. He was also an anti-Semite and a snob.

Like children proud of their anal precocity, Attridge held himself "above it all." Not he, *he* was not guilty of disgusting human frailties! Unlike his Jewish neighbor, *he* was a "tidy" person, being tidy was simply "part of his nature." Nevertheless, as a result of his experience with Mrs. Matara and the revival of memories of his ex-wife, some real growth did take place in Mr. Attridge, whose ego ideal now included "warmth and compassion."

On another level, it is interesting to note how often Attridge referred to his ex-wife's comments in so short a story. He did so not because he loved her—such a person is not capable of love—but because he never got over the rage, wounded pride, and narcissistic injury he felt at her rejection. Unsympathetic to the feelings of others, he was very sensitive indeed to slights against himself.

7

A DISTANT EPISODE

PAUL BOWLES

The September sunsets were at their reddest the week the Professor decided to visit Ain Tadouirt, which is in the warm country. He came down out of the high, flat region in the evening by bus, with two small overnight bags full of maps, sun lotions and medicines. Ten years ago he had been in the village for three days; long enough to establish a fairly firm friendship with the cafe-keeper, who had written him several times during the first year after his visit, if never since. "Hassan Ramani," the professor said over and over, as the bus bumped downward through ever warmer layers of air. Now facing the flaming sky in the west, and now facing the sharp mountains, the car followed the dusty trail down the canyons into air which began to smell of other things besides the endless ozone of the heights: orange blossoms, pepper, sunbaked excrement, burning olive oil, rotten fruit. He closed his eyes happily and lived for an instant in a purely olfactory world. The distant past returned—what part of it, he could not decide.

The chauffeur, whose seat the Professor shared, spoke to him without taking his eyes from the road. "*Vous etes geologue?*"

"A geologist? Ah, no! I am a linguist."

"There are no languages here. Only dialects."

"Exactly. I'm making a survey of variations on Moghrebi."

The chauffeur was scornful. "Keep on going south," he said. "You'll find some languages you never heard of before."

As they drove through the town gate, the usual swarm of urchins rose up out of the dust and ran screaming beside the bus. The Professor folded his dark glasses, put them in his pocket; and as soon as the vehicle had come to a standstill he jumped out, pushing his way through the indignant boys who clutched at his luggage in vain, and walked quickly into the Grand Hotel Saharien. Out of its eight rooms there were two available—one facing the market and the other, a smaller and cheaper one, giving onto a tiny yard full of refuse and barrels, where two gazelles wandered about. He took the smaller room, and pouring the entire pitcher of water into the tin basin, began to wash the grit from his face and ears. The afterglow was nearly gone from the sky, and the pinkness in objects was disappearing, almost as he watched. He lit the carbide lamp and winced at its odor.

After dinner the Professor walked slowly through the streets to Hassan Ramani's café, whose back room hung hazardously out above the river. The entrance was very low, and he had to bend down slightly to get in. A man was tending the fire. There was one guest sipping tea. The *qaouaji* tried to make him take a seat at the other table in the front room, but the Professor walked airily ahead into the back room and sat down. The moon was shining through the reed latticework and there was not a sound outside but the occasional distant bark of a dog. He changed tables so he could see the river. It was dry, but there was a pool here and there that reflected the bright night sky. The *qaouaji* came in and wiped off the table.

"Does this café still belong to Hassan Ramani?" he asked him in the Moghrebi he had taken four years to learn.

The man replied in bad French, "He is deceased."

"Deceased?" repeated the Professor, without noticing the absurdity of the word. "Really? When?"

"I don't know," said the *qaouaji*. "One tea?"

"Yes. But I don't understand."

The man was already out of the room, fanning the fire. The Professor sat still, feeling lonely, and arguing with himself that to do so was ridiculous. Soon the *qaouaji* returned with the tea. He paid him and gave him an enormous tip, for which he received a grave bow.

"Tell me," he said, as the other started away. "Can one still get those little boxes made from camel udders?"

The man looked angry. "Sometimes the Reguibat bring in those things. We do not buy them here." Then insolently, in Arabic: "And why a camel-udder box?"

"Because I like them," retorted the professor. And then because he was feeling a little exalted, he added, "I like them so much I want to make a collection of them, and I will pay you ten francs for every one you can get me."

"*Khamstache*," said the *qaouaji*, opening his left hand rapidly three times in succession.

"Never. Ten."

"Not possible. But wait until later and come with me. You can give me what you like. And you will get camel-udder boxes if there are any."

He went out into the front room, leaving the professor to drink his tea and listen to the growing chorus of dogs that barked and howled as the moon rose higher into the sky. A group of customers came into the front room and sat talking for an hour or so. When they had left, the *qaouaji* put out the fire and stood in the doorway putting on his burnous. "Come," he said.

Outside in the street there was very little movement. The booths were all closed and the only light came from the moon. An occasional pedestrian passed, and grunted a brief greeting to the *qaouaji*.

"Everyone knows you," said the professor, to cut the silence between them.

"Yes."

"I wish everyone knew me," said the Professor, before he realized how infantile such a remark must sound.

"No one knows you," said his companion gruffly.

They had come to the other side of the town, on the promontory above the desert, and through a great rift in the wall the professor saw the white endlessness, broken in the foreground by dark spots of oasis. They walked through the opening and followed a winding road between rocks, downward toward the nearest small forest of palms. The professor thought: "He may cut my throat. But his café—he would surely be found out."

"Is it far?" he asked, casually.

"Are you tired?" countered the *qaouaji*.

"They are expecting me back at the Hotel Saharien," he lied.

"You can't be there and here," said the *qaouaji*.

The professor laughed. He wondered if it sounded uneasy to the other.

"Have you owned Ramani's café long?"

"I work there for a friend." The reply made the professor more unhappy than he had imagined it would.

"Oh. Will you work tomorrow?"

"That is impossible to say."

The professor stumbled on a stone, and fell, scraping his hand. The *qaouaji* said, "Be careful."

The sweet black odor of rotten meat hung in the air suddenly.

"Agh!" said the professor, choking. "What is it?"

The *qaouaji* had covered his face with his burnous and did not answer. Soon the stench had been left behind. They were on flat ground. Ahead the path was bordered on each side by a high mud wall. There was no breeze and the palms were quite still, but behind the walls was the sound of running water. Also, the odor of human excrement was almost constant as they walked between the walls.

The professor waited until he thought it seemed logical for him to ask with a certain degree of annoyance: "But where are we going?"

"Soon," said the guide, pausing to gather some stones in the ditch.

"Pick up some stones," he advised. "Here are bad dogs."

"Where?" asked the professor, but he stooped and got three large ones with pointed edges.

They continued very quietly. The walls came to an end and the bright desert lay ahead. Nearby was a ruined marabout, with its tiny doe only half standing, and the front wall entirely destroyed. Behind it were clumps of stunted, useless palms. A dog came running crazily toward them on three legs. Not until it got quite close did the professor hear its steady low growl. The *qaouaji* let fly a large stone at it, striking it square in the muzzle. There was a strange snapping of jaws and the dog ran sideways in another direction, falling blindly against rocks and scrambling haphazardly about like an injured insect.

Turning off the road, they walked across the earth strewn with sharp stones, past the little ruin, through the trees, until they came to a place where the ground dropped abruptly away in front of them.

"It looks like a quarry," said the professor, resorting to French for the word "quarry," whose Arabic equivalent he could not call to mind at the moment. The *qaouaji* did not answer. Instead he stood still and turned his head, as if listening. And indeed, from somewhere down below, but very far below, came the faint sound of a low flute. The *qaouaji* nodded his head slowly several times. Then he said: "The path begins here. You can see it well all the way. The rock is white and the moon is strong. So you can see well. I am going back now and sleep. It is late. You can give me what you like."

Standing there at the edge of the abyss which at each moment looked deeper, with the dark face of the *qaouaji* framed in its moonlit burnous close to his own face, the professor asked himself exactly what he felt. Indignation, curiosity, fear, perhaps, but most of all relief and the hope that this was not a trick, the hope that the *qaouaji* would really leave him alone and turn back without him.

He stepped back a little from the edge, and fumbled in his pocket for a loose note, because he did not want to show his wal-

let. Fortunately there was a fifty-franc bill there, which he took out
and handed to the man. He knew the *qaouaji* was pleased, and so
he paid no attention when he heard him saying: "It is not enough.
I have to walk a long way home and there are dogs...."

"Thank you and good night," said the professor, sitting down
with his legs drawn up under him and lighting a cigarette. He felt
almost happy.

"Give me only one cigarette," pleaded the man.

"Of course," he said, a bit curtly, and he held up the pack.

The *qaouaji* squatted close beside him. His face was not pleasant to see. "*What is it?*" thought the professor, terrified again, as he
held out his lighted cigarette toward him.

The man's eyes were almost closed. It was the most obvious
registering of concentrated scheming the professor had ever seen.
When the second cigarette was burning, he ventured to say to the
still-squatting Arab: "What are you thinking about?"

The other drew on his cigarette deliberately, and seemed about
to speak. Then his expression changed to one of satisfaction, but
he did not speak. A cool wind had risen in the air, and the Professor shivered. The sound of the flute came up from the depths below at intervals, sometimes mingled with the scraping of nearby
palm fronds one against the other. "*These people are not primi-
tives,*" the professor found himself saying in his mind.

"Good," said the *qaouaji*, rising slowly. "Keep your money. Fifty
francs is enough. It is an honor." Then he went back into French:
"*Ti m'as qu'a discendre, to' droit.*" He spat, chuckled (or was the
professor hysterical?), and strode away quickly.

The professor was in a state of nerves. He lit another cigarette,
and found his lips moving automatically. They were saying, "Is
this a situation or a predicament? This is ridiculous." He sat very
still for several minutes, waiting for a sense of reality to come to
him. He stretched out on the hard, cold ground and looked up at
the moon. It was almost like looking straight at the sun. If he shifted
his gaze a little at a time, he could make a string of weaker moons
across the sky. "Incredible," he whispered. Then he sat up quickly

and looked about. There was no guarantee that the *qaouaji* really
had gone back to town. He got to his feet and looked over the edge
of the precipice. In the moonlight the bottom seemed miles away.
And there was nothing to give it scale; not a tree, not a house, not
a person....He listened for the flute, and heard only the wind going by his ears. A sudden violent desire to run back to the road
seized him, and he turned and looked in the direction the *qaouaji*
had taken. At the same time he felt softly of his wallet in his breast
pocket. Then he spat over the edge of the cliff. Then he made
water over it, and listened intently, like a child. This gave him the
impetus to start down the path into the abyss. Curiously enough,
he was not dizzy. But prudently he kept from peering to his right,
over the edge. It was a steady and steep downward climb. The
monotony of it put him into a frame of mind not unlike that which
had been induced by the bus ride. He was murmuring "Hassan
Ramani" again, repeatedly and in rhythm. He stopped, furious
with himself for the sinister overtones the name now suggested to
him. He decided he was exhausted from the trip. "And the walk,"
he added.

It occurred to him that he ought to ask himself why he was
doing this irrational thing, but he was intelligent enough to know
that since he was doing it, it was not so important to probe for
explanations at that moment.

Suddenly the earth was flat beneath his feet. He had reached
the bottom sooner than he expected. He stepped ahead distrustfully still, as if he expected another treacherous drop. It was so
hard to know in this uniform, dim brightness. Before he knew what
had happened the dog was upon him, a heavy mass of fur trying to
push him backwards, a sharp nail rubbing down his chest, a straining of muscles against him to get the teeth into his neck. The professor thought, "*I refuse to die this way.*" The dog fell back; it looked
like an Eskimo dog. As it sprang again, he called out, very loud:
"Ay!" It fell against him, there was a confusion of sensations and a
pain somewhere. There was also the sound of voices very near to
him, and he could not understand what they were saying. Some-

thing cold and metallic was pushed brutally against his spine as
the dog still hung for a second by his teeth from a mass of clothing
and perhaps flesh. The Professor knew it was a gun, and he raised
his hands, shouting in Moghrebi: "Take away the dog!" But the
gun merely pushed him forward, and since the dog, once it was
back on the ground, did not leap again, he took a step ahead. The
gun kept pushing; he kept taking steps. Again he heard voices, but
the person directly behind him said nothing. People seemed to be
running about; it sounded that way, at least. For his eyes, he discovered, were still shut tight against the dog's attack. He opened
them. A group of men was advancing toward him. They were
dressed in the black clothes of the Reguibat. "The Reguiba is a
cloud across the face of the sun." "When the Reguiba appears the
righteous man turns away." In how many shops and market places
he had heard these maxims uttered banteringly among friends.
Never to a Reguiba, to be sure, for these men do not frequent
towns. They send a representative in disguise, to arrange with shady
elements there for the disposal of captured goods. "*An opportunity,*" he thought quickly, "*of testing the accuracy of such statements.*" He did not doubt for a moment that the adventure would
prove to be a kind of warning which in retrospect would be half
sinister, half farcical.

    Two snarling dogs came running from behind the oncoming
men and threw themselves at his legs. He was scandalized to note
that no one paid any attention to this breach of etiquette. The gun
pushed him harder as he tried to sidestep the animals' noisy assault. Again he cried: "The dogs! Take them away!" The gun shoved
him forward with great force and he fell, almost at the feet of the
crowd of men facing him. The dogs were wrenching at his hands
and arms. A boot kicked them aside, yelping, and then with increased vigor it kicked the professor in the hip. Then came a chorus of kicks from different sides, and he was rolled violently about
on the earth for a while. During this time he was conscious of
hands reaching into his pockets and removing everything from
them. He tried to say: "You have all my money; stop kicking me!"

But his bruised facial muscles would not work; he felt himself pouting and that was all. Someone dealt him a terrific blow on the head, and he thought: "*Now at least I shall leave consciousness, thank Heaven.*" Still he went on being aware of the guttural voices he could not understand, and of being bound tightly about the ankles and chest. Then there was black silence that opened like a wound from time to time, to let in the soft, deep notes of the flute playing the same succession of notes again and again. Suddenly he felt excruciating pain everywhere—pain and cold. "So I have been unconscious after all," he thought. In spite of that, the present seemed only like a direct continuation of what had gone before.

It was growing faintly light. There were camels near where he was lying; he could hear their gurgling and their heavy breathing. He could not bring himself to attempt opening his eyes, just in case it should turn out to be impossible. However, when he heard someone approaching, he found that he had no difficulty in seeing. The man looked at him dispassionately in the gray, morning light. With one hand he pinched together the professor's nostrils. When the professor opened his mouth to breathe, the man swiftly seized his tongue and pulled on it with all his might. The professor was gagging and catching his breath; he did not see what was happening. He could not distinguish the pain of the brutal yanking from that of the sharp knife. Then there was an endless choking and spitting that went on automatically, as though he were scarcely a part of it. The word "operation" kept going through his mind; it calmed his terror somewhat as he sank back into darkness.

The caravan left sometime toward midmorning. The professor, not unconscious, but in a state of utter stupor, still gagging and drooling blood, was dumped doubled-up into a sack and tied at one side of a camel. The lower end of the enormous amphitheater contained a natural gate in the rocks. The camels, swift *mehara*, were lightly laden on this trip. They passed through single file, and slowly mounted the gentle slope that led up into the beginning of the desert. That night, at a stop behind some low hills, the men took him out, still in a state which permitted no thought, and over the dusty rags that remained of his clothing they fastened a series of curious belts made of the bottoms of tin cans strung together. One after another of these bright girdles was wired about his torso, his arms and legs, even across his face, until he was entirely within a suit of armor that covered him with its circular metal scales. There was a good deal of merriment during the decking-out of the professor. One man brought out a flute and a younger one did a not ungraceful caricature of an Ouled Nail executing a cane dance. The professor was no longer conscious; to be exact, he existed in the middle of the movements made by these other men. When they had finished dressing him the way they wished him to look, they stuffed some food under the tin bangles hanging over his face. Even though he chewed mechanically, most of it eventually fell out onto the ground. They put him back into the sack and left him there.

Two days later they arrived at one of their own encampments. There were women and children here in the tents, and the men had to drive away the snarling dogs they had left there to guard them. When they emptied the professor out of his sack there were screams of fright, and it took several hours to convince the women that he was harmless, although there had been no doubt from the start that he was a valuable possession. After a few days, they began to move on again, taking everything with them, and traveling only at night as the terrain grew warmer.

Even when all his wounds had healed and he felt no more pain, the professor did not begin to think again; he ate and defecated, and he danced when he was bidden, a senseless hopping up and down that delighted the children, principally because of the wonderful jangling racket it made. And he generally slept through the heat of the day among the camels.

Wending its way southeast, the caravan avoided all stationary civilization. In a few weeks they reached a new plateau, wholly wild and with a sparse vegetation. Here they pitched camp and remained, while the *mehara* were turned loose to graze. Everyone was happy here; the weather was cooler and there was a well only a few hours away on a seldom-frequented trail. It was here they conceived the idea of taking the professor to Fogara and selling him to the Touareg.

It was a full year before they carried out this project. By this time the professor was much better trained. He could do a hand-spring, make a series of fearful growling noises which had, nevertheless, a certain element of humor; and when the Reguibat removed the tin from his face they discovered he could grimace admirably while he danced. They also taught him a few basic obscene gestures which never failed to elicit delighted shrieks from the women. He was now brought forth only after especially abundant meals, when there was music and festivity. He easily fell in with their sense of ritual, and evolved an elementary sort of "program" to present when he was called for: dancing, rolling on the ground, imitating certain animals, and finally rushing toward the group in feigned anger, to see the resultant confusion and hilarity.

When three of the men set out for Fogara with him, they took four *mehara* with them, and he rode astride his quite naturally. No precautions were taken to guard him, save that he was kept among them, one man always staying at the rear of the party. They came within sight of the walls at dawn, and they waited among the rocks all day. At dusk the youngest started out, and in three hours he returned with a friend who carried a stout cane. They tried to put the professor through his routine then and there, but the man from Fogara was in a hurry to get back to town, so they all set out on the *mehara*.

In the town they went directly to the villager's home, where they had coffee in the courtyard sitting among the camels. Here the professor went into his act again, and this time there was prolonged merriment and much rubbing together of hands. An agreement was reached, a sum of money paid, and the Reguibat withdrew, leaving the professor in the house of the man with the cane, who did not delay in locking him into a tiny enclosure off the courtyard.

The next day was an important one in the professor's life, for it was then that pain began to stir again in his being. A group of men came to the house, among whom was a venerable gentleman, better clothed than those others who spent their time flattering him, setting fervent kisses upon his hands and the edges of his garments. This person made a point of going into classical Arabic from time to time, to impress the others, who had not learned a word of the Koran. Thus his conversation would run more or less as follows: "Perhaps at in Salah. The French there are stupid. Celestial vengeance is approaching. Let us not hasten it. Praise the highest and cast thine anathema against idols. With paint on his face. In case the police wish to look close." The others listened and agreed, nodding their heads slowly and solemnly. And the professor in his stall beside them listened, too. That is, he was *conscious* of the sound of the old man's Arabic. The words penetrated for the first time in many months. Noises, then: "Celestial vengeance is approaching." Then: "It is an honor. Fifty francs is enough. Keep your money. Good." And the *qaouaji* squatting near him at the edge of the precipice. Then "anathema against idols" and more gibberish. He turned over panting on the sand and forgot about it. But the pain had begun. It operated in a kind of delirium, because he had begun to enter into consciousness again. When the man opened the door and prodded him with his cane, he cried out in a rage, and everyone laughed.

They got him onto his feet, but he would not dance. He stood before them, staring at the ground, stubbornly refusing to move. The owner was furious, and so annoyed by the laughter of the others that he felt obliged to send them away, saying that he would await a more propitious time for exhibiting his property, because he dared not show his anger before the elder. However, when they had left he dealt the professor a violent blow on the shoulder with his cane, called him various obscene things, and went out into the street, slamming the gate behind him. He walked straight to the street of the Ouled Nail, because he was sure of finding the Reguibat there among the girls, spending the money. And there in a tent he found one of them still abed, while an Ouled Nail washed the tea glasses. He walked in and almost decapitated the man before the latter had even attempted to sit up. Then he threw his razor on the bed and ran out.

The Ouled Nail saw the blood, screamed, ran out of her tent into the next, and soon emerged from that with four girls who rushed together into the coffeehouse and told the *qaouaji* who had killed the Reguiba. It was only a matter of an hour before the French military police had caught him at a friend's house, and dragged him off to the barracks. That night the professor had nothing to eat, and the next afternoon, in the slow sharpening of his consciousness caused by increasing hunger, he walked aimlessly about the courtyard and the rooms that gave onto it. There was no one. In one room a calendar hung on the wall. The professor watched nervously, like a dog watching a fly in front of its nose. On the white paper were black objects that made sounds in his head. He heard them: "*Grande Epicerie du Sahel. Juin. Lundi, Mardi, Mercredi....*"

The tiny ink marks of which a symphony consists may have been made long ago, but when they are fulfilled in sound they become imminent and mighty. So a kind of music of feeling began to play in the professor's head, increasing in volume as he looked at the mud wall, and he had the feeling that he was performing what had been written for him long ago. He felt like weeping; he felt like roaring through the little house, upsetting and smashing the few breakable objects. His emotion got no further than this one overwhelming desire. So, bellowing as loud as he could, he attacked the house and its belongings. Then he attacked the door into the street, which resisted for a while and finally broke. He climbed through the opening made by the boards he had ripped apart, and still bellowing and shaking his arms in the air to make as loud a jangling as possible, he began to gallop along the quiet street toward the gateway of the town. A few people looked at him with great curiosity. As he passed the garage, the last building before the high mud archway that framed the desert beyond, a French soldier saw him. "*Tiens*," he said to himself, "a holy maniac."

Again it was sunset time. The professor ran beneath the arched gate, turned his face toward the red sky, and began to trot along the Piste d'In Salah, straight into the setting sun. Behind him, from the garage, the soldier took a potshot at him for good luck. The bullet whistled dangerously near the professor's head, and his yelling rose into an indignant lament as he waved his arms more wildly, and hopped high into the air at every few steps, in a access of terror.

The soldier watched a while, smiling, as the cavorting figure grew smaller in the oncoming evening darkness, and the rattling of the tin became a part of the great silence out there beyond the gate. The wall of the garage as he leaned against it still gave forth heat. left there by the sun, but even then the lunar chill was growing in the air.

A *Distant Episode* by Paul Bowles illustrates with blinding insight some of Freud's most consequential findings. I first read the story in college many years ago, and have been haunted by it ever since. In it, a professor was captured by renegades near Ain Tadouirt, where a horrendous incident occurred which illustrates everyman's most frightening nightmare. Although I have read and reread the story many times, I still approach the description of his torturous treatment with apprehension and leave it shaking, an experience I have never had in all my years of reading. The passage is perhaps the most horrible in all of literature. Bound tightly about his ankles and chest, the professor awoke from an unconscious state to hear the gurgling and heavy breathing of camels. A native approached and "looked at him dispassionately in the gray morning light." With one hand he pinched together the professor's nostrils. When the professor opened his mouth to breathe, the man swiftly seized his tongue and pulled on it with all his might. The professor was gagging and catching his breath; he did not see what was happening. He could not distinguish the pain of the brutal yanking from that of the sharp knife. Then there was an endless choking and spitting that went on automatically, as though he were scarcely a part of it. The word "operation" kept going through his mind. It calmed his terror somewhat as he sank back into darkness.

Underneath the actual horror of having one's tongue amputated, there must have lurked a deep unconscious dread in the mind of the professor, that of castration, which Freud believed is the bedrock of all psychic terror in men. As if to accentuate this aspect of castration, Bowles in his brilliance made the professor a linguist, who by losing his tongue also lost the organ with which he earned a living. His manhood, so as to speak, was castrated symbolically, as well as orally.

While many people in this day and age are aware of Freud's emphasis on castration anxiety, his concept of warding off pain and anxiety through mechanisms of defense is still relatively unfamiliar. An obsessive defense was customary for the professor, even in moments in which he experienced a normal amount of anxiety, as suggested by his repetition of "Hassan Ramani" over and over, as the bus bumped along, early in his visit to the strange land. What made so deep an impression on me that I still dwell on it 50 years later, however, is the manner in which the professor coped with acute terror. He removed himself psychologically from the scene, "as though he were scarcely a part of it." Then in an obsessional manner, the word "operation" ripped through his mind over and over again, as though giving a name to a horrifying experience can mitigate terror and make sense of it. In moments of panic in my own life, the professor's means of handling his anguish have entered my mind, and I found myself repeating "operation, operation" until the alarming circumstances were over. Thus I knew I had been warding off a state of mind which seemed too painful to bear.

While his obsessive defense helped the professor hold his panic at bay, he did so at the cost of all feelings and insight. This mindless state continued for a year or two until he heard an intelligent "gentleman" speak in classic Arabic. He was trying to impress the natives, who were listening and solemnly nodding their heads. The professor suddenly understood that the "gentleman" was speaking gibberish. The realization jolted him out of his state of denial, and gave him the first awareness of the reality of his situation. "It was then," Bowles writes, "that pain began to stir again in his being." In psychoanalysis such an insurgence of buried affect into consciousness is called "the return of the repressed."

When the professor further recognized that the little black objects on white paper on a calendar were familiar to him, his defenses shattered, and he was deluged by the feelings of terror and rage he had blocked out of his mind for so long. He was then flooded with the unspeakable horror of the situation. Bellowing as loudly as he could, he burst on a rampage through the house, destroying it and its belongings. Then smashing down the door,he galloped along the street toward the gateway of the town.

8

VERONA: A YOUNG WOMAN SPEAKS

HAROLD BRODKEY

I know a lot! I know about happiness! I don't mean the love of God, either. I mean I know the human happiness with the crimes in it.

Even the happiness of childhood.

I think of it now as a cruel, middle-class happiness.

Let me describe one time—one day, one night.

I was quite young, and my parents and I—there were just the three of us—were traveling from Rome to Salzburg, a journey across a quarter of Europe to be in Salzburg for Christmas, for the music and the snow. We went by train because planes were erratic, and my father wanted us to stop in half a dozen Italian towns and see paintings and buy things. It was absurd, but we were all three drunk with this; it was very strange: we woke every morning in a strange hotel, in a strange city. I would be the first to wake; and I would go to the window and see some tower or palace; and then I would wake my mother and be justified in my sense of wildness and belief and adventure by the way she acted, her sense of romance at being in a city as strange as I had thought it was when I had looked out the window and seen the palace or the tower.

We had to change trains in Verona, a darkish, smallish city at the edge of the Alps. By the time we got there, we'd bought and bought our way up the Italian peninsula. I was dizzy with shopping and new possessions. I hardly knew who I was, I owned so many new things. My reflection in any mirror or shopwindow was resplendently fresh and new, disguised even, glittering, I thought. I was seven or eight years old. It seemed to me we were almost in a movie or in the pages of a book: only the simplest and most light-filled words and images can suggest what I thought we were then. We went around shiningly: we shone everywhere. *Those clothes.* It's easy to buy a child. I had a new dress, knitted, blue and red, expensive as hell, I think; leggings, also red, a red loden-cloth coat with a hood and a knitted cap for under the hood; marvelous lined gloves; fur-lined boots and a fur purse or carryall, and a tartan skirt—and shirts and a scarf, and there was even more; a watch, a bracelet; more and more.

On the train we had private rooms, and Momma carried games in her purse and things to eat, and Daddy sang carols off-key to me; and sometimes I became so intent on my happiness I would suddenly be in real danger of wetting myself; and Momma, who understood such emergencies, would catch the urgency in my face; and she—a large, good-looking woman—would whisk me to a toilet with amazing competence and unstoppability, murmuring to me, "Just hold on for a while," and she would hold my hand while I did it.

So we came to Verona, where it was snowing, and the people had stern, sad faces, beautiful, unlaughing faces. But if they looked at me, those serious faces would lighten, they would smile at me in my splendor. Strangers offered me candy, sometimes with the most excruciating sadness, kneeling or stooping to look directly into my face, into my eyes; and Momma or Papa would judge them, the people, and say in Italian we were late, we had to hurry, or pause, and let the stranger touch me, talk to me, look into my

face for a while. I would see myself in the eyes of some strange
man or woman; sometimes they stared so gently I would want to
touch their eyelashes, stroke those strange, large, glistering eyes. I
knew I decorated life. I took my duties with great seriousness. An
Italian count in Siena said I had the manners of an English prin-
cess—at times—and then he laughed because it was true I would
be quite lurid: I ran shouting in his *galleria,* a long room, hung
with pictures, and with a frescoed ceiling, and I sat on his lap and
wriggled. I was a wicked child, and I liked myself very much; and
almost everywhere, almost every day, there was someone new to
love me, briefly, while we traveled.

I understood I was special. I understood it *then.*

I knew that what we were doing, everything we did, involved
money. I did not know if it involved mind or not, or style. But I
knew about money somehow, checks and traveler's checks and
the clink of coins. Daddy was a fountain of money: he said it was a
spree; he meant for us to be amazed; he had saved money—we
weren't really rich but we were to be for this trip. I remember a
conservatory in a large house outside Florence and orange trees in
tubs; and I ran there too. A servant, a man dressed in black, a very
old man, mean-faced—he did not like being a servant anymore
after the days of servants were over—and he scowled but he smiled
at me, and at my mother, and even once at my father. We were
clearly so separate from the griefs and wearinesses and cruelties of
the world. We were at play, we were at our joys, and Momma was
glad, with a terrible and naive inner gladness, and she relied on
Daddy to make it work. Oh, she worked too, but she didn't know
the secret of such—unreality: is that what I want to say? Of such a
game, of such an extraordinary game.

There was a picture in Verona Daddy wanted to see; a painting; I remember the painter because the name Pisanello reminded
me I had to go to the bathroom when we were in the museum,
which was an old castle, Guelf or Ghibelline, I don't remember
which; and I also remember the painting because it showed the
hind end of the horse, and I thought that was not nice and rather

funny, but Daddy was admiring; and so I said nothing. He held my hand and told me a story so I wouldn't be bored as we walked from room to room in the museum/castle, and then we went outside into the snow, into the soft light when it snows, light coming through snow; and I was dressed in red and had on boots, and my parents were young and pretty and had on boots too, and we could stay out in the snow if we wanted; and we did. We went to a square, a piazza—the Scaligera, I think; I don't remember—and just as we got there, the snowing began to bellow and then subside, to fall heavily and then sparsely, and then it stopped: and it was very cold, and there were pigeons everywhere in the piazza, on every cornice and roof, and all over the snow on the ground, leaving little tracks as they walked, while the air trembled in its just-after-snow and just-before-snow weight and thickness and grey seriousness of purpose. I had never seen so many pigeons or such a private and haunted place as that piazza, me in my new coat at the far rim of the world, the far rim of who knew what story, the rim of foreign beauty and Daddy's games, the edge, the white border of a season.

I was half mad with pleasure, anyway, and now Daddy brought five or six cones made of newspaper, wrapped, twisted; and they held grains of something like corn, yellow and white kernels of something; and he poured some on my hand and told me to hold my hand out, and then he backed away.

At first there was nothing, but I trusted him and I waited; and then the pigeons came. On heavy wings. Clumsy pigeony bodies. And red, unreal bird's feet. They flew at me, slowing at the last minute; they lit on my arm and fed from my hand. I wanted to flinch, but I didn't. I closed my eyes and held my arm stiffly; and felt them peck and eat—from my hand, these free creatures, these flying things. I liked that moment. I liked my happiness. If I were mistaken about life and pigeons and my own nature, it didn't matter then.

The piazza was very silent, with snow; and Daddy poured grains on both my hands and then on the sleeves of my coat and on the shoulders of the coat, and I was entranced with yet more stillness, with this idea of his. The pigeons fluttered heavily in the heavy air, more and more of them, and sat on my arms and on my shoulders; and I looked at Momma and then at my father and then at the birds on me.

Oh, I'm sick of everything as I talk. There is happiness. It always makes me slightly ill. I lose my balance because of it.

The heavy birds, and the strange buildings, and Momma near, and Daddy too: Momma is pleased that I am happy and she is a little jealous; she is jealous of everything Daddy does; she is a woman of enormous spirit; life is hardly big enough for her; she is drenched in wastefulness and prettiness. She knows things. She gets inflexible, though, and foolish at times, and temperamental; but she is a somebody, and she gets away with a lot, and if she is near, you can feel her, you can't escape her, she's that important, that echoing, her spirit is that powerful in the space around her.

If she weren't restrained by Daddy, if she weren't in love with him, there is no knowing what she might do; he is incredibly watchful and changeable and he gets tired; he talks and charms people; sometimes, then, Momma and I stand nearby, like moons; we brighten and wane; and after a while, he comes to us, to the moons, the big one, and the little one, and we welcome him, and he is always, to my surprise, he is always surprised, as if he didn't deserve to be loved, as if it were time he was found out.

Daddy is very tall, and Momma is watching us, and Daddy anoints me again and again with the grain. I cannot bear it much longer. I feel joy or amusement or I don't know what; it is all through me, like a nausea—I am ready to scream and laugh, that laughter that comes out like magical, drunken, awful and yet pure spit or vomit or God knows what, that makes me a child mad with laughter. I become brilliant, gleaming, soft; an angel, a great birdchild of laughter. I am ready to be like that, but I hold myself back.

There are more and more birds near me. They march around my feet and peck at falling and fallen grains. One is on my head. Of those on my arms, some move their wings, fluff those frail, feather-loaded wings, stretch them. I cannot bear it, they are so frail, and I am, at the moment, the kindness of the world that feeds them in the snow.

All at once, I let out a splurt of laughter: I can't stop myself and the birds fly away but not far; they circle around me, above me, some wheel high in the air and drop as they return; they all returned, some in clouds and clusters driftingly, some alone and angry, pecking at others; some with a blind, animal-strutting abruptness. They gripped my coat and fed themselves. It started to snow again.

I was there in my kindness, in that piazza, within reach of my mother and father.

Oh, how will the world continue? Daddy suddenly understood I'd had enough, I was at the end of my strength — Christ, he was alert — and he picked me up, and I went limp, my arm around his neck, and the snow fell. Momma came near and pulled the hood lower and said there were snowflakes in my eyelashes. She knew he had understood, and she wasn't sure she had; she wasn't sure he ever watched her so carefully. She became slightly unhappy; and so she walked like a clumsy boy beside us, but she was so pretty: she had powers, anyway.

We went to a restaurant , and I behaved very well, but I couldn't eat, and then we went to the train and people looked at us, but I couldn't smile; I was too dignified, too sated; some leftover — pleasure, let's call it — made my dignity very deep, I could not stop remembering the pigeons, or that Daddy loved me in a way he did not love Momma; and Daddy was alert, watching the luggage, watching strangers for assassination attempts or whatever; he was on duty; and Momma was pretty and alone and *happy*, defiant in that way.

And then, you see, what she did was wake me in the middle of the night when the train was chugging up a very steep mountainside; and outside the window, visible because our compartment was dark and the sky was clear and there was a full moon, were mountains, a landscape of mountains everywhere, big mountains, huge ones, impossible, all slanted and pointed and white with snow, and absurd, sticking up into an ink-blue sky and down into blue, blue shadows, miraculously deep. I don't know how to say what it was like; they were not like anything I knew. They were high things and we were up high in the train and we were climbing higher, and it was not at all true, but it was, you see. I put my hands on the window and stared at the wild, slanting, unlikely marvels, whiteness and dizziness and moonlight and shadows cast by moonlight, not real, not familiar, not pigeons, but a clean world.

We sat for a long time, Momma and I, and stared, and then Daddy woke up and came and looked too. "It's pretty," he said, but he didn't really understand. Only Momma and I did. She said to him, "When I was a child, I was bored all the time, my love—I thought nothing would ever happen to me—and now these things are happening—and you have happened." I think he was flabbergasted by her love in the middle of the night; he smiled at her, oh, so swiftly that I was jealous, but I stayed quiet, and after a while, in his silence and amazement at her, at us, he began to seem different from us, from Momma and me; and then he fell asleep again; Momma and I didn't; we sat at the window and watched all night, watched the mountains and the moon, the clean world. We watched together.

Momma was the winner.

We were silent, and in silence we spoke of how we loved men and how dangerous men were and how they stole everything from you no matter how much you gave—but we didn't say it aloud.

We looked at mountains until dawn, and then when dawn came, it was too pretty for me—there was pink and blue and gold, in the sky, and on icy places, brilliant pink and gold flashes, and the snow colored too, and I said, "Oh," and sighed; and each moment was more beautiful than the one before; and I said, "I love you, Momma." Then I fell asleep in her arms.

That was happiness then.

Harold Brodkey's *Verona: A Young Woman Speaks* is included in this book because I had never before read a story about pure happiness in childhood. After reading this story, I know why very few have been written.

The daughter in the tale was seven or eight years old when she was taken on a trip across a quarter of Europe by her parents. They went by train because planes were erratic, and the adoring father wanted to stop at half a dozen Italian towns to show his family paintings and to buy things.

The child had young, attractive, charming parents. She had them all to herself, and she had their full attention. He was an indulgent father with a fountain of money, if only on the spree, who bought her beautiful clothes, watches, bracelets, and whatever else she wanted. An adventurous man, he introduced her to "the secret of unreality," separate from the "griefs and wearinesses and cruelties of the world." She had someone new to love her, briefly, every day. To top it all off, with this child the dream of every girl came true: She believed that her father, in sharing with her the secret of unreality, secretly preferred her to his wife. But this loving family also brought about a healthy resolution to the Oedipus Complex. Despite the child's feeling that her father loved her more than he did her mother, it became apparent that Momma in reality was first in Father's eyes. At this realization, the child first felt jealous. But she had a loving, understanding mother who was willing to wake her in the middle of the night to show her the beautiful moonlight on the mountains and talk in silence about important things like men. She allowed her daughter to fall asleep in her arms, and let her know that she loved her more than her father. With so glorious a mother, the child was able to relinquish her father as a lover and give him back to her mother.

With such parents on a trip like that, wouldn't any child be ecstatic?

P.S. It also helps to have a vibrant, sensual infancy, where the milk flows endlessly, in which one is rocked and held to a state of complete contentment and falls asleep in a loving mother's arms. Such memories, conscious or otherwise, will infuse many circumstances and saturate vacations such as the one in the story with delirious joy throughout one's life. The Bible said "To him that hath shall be given...." Life is not fair.

9

THE MIDDLE YEARS

HENRY JAMES

The April day was soft and bright, and poor Dencombe, happy in the conceit of reasserted strength, stood in the garden of the hotel, comparing, with a deliberation in which however there was still something of languor, the attractions of easy strolls. He liked the feeling of the south so far as you could have it in the north, he liked the sandy cliffs and the clustered pines, he liked even the colourless sea. "Bournemouth as a health-resort" had sounded like a mere advertisement, but he was thankful now for the commonest conveniences. The sociable country postman, passing through the garden, had just given him a small parcel which he took out with him, leaving the hotel to the right and creeping to a bench he had already haunted, a safe recess in the cliff. It looked to the south, to the tinted walls of the Island, and was protected behind by the sloping shoulder of the down. He was tired enough when he reached it, and for a moment was disappointed: he was better of course, but better, after all, than what? He should never again, as at one or two great moments of the past, be better than himself. The infinite of life was gone, and what remained of the dose a small glass scored like a thermometer by the apothecary. He sat and stared at the sea, which appeared all surface and twinkle, far shallower than the spirit of man. It was the

The Middle Years, by Henry James. From *Short Stories of Henry James*, 1864.

abyss of human illusion that was the real, the tideless deep. He held his packet, which had come by book-post, unopened on his knee, liking, in the lapse of so many joys—his illness had made him feel his age—to know it was there, but taking for granted there could be no complete renewal of the pleasure, dear to young experience, of seeing one's self "just out." Dencombe, who had a reputation, had come out too often and knew too well in advance how he should look.

His postponement associated itself vaguely, after a little, with a group of three persons, two ladies and a young man, whom, beneath him, straggling and seemingly silent, he could see move slowly together along the sands. The gentleman had his head bent over a book and was occasionally brought to a stop by the charm of this volume, which, as Dencombe could perceive even at a distance, had a cover alluringly red. Then his companions, going a little further, waited for him to come up, poking their parasols into the beach, looking around them at the sea and sky and clearly sensible of the beauty of the day. To these things the young man with the book was still more clearly indifferent, lingering, credulous, absorbed, he was an object of envy to an observer from whose connexion with literature all such artlessness had faded. One of the ladies was large and mature; the other had the spareness of comparative youth and of a social situation possibly inferior. The large lady carried back Dencombe's imagination to the age of crinoline; she wore a hat of the shape of a mushroom, decorated with a blue veil, and had the air, in her aggressive amplitude, of clinging to a vanished fashion or even a lost cause. Presently her companion produced from under the folds of a mantle a limp portable chair which she stiffened out and of which the large lady took possession. This act, and something in the movement of either party, at once characterized the performers—they performed for Dencombe's recreation—as opulent matron and humble dependent. Where moreover was the virtue of an approved novelist if one couldn't establish a relation between such figures? The clever theory for instance that the young man was the son of the opulent

matron and that the humble dependent, the daughter of a clergy-
man or an officer, nourished a secret passion for him. Was that not
visible from the way she stole behind her protectress to look back
at him?—back to where he had let himself come to a full stop
when his mother sat down to rest. His book was a novel, it had the
catchpenny binding; so that while the romance of life stood neglected at his side he lost himself in that of the circulating library.
He moved mechanically to where the sand was softer and ended
by plumping down in it to finish his chapter at his ease. The humble
dependent, discouraged by his remoteness, wandered with a
martyred droop of the head in another direction, and the exorbi-
tant lady, watching the waves, offered a confused resemblance to
a dying-machine that had broken down.

When his drama began to fail Dencombe remembered that
he had after all another pastime. Though such promptitude on
the part of the publisher was rare he was already able to draw from
its wrapper his "latest," perhaps his last. The cover of "The Middle
Years" was duly meretricious, the smell of the fresh pages the very
odour of sanctity, but for the moment he went no further—he had
become conscious of a strange alienation. He had forgotten what
his book was about. Had the assault of his old ailment, which he
had so fallaciously come to Bournemouth to ward off, interposed
utter blankness as to what had preceded it? He had finished the
revision of proof before quitting London, but his subsequent fortnight in bed had passed the sponge over colour. He couldn't have
chanted to himself a single sentence, couldn't have turned with
curiosity or confidence to any particular page. His subject had
already gone from him, leaving scarce a superstition behind. He
uttered a low moan as he breathed the chill of this dark void, so
desperately it seemed to represent the completion of a sinister process. The tears filled his mild eyes; something precious had passed
away. This was the pang that had been sharpest during the last few
years—the sense of ebbing time, of shrinking opportunity, and now
he felt not so much that his last chance was going as that it was
gone indeed. He had done all he should ever do, and yet hadn't

done what he wanted. This was the laceration—that practically his career was over: it was as violent as a grip at his throat. He rose from his seat—a creature hunted by a dread; then he fell back in his weakness and nervously opened his book. It was a single volume; he preferred single volumes and aimed at a rare compression. He began to read and, little by little, in this occupation, was pacified and reassured. Everything came back to him, but came back with a wonder, came back above all with a high and magnificent beauty. He read his own prose, he turned his own leaves, and had as he sat there with the spring sunshine on the page an emotion, peculiar and intense. His career was over, no doubt, but it was over, when all was said, with *that*.

He had forgotten during his illness the work of the previous year; but what he had chiefly forgotten was that it was extraordinarily good. He dived once more into his story and was drawn down, as by a siren's hand, to where, in the dim underworld of fiction, the great glazed tank of art, strange, silent subjects float. He recognized his motive and surrendered to his talent. Never probably had that talent, such as it was, been so fine. His difficulties were still there, but what was also there, to his perception, though probably, alas! to nobody's else, was the art that in most cases had surmounted them. In his surprised enjoyment of this ability he had a glimpse of a possible reprieve. Surely its force wasn't spent—there was life and service in it yet. It hadn't come to him easily. It had been backward and roundabout. It was the child of time, the nursling of delay, he had struggled and suffered for it, making sacrifices not to be counted, and now that it was really mature was it to cease to yield, to confess itself brutally beaten? There was an infinite charm for Dencombe in feeling as he had never felt before that diligence *vincit omnia*. The result produced in his little book was somehow a result beyond his conscious intention: it was as if he had planted his genius, had trusted his method, and they had grown up and flowered with this sweetness. If the achievement had been real, however, the process had been painful enough. What he saw so intensely today, what he felt as a nail driven in, was that only now, at the very last, had he come into possession. His development had been abnormally slow, almost grotesquely gradual. He had been hindered and retarded by experience, he had for long periods only groped his way. It had taken too much of his life to produce too little of his art. The art had come, but it had come after everything else. At such a rate a first existence was too short—long enough only to collect material; so that to fructify, to use the material, one should have a second age, an extension. This extension was what poor Dencombe sighed for. As he turned the last leaves of his volume he murmured "Ah for another go, ah for better chance!"

The three persons drawing his attention to the sands had vanished and then reappeared. They had now wandered up a path, an artificial and easy ascent, which led to the top of the cliff. Dencombe's bench was halfway down, on a sheltered ledge, and a large lady, a massive heterogeneous person with bold, black eyes and kind red cheeks, now took a few moments to rest. She wore dirty gauntlets and immense diamond earrings. At first she looked vulgar, but she contradicted this announcement in an agreeable off-hand tone. While her companions stood waiting for her, she spread her skirts on the end of Dencombe's seat. The young man had gold spectacles, through which, with his finger still in his red-covered book, he glanced at the volume, bound in the same shade of the same colour, lying on the lap of the original occupant of the bench. After an instant Dencombe felt him struck with a resemblance. He had recognized the gilt on the crimson cloth, was reading "The Middle Years" and now noted that somebody else had kept pace with him. The stranger was startled, possibly even a little ruffled, to find himself not the only person favoured with an early copy. The eyes of the two proprietors met a moment, and Dencombe borrowed amusement from the expression of those of his competitor, those, it might even be inferred, of his admirer. They confessed to some resentment—they seemed to say: "Hang it, has he got it *already*? Of course he's a brute of a reviewer!" Dencombe shuffled his copy out of sight while the opulent matron, rising from her repose, broke out: "I feel already the good of this air!"

"I can't say I do," sad the angular lady. "I find myself quite let down."

"I find myself horribly hungry. At what time did you order luncheon?" her protectress, pursued.

The young person put the question by. "Doctor Hugh always orders it."

"I ordered nothing today—I'm going to make you diet," said their comrade.

"Then I shall go home and sleep. *Qui dort vine!*"

"Can I trust you to Miss Vernham?" asked Dr. Hugh of his elder companion.

"Don't I trust *you?*" she archly enquired.

"Not too much!" Miss Vernham, with her eyes on the ground, permitted herself to declare. "You must come with us at least to the house," she went on while the personage on whom they appeared to be in attendance began to mount higher. She had got a little out of earshot; nevertheless Miss Vernham became, so far as Dencombe was concerned, less distinctly audible to murmur to the young man: "I don't think you realize all you owe the Countess!"

Absently, a moment, Dr. Hugh caused his gold-rimmed spectacles to shine at her. "Is that the way I strike you? Then I see—I see!"

"She's awfully good to us," continued Miss Vernham, compelled by the lapse of the other's motion to stand there in spite of his discussion of private matters. Of what use would it have been that Dencombe should be sensitive to shades, hadn't he detected in that arrest a strange influence from the quiet old convalescent in the great tweed cape? Miss Vernham appeared suddenly to become aware of some such connexion, for she added in a moment: "If you want to sun yourself here you can come back after you've seen us home."

Doctor Hugh, at this, hesitated, and Dencombe, in spite of a

desire to pass for unconscious, risked a covert glance at him. What
his eyes met this time, as happened, was, on the part of the young
lady, a queer stare, naturally vitreous, which made her remind him
of some figure—he couldn't name it—in a play or a novel, some
sinister governess or tragic old maid. She seemed to scan him, to
challenge him, to say out of general spite: "What have you got to
do with us?" At the same instant the rich humour of the Countess
reached them from above. "Come, come, my little lambs; you
should follow your old *bergere!*" Miss Vernham turned away for it,
pursuing the ascent, and Doctor Hugh, after another mute appeal
to Dencombe and a minute's evident demur, deposited his book
on the bench as if to keep his place, or even as a gage of earnest
return, and bounded without difficulty up the rougher part of the
cliff.

Equally innocent and infinite are the pleasures of observation
and the resources engendered by the trick of analyzing life. It
amused poor Dencombe as he dawdled in his tepid air-bath, to
believe himself awaiting a revelation of something at the back of a
fine young mind. He looked hard at the book on the end of the
bench, but wouldn't have touched it for the world.

It served his purpose to have a theory that shouldn't be exposed to refutation. He already felt better of his melancholy; he
had, according to his old formula, put his head at the window. A
passing Countess could draw off the fancy when, like the elder of
the ladies who had just retreated, she was as obvious as the giant-
ess of a caravan. It was indeed general views that were terrible;
short ones, contrary to an opinion sometimes expressed, were the
refuge, were the remedy. Doctor Hugh couldn't possibly be anything but a reviewer who had understandings for early copies with
publishers or with newspapers. He reappeared in a quarter of an
hour with visible relief at finding Dencombe on the spot and the
gleam of white teeth in an embarrassed but generous smile. He
was perceptibly disappointed at the eclipse of the other copy of the
book: it made a pretext the less for speaking to the quiet gentleman. But he spoke notwithstanding. He held up his own copy and

broke out pleadingly: "*Do* say, if you have occasion to speak of it, that it's the best thing he has done yet!"

Dencombe responded with a laugh: "Done yet" was so amusing to him, made such a grand avenue of the future. Better still, the young man took *him* for a reviewer. He pulled out "The Middle Years" from under his cape, but instinctively concealed any telltale look of fatherhood. This was partly because a person was always a fool for insisting to others on his work. "Is that what you're going to say yourself?" he put to his visitor.

"I'm not quite sure I shall write anything. I don't, as a regular thing—I enjoy in peace. But it's awfully fine."

Dencombe just abated. If the young man had begun to abuse him he would have confessed on the spot to his identity, but there was no harm in drawing out any impulse to praise. He drew it out with such success that in a few moments his new acquaintance, seated by his side, was confessing candidly that the works of the author of the volumes before them were the only ones he could read a second time. He had come the day before from London, where a friend of his, a journalist, had lent him his copy of the last, the copy sent to the office of the journal and already the subject of a "notice" which, as was pretended there—but one had to allow for "swagger"—it had taken a full quarter of an hour to prepare. He intimated that he was ashamed for his friend, and in the case of a work demanding and repaying study, of such inferior manners, and with his fresh appreciation and his so irregular wish to express it, he speedily became for poor Dencombe a remarkable, a delightful apparition. Chance had brought the weary man of letters face to face with the greatest admirer in the new generation of whom it was supposable he might boast. The admirer in truth was mystifying, so rare a case was it to find a bristling young doctor—he looked like a German physiologist—enamoured of literary form. It was an accident, but happier than most accidents, so that Dencombe, exhilarated as well as confounded, spent half an hour in making his visitor talk while he kept himself quiet. He explained his premature possession of "The Middle Years" by an

allusion to the friendship of the publisher, who, knowing he was
at Bournemouth for his health, had paid him this graceful attention. He allowed he had been ill, for Doctor Hugh would infalli-
bly have guessed it; he even went so far as to wonder if he mightn't
look for some "hygienic" tip from a personage combining so bright
an enthusiasm with a presumable knowledge of the remedies now
in vogue. It would shake his faith a little perhaps to have to take a
doctor seriously who would take *him* so seriously, but he enjoyed
this gushing modern youth and felt with an acute pang that there
would still be work to do in a world in which such odd combinations were presented. It wasn't true, what he had tried for
remuneration's sake to believe, that all the combinations were exhausted. They weren't by any means—they were infinite: the exhaustion was in the miserable artist.

Doctor Hugh, an ardent physiologist, was saturated with the
spirit of the age—in other words he had just taken his degree: but
he was independent and various, he talked like a man who would
have preferred to love literature best. He fain would have made
fine phrases, but nature had denied him the trick. Some of the
finest in "The Middle Years" had struck him inordinately, and he
took the liberty of reading them to Dencombe in support of his
plea. He grew vivid, in the balmy air, to his companion, for whose
deep refreshment he seemed to have been sent; and was particularly ingenious in describing how recently he had become ac-
quainted and how instantly infatuated, with the only man who
had put flesh between the ribs of an art that was starving on superstitions. He hadn't yet written to him—he was deterred by a strain
of respect. Dencombe at this moment rejoiced more inwardly than
ever that he had never answered the photographers. His visitor's
attitude promised him a luxury of intercourse, though he was sure
a due freedom for Doctor Hugh would depend not a little on the
Countess. He learned without delay what type of Countess was
involved, mastering as well the nature of the tie that united the
curious trio. The large lady, an Englishwoman by birth and the
daughter of a celebrated baritone, who's taste *minus* his talent she

had inherited, was the widow of a French nobleman and mistress of all that remained of the handsome fortune, the fruit of her father's earnings that had constituted her dower. Miss Vernham, an odd creature but an accomplished pianist, was attached to her person at a salary. The Countess was generous, independent, eccentric; She traveled with her minstrel and her medical man. Ignorant and passionate she had nevertheless moments in which she was almost irresistible. Dencombe saw her sit for her portrait in Doctor Hugh's free sketch, and felt the picture of his young friend's relation to her frame itself in his mind. This young friend, for a representative of the new psychology, was himself easily hypnotized, and if he became abnormally communicative it was only a sign of his real subjection. Dencombe did accordingly what he wanted with him even without being known as Dencombe.

Taken ill on a journey in Switzerland the Countess had picked him up at an hotel, and the accident of his happening to please her had made her offer him, with her imperious liberality, terms that couldn't fail to dazzle a practitioner without patients and whose resources had been drained dry by his studies. It wasn't the way he would have proposed to spend his time, but it was time that would pass quickly, and meanwhile she was wonderfully kind. She exacted perpetual attention, but it was impossible not to like her. He gave details about his queer patient, a "type" if there ever was one, who had in connexion with her flushed obesity, and in addition to the morbid strain of a violent and aimless will, a grave organic disorder. But he came back to his loved novelist, whom he was so good as to pronounce more essentially a poet than many of those who went in for verse, with a zeal excited, as all his indiscretion had been excited, by the happy chance of Dencombe's sympathy and the coincidence of their occupation. Dencombe had confessed to a slight personal acquaintance with the author of "The Middle Years," but had not felt himself as ready as he could have wished when his companion, who had never yet encountered a being so privileged, began to be eager for particulars. He even divined in Doctor Hugh's eye at that moment a glimmer of suspicion. But the young man was too influenced to be shrewd and repeatedly caught up in the book to exclaim: "Did you notice this?" or "Weren't you immensely struck with that?" "There's a beautiful passage toward the end," he broke out, and again he laid his hand on the volume. As he turned the pages he came upon something else, while Dencombe saw him suddenly change colour. He had taken up as it lay on the bench Dencombe's copy instead of his own, and his neighbor at once guessed the reason of his start. Doctor Hugh looked grave an instant; then he said: "I see you've been altering the text!" Dencombe was a passionate corrector, a fingerer of style; the last thing he ever arrived at was a form final for himself. His ideal would have been to publish secretly, and then, on the published text, treat himself to the terrified revise, sacrificing always a first edition and beginning for posterity and even for the collectors, poor dears, with a second. This morning, in "The Middle Years," his pencil had pricked a dozen lights. He was amused at the effect of the young man's reproach; for an instant it made him change colour. He stammered at any rate ambiguously, then through a blur of ebbing consciousness saw Doctor Hugh's mystified eyes. He only had time to feel he was about to be ill again — that emotion, excitement, fatigue, the heat of the sun, the solicitation of the air, had combined to play him a trick, before, stretching out a hand to his visitor with a plaintive cry, he lost his senses altogether.

Later he knew he had fainted and that Doctor Hugh had got him home in a Bath-chair, the conductor of which, prowling within hail for custom, had happened to remember seeing him in the garden of the hotel. He had recovered his perception on the way, and had, in bed that afternoon, a vague recollection of Doctor Hugh's young face, as they went together, bent over him in a comforting laugh and expressive of something more than a suspicion of his identity. That identity was ineffaceable now, and all the more that he was rueful and sore. He had been rash, been stupid, had gone out too soon, stayed out too long. He oughtn't to have exposed himself to strangers, he ought to have taken his servant. He felt as if he had fallen into a hole too deep to descry any little patch of heaven. He was confused about the time that had passed—he pieced the fragments together. He had seen his doctor, the real one, the one who had treated him from the first and who had again been very kind. His servant was in and out on tiptoe, looking very wise after the fact. He said more than once something about the sharp young gentleman. The rest was vagueness in so far as it wasn't despair. The vagueness, however, justified itself by dreams, dozing anxieties from which he finally emerged to the consciousness of a dark room and a shaded candle.

"You'll be all right again—I know all about you now," said a voice near him that he felt to be young. Then his meeting with Doctor Hugh came back. He was too discouraged to joke about it yet, but made out after a little that the interest was intense for his visitor. "Of course I can't attend you professionally—you've got your own man, with whom I've talked and who's excellent." Doctor Hugh went on, "But you must let me come to see you as a good friend. I've just looked in before going to bed. You're doing beautifully, but it's a good job I was with you on the cliff. I shall come in early tomorrow. I want to do something for you. I want to do everything. You've done a tremendous lot for me." The young man held his hand, hanging over him, and poor Dencombe, weakly aware of this living pressure, simply lay there and accepted his devotion. He couldn't do anything less—he needed help too much.

The idea of the help he needed was very present to him that night, which he spent in a lucid stillness, an intensity of thought that constituted a reaction from his hours of stupor. He was lost, he was lost—he was lost if he couldn't be saved. He wasn't afraid of suffering, of death, wasn't even in love with life; but he had had a deep demonstration of desire. It came over him in the long quiet hours that only with "The Middle Years" had he taken his flight; and only on that day, visited by soundless processions, had he recognized his kingdom. He had had a revelation of his range. What he dreaded was the idea that his reputation should stand on the unfinished. It wasn't with his past but with his future that it should properly be concerned. Illness and age rose before him like spectres with pitiless eyes: how was he to bribe such fates to give him the second chance? He had had the one chance that all men have—he had had the chance of life. He went to sleep again very late, and when he awoke Doctor Hugh was sitting at hand. There was already by this time something beautifully familiar in him.

"Don't think I've turned out your physician," he said. "I'm acting with his consent. He has been here and seen you. Somehow he seems to trust me. I told him how we happened to come together yesterday, and he recognizes that I've a peculiar right."

Dencombe felt his own face pressing. "How have you squared the Countess?"

The young man blushed a little, but turned it off. "Oh never mind the Countess!"

"You told me she was very exacting."

Doctor Hugh had a wait. "So she is."

"And Miss Vernham's an *intricante*."

"How do you know that?"

"I know everything. One *has* to, to write decently."

"I think she's mad," said limpid Doctor Hugh.

"Well, don't quarrel with the Countess—she's a present help to you."

"I don't quarrel," Doctor Hugh returned. "But I don't get on with silly women." Presently he added, "You seem very much alone."

"That often happens at my age. I've outlived, I've lost by the way."

Doctor Hugh faltered, then surmounting a soft scruple: "Whom have you lost?"

"Every one."

"Ah no," the young man breathed, laying a hand on his arm.

"I once had a wife—I once had a son. My wife died when my child was born, and my boy, at school, was carried off by typhoid."

"I wish I'd been there!" cried Doctor Hugh.

"Well—if you're here!" Dencombe answered with a smile that,

in spite of dimness, showed how he valued being sure of his companion's whereabouts.

"You talk strangely of your age. You're not old."

"Hypocrite—so early?"

"I speak psychologically."

"That's the way I've been speaking for the last five years, and it's exactly what I've been saying to myself. It isn't till we *are* old that we begin to tell ourselves we're not."

"Yet I know I myself am young," Doctor Hugh returned.

"Not so well as I!" laughed his patient, whose visitor indeed would have established the truth in question by the honesty with which he changed the point of view, remarking that it must be one of the charms of age—at any rate in the case of high distinction— to feel that one has laboured and achieved. Doctor Hugh employed the common phrase about earning one's rest, and it made poor Dencombe for an instant almost angry. He recovered himself, however, to explain, lucidly enough, that if, ungraciously, he knew nothing of such a balm, it was doubtless because he had wasted inestimable years. He had followed literature from the first, but he had taken a lifetime to get abreast of her. Only today at last had he begun to *see*, so that all he had hitherto shown was a movement without a direction. He had ripened too late, and was so clumsily constituted that he had had to teach himself by mistakes.

"I prefer your flowers then to other people's fruits, and your mistakes to other people's successes," said gallant Doctor Hugh. "It's for your mistakes I admire you."

"You're happy—you don't know," Dencombe answered.

Looking at his watch the young man had got up; he named the hour of the afternoon at which he would return. Dencombe warned him against committing himself too deeply, and expressed again all his dread of making him neglect the Countess—perhaps incur her displeasure.

"I want to be like you—I want to learn by mistakes!" Dr. Hugh laughed.

"Take care you don't make too grave a one! But do come back,"

Dencombe added with the glimmer of a new idea.

"You should have had more vanity!" His friend spoke as if he knew the exact amount required to make a man of letters normal.

"No, no—I only should have had more time. I want another go."

"Another go?"

"I want an extension."

"An extension?" Again Doctor Hugh repeated Dencombe's words, with which he seemed to have been struck.

"Don't you know?—I want to do what they call 'live.'"

The young man, for good-bye, had taken his hand, which closed with a certain force. They looked at each other hard. "You *will* live," said Doctor Hugh.

"Don't be superficial. It's too serious!"

"You *shall* live!" Dencombe's visitor declared, turning pale.

"Ah, that's better!" And as he retired the invalid, with a troubled laugh, sank gratefully back.

All that day and all the following night he wondered if it mightn't be arranged. His doctor came again, his servant was attentive, but it was to his confident young friend that he felt himself mentally appeal. His collapse on the cliff was plausibly explained and his liberation, on a better basis, promised for the morrow; meanwhile, however, the intensity of his meditations kept him tranquil and made him indifferent. The idea that occupied him was none the less absorbing because it was a morbid fancy. Here was a clever son of the age, ingenious and ardent, who happened to have set him up for connoisseurs to worship. This servant of his altar had all the new learning in science and all the old reverence in faith; wouldn't he therefore put his knowledge at the disposal of his sympathy, his craft at the disposal of his love? Couldn't he be trusted to invent a remedy for a poor artist to whose art he had paid a tribute? If he couldn't the alternative was hard: Dencombe would have to surrender to silence unvindicated and undivined. The rest of the day and all the next he toyed in secret with this sweet futility. Who would work the miracle for him but the young man who could combine such lucidity with such passion? He thought of the fairytales of science and charmed himself into forgetting that he looked for a magic that was not of this world. Doctor Hugh was an apparition, and that placed him above the law. He came and went while his patient, who now sat up, followed him with supplicating eyes. The interest of knowing the great author had made the young man begin "The Middle Years" afresh and would help him to find a richer sense between its covers. Dencombe had told him what he "tried for"; with all his intelligence, on a first perusal, Doctor Hugh had failed to guess it. The baffled celebrity wondered then who in the world *would* guess it. He was amused once more at the diffused massive weight that could be thrown into the missing of an intention. Yet he wouldn't rail at the general mind—today—consoling as that ever had been; the revelation of his own slowness had seemed to make all stupidity sacred.

Doctor Hugh, after a little, was visibly worried, confessing, on enquiry, to a source of embarrassment at home. "Stick to the Countess—don't mind me," Dencombe said repeatedly, for his companion was frank enough about the large lady's attitude. She was so jealous that she had fallen ill—she resented such a breach of allegiance. She paid so much for his fidelity that she must have it all: she refused him the right to her sympathies, charged him with scheming to make her die alone, for it was needless to point out how little Miss Vernham was a resource in trouble. When Doctor Hugh mentioned that the Countess would already have left Bournemouth if he hadn't kept her in bed, poor Dencombe held his arm tighter and said with decision; "Take her straight away." They had gone out together, walking back to the sheltered nook in which, the other day, they had met. The young man, who had given his companion a personal support, declared with emphasis that his conscience was clear—he could ride two horses at once. Didn't he dream for his future of a time when he should have to ride five hundred? Longing equally for virtue, Dencombe replied that in that golden age no patient would pretend to have contracted with him for his whole attention. On the part of the Countess wasn't such an avidity lawful? Doctor Hugh denied it, and said there was no contract, but only a free understanding, and that a sordid servitude was impossible to a generous spirit: he liked moreover to talk about art, and that was the subject on which, this time, as they sat together on the sunny bench, he tried most to engage the author of "The Middle Years." Dencombe, soaring again a little on the weak wings of convalescence and still haunted by that happy notion of an organized rescue, found another strain of eloquence to plead the cause of a certain splendid "last manner": the very citadel, as it would prove, of his reputation, the stronghold into which his real treasure would be gathered. While his listener gave up the morning and the great still sea ostensibly waited he had a wondrous explanatory hour. Even for himself he was inspired as he told what his treasure would consist of; the precious metals he would dig from the mine, the jewels rare, strings of pearls, he would hang between the columns of his temple. He was wondrous for himself, so thick his convictions crowded, but still more wondrous for Doctor Hugh, who had assured him none the less that the very pages he had just published were already encrusted with gems. This admirer, however, panted for the combinations to come and before the face of the beautiful day, renewed to Dencombe his guarantee that his profession would hold itself responsible for such a life. Then he suddenly clapped his hand upon his watch-pocket and asked leave to absent himself for half an hour. Dencombe waited there for his return, but was at last recalled to the actual by the fall of a shadow across the ground. The shadow darkened into that of Miss Vernham, the young lady in attendance on the Countess, whom Dencombe, recognizing her, perceived so clearly to have come to speak to him that he rose from his bench to acknowledge the civility. Miss Vernham indeed proved not particularly civil; she looked strangely agitated, and her type was now unmistakable.

"Excuse me if I do ask," she said, "whether it's too much to hope that you may be induced to leave Doctor Hugh alone." Then before our poor friend, greatly disconcerted, could protest: "You ought to be informed that you stand in his light—that you may do him a terrible injury."

"Do you mean by causing the Countess to dispense with his services?"

"By causing her to disinherit him." Dencombe stared at this, and Miss Vernham pursued, in the gratification of seeing she could produce an impression: "It has depended on himself to come into something very handsome. He has had a grand prospect, but I think you've succeeded in spoiling it."

"Not intentionally, I assure you. Is there no hope the accident may be repaired?" Dencombe asked.

"She was ready to do anything for him. She takes great fancies, she lets herself go—it's her way. She has no relations, she's free to dispose of her money, and she's very ill," said Miss Vernham for a climax.

"I'm very sorry to hear it," Dencombe stammered.

"Wouldn't it be possible for you to leave Bournemouth? That's what I've come to see about."

He sank to his bench. "I'm very ill myself, but I'll try."

Miss Vernham still stood there with her colourless eyes and the brutality of her good conscience. "Before it's too late, please!" she said, and with this she turned her back, in order, quickly, as if it had been a business to which she could spare but a precious moment, to pass out of his sight.

Oh yes, after this Dencombe was certainly very ill. Miss Vernham had upset him with her rough fierce news; it was the sharpest shock to him to discover what was at stake for a penniless young man of fine parts. He sat trembling on his bench, staring at the waste of waters, feeling sick with the directness of the blow. He was indeed too weak, too unsteady, too alarmed; but he would make the effort to get away, for he couldn't accept the guilt of interference and his honour was really involved. He would hobble home, at any rate, and then think what was to be done. He made his way back to the hotel and, as he went, had a characteristic vision of Miss Vernham's great motive. The Countess hated women of course—Dencombe was lucid about that; so that the hungry pianist had no personal hopes, and could only console herself with the bold conception of helping Doctor Hugh in order to marry him after he should get his money or else induce him to recognize her claim for compensation and buy her off. If she had befriended him at a fruitful crisis he would really, as a man of delicacy—and she knew what to think of that point—have to reckon with her.

At the hotel Dencombe's servant insisted on his going back to bed. The invalid had talked about catching a train and had begun with orders to pack, after which his racked nerves had yielded to a sense of sickness. He consented to see his physician, who immediately was sent for, but he wished it to be understood that his door was irrevocably closed to Doctor Hugh. He had his plan, which was so fine that he rejoiced in it after getting back to bed. Doctor Hugh, suddenly finding himself snubbed without mercy, would, in natural disgust and to the joy of Miss Vernham, renew his allegiance to the Countess. When his physician arrived Dencombe learned that he was feverish and that this was very wrong: he was to cultivate calmness and try, if possible, not to think. For the rest of the day he wooed stupidity; but there was an ache that kept him sentient, the probable sacrifice of his "extension," the limit of his course. His medical adviser was anything but pleased: his successive relapses were ominous. He charged this personage to put out a strong hand and take Doctor Hugh off his mind—it would contribute so much to his being quiet. The agitating name, in his room, was not mentioned again, but his security was a smothered fear, and it was not confirmed by the receipt, at ten o'clock that evening, of a telegram which his servant opened and read him and to which, with an address in London, the signature of Miss Vernham was attached. "Beseech you to use all influence to make our friend join us here in the morning. Countess much the worse for dreadful journey, but everything may still be saved." The two ladies had gathered themselves up and had been capable in the afternoon of a spiteful revolution. They had started for the capital, and if the elder one, as Miss Vernham had announced, was very ill, she had wished to make it clear that she was proportionately reckless. Poor Dencombe, who was not reckless and who only desired that everything should indeed be "saved," sent this missive straight off to the young man's lodging and had on the morrow the pleasure of knowing that he had quitted Bournemouth by an early train.

Two days later he pressed in with a copy of a literary journal in his hand. He had returned because he was anxious and for the pleasure of flourishing the great review of "The Middle Years." Here, at least, was something adequate — it rose to the occasion, it was an acclamation, a reparation, a critical attempt to place the author in the niche he had fairly won. Dencombe accepted and submitted, he made neither objection nor enquiry, for old complications had returned and he had had two dismal days. He was convinced not only that he should never again leave his bed, so that his young friend might pardonably remain, but that the demand he should make on the patience of beholders would be of the most moderate. Doctor Hugh had been to town, and he tried to find in his eyes some confession that the Countess was pacified. and his legacy clinched; but all he could see there was the light of his juvenile joy in two or three of the phrases of the newspaper. Dencombe couldn't read them, but when his visitor had insisted on repeating them more than once he was able to shake an unintoxicated head. "Ah no — but they would have been true of what I *could* have done!"

"What people 'could have done' is mainly what they've in fact done," Doctor Hugh contended.

"Mainly, yes, but I've been an idiot!" Dencombe said.

Doctor Hugh did remain; the end was coming fast. Two days later his patient observed to him, by way of the feeblest of jokes, that there would now be no question whatever of a second chance. At this the young man stared; then he exclaimed: "Why it has come to pass — it has come to pass. The second chance has been the public's — the chance to find the point of view, to pick up the pearl!"

"Oh the pearl!" poor Dencombe uneasily sighed. A smile as cold as a winter sunset flickered on his drawn lips as he added: "The pearl is the unwritten—the pearl is the unalloyed, the *rest,* the lost!"

From that hour he was less and less present, heedless to all appearance of what went on round him. His disease was definitely mortal, of an action as relentless, after the short arrest that had enabled him to fall in with Doctor Hugh, as a leak in a great ship. Sinking steadily, though this visitor, a man of great resources, now cordially approved by his physician, showed endless art in guarding him from pain, poor Dencombe kept no reckoning or speculation. Yet toward the last he gave a sign of having noticed how for two days Doctor Hugh hadn't been in his room, a sign that consisted of his suddenly opening his eyes to put a question. Had he spent those days with the Countess?

"The Countess is dead," said Dr. Hugh. "I knew that in a particular contingency she wouldn't resist. I went to her grave."

Dencombe's eyes opened wider. "She left you 'something handsome?'"

The young man gave a laugh almost too light for a chamber of woe. "Never a penny. She roundly cursed me."

"Cursed you?" Dencombe wailed.

"For giving her up. I gave her up for *you.* I had to choose," his companion explained.

"You choose to let a fortune go?"

"I chose to accept, whatever they might be, the consequences of my infatuation," smiled Doctor Hugh. Then as a larger pleasantry: "The fortune be hanged! It's your own fault if I can't get your things out of my head." The immediate tribute to his humour was a long bewildered moan; after which, for many hours, many days, Dencombe lay motionless and absent. A response so absolute, such a glimpse of a definite result and such a sense of credit, worked together in his mind and, producing a strange commotion, slowly altered and transfigured his despair. The sense of cold submersion left him—he seemed to float without an effort. The incident was extraordinary as evidence, and it shed an intenser light. At the last he signed to Doctor Hugh to listen and, when he was down on his knees by the pillow, brought him very near. "You've made me think it all a delusion."

"Not your glory, my dear friend," stammered the young man. "Not my glory—what there is of it! It is glory—to have been tested, to have had our little quality and cast our little spell. The thing is to have made somebody care. You happen to be crazy of course, but that doesn't affect the law."

"You're a great success!" said Doctor Hugh, putting into his young voice the ring of a marriage bell.

Dencombe lay taking this in, then he gathered strength to speak once more. "A second chance—*That's* the delusion. There never was to be but one. We work in the dark—we do what we can—we give what we have. Our doubt is our passion and our passion is our task. The rest is the madness of art."

"If you've doubted, if you've despaired, you've always 'done' it," his visitor subtly argued.

"We've done something or other," Dencombe conceded.

"Something or other is everything. It's the feasible. It's you!"

"Comforter!" Poor Dencombe ironically sighed.

"But it's true," insisted his friend.

"It's true. It's frustration that doesn't count."

"Frustration's only life," said Doctor Hugh.

"Yes, it's what passes." Poor Dencombe was barely audible, but he had marked with the words the virtual end of his first and only chance.

The Middle Years, by Henry James, is the story of a mid-life crisis before that term came into use. Although Dencombe is a writer, the story contains profound insights into the feelings faced by many people at his time of life. He felt that he "should never again, as at one or two great moments of the past, be better than himself." As a patient of mine put it, "Is this all there will ever be for me?" Although Dencombe's last book had just been published, he felt alienated from it, had actually forgotten what it was about, and took it for granted that he would never again recapture the pleasure of seeing his first book published. He had to mourn that loss, in order to be well. So all "middle-agers" must grieve for the intensity of youthful pleasures never to be regained, for lost loves, lost friends, lost joys, lost passions, lost triumphs, lost time, disappointed fantasies.

Dencombe was tormented by thoughts that time was ebbing, opportunities were shrinking, and despite his success as a writer, he had never really written what he wanted to. It disturbed him that his reputation would rest on work he had done in the past, when he had come into his full power only recently. Because he now felt capable of writing so much better, he needed a "second age," "an extension" of life in order to put into practice all the material he had collected. Who among us in this age group has not felt the same way? "If only I had gone to school more, I could have been a second Einstein," one man told me. The doctor in the story has a perfect answer to my friend. "What people 'could have done' is mainly what they have in fact done."

Dencombe is fortunate in coming across Dr. Hugh, a young doctor who worships the writer's work, and in actuality serves as his psychotherapist. Dencombe is able to express his feelings to the doctor, who values the writer's artistry above all other authors, no matter how much of a failure he has been in his own mind. Such is the process of psychotherapy, which has helped many depressives survive similar periods.

As in many mid-life crises, Dencombe comes to see the truth of what he has hitherto denied. In a famous passage, he says, "A second chance—*that's* the delusion. There never was to be one. We work in the dark—we do what we can—we give what we have.

Our doubt is our passion and our passion is our task."

Although our "diagnosis" is complicated by the fact that Dencombe is ill, and indeed, is dying, his "mid-life crisis" is successfully resolved. When the young doctor tells the dying man that he has been a great success, that whatever his doubts, he has always "done it," Dencombe is able to admit that the frustration he has experienced in his writing doesn't count, that "frustration is only life." This is an excellent solution to the "mid-life crisis," when the aging person is able to come to the realization that although his accomplishments have not been all that he would wish for himself, what matters is what he truly has done.

10

SILENT SNOW, SECRET SNOW

CONRAD AIKEN

Just why it should have happened, or why it should have happened just when it did, he could not, of course, possibly have said; nor perhaps would it even have occurred to him to ask. The thing was above all a secret, something to be preciously concealed from Mother and Father; and to that very fact it owed an enormous part of its deliciousness. It was like a peculiarly beautiful trinket to be carried unmentioned in one's trouser pocket—a rare stamp, an old coin, a few tiny gold links found trodden out of shape on the path in the park, a pebble of carnelian, a seashell distinguishable from all others by an unusual spot or stripe—and, as if it were any one these, he carried around with him everywhere a warm and persistent and increasingly beautiful sense of obsession. Nor was it only a sense of possession—it was also a sense of protection. It was as if, in some delightful way, his secret gave him a fortress, a wall behind which he could retreat into heavenly seclusion. This was almost the first thing he had noticed about it— apart from the oddness of the thing itself—and it was this that now again, for the fiftieth time, occurred to him, as he sat in the little schoolroom. It was the half-hour for geography. Miss Buell was revolving with one finger, slowly, a huge terrestrial globe which had been placed on her desk. The green and yellow continents passed and repassed, questions were asked and answered, and now the little girl in front of him, Deirdre, who had a funny little constellation of freckles on the back of her neck, exactly like the Big Dipper, was standing up and telling Miss Buell that the equator was the line that ran round the middle.

Miss Buell's face, which was old and grayish and kindly, with gray stiff curls beside the cheeks, and eyes that swam very brightly, like little minnows, behind thick glasses, wrinkled itself into a complication of amusements.

"Ah, I see. The earth is wearing a belt, or a sash. Or someone drew a line round it."

"Oh no—not that—I mean—"

In the general laughter, he did not share, or only a very little. He was thinking about the Arctic and Antarctic regions, which of course, on the globe, were white. Miss Buell was not telling them about the tropics, the jungles, the steamy heat of equatorial swamps, where the birds and butterflies, and even the snakes, were like living jewels. As he listened to these things, he was already, with a pleasant sense of half-effort, putting his secret between himself and the words. Was it really an effort at all? For effort implied something voluntary, and perhaps even something one did not especially want; whereas this was distinctly pleasant, and came almost of its own accord. All he needed to do was to think of that morning, the first one, and then of all the others—.

But it was all so absurdly simple! It had amounted to so little. It was nothing, just an idea—and just why it should have become so wonderful, so permanent, was a mystery—a very pleasant one, to be sure, but also, in an amusing way, foolish. However, without ceasing to listen to Miss Buell, who had now moved up to the north temperate zones, he deliberately invited his memory of the first morning. It was only a moment or two after he had waked up—or perhaps the moment itself. But was there, to be exact, an exact moment? Was one awake all at once? Or was it gradual?

Anyway, it was after he had stretched a lazy hand up toward the headrail, and yawned, and then relaxed again among his warm covers, all the more grateful on a December morning, that the thing had happened. Suddenly, for no reason, he had thought of the postman, he remembered the postman. Perhaps there was nothing so odd in that. After all, he heard the postman almost every morning in his life—his heavy boots could be heard clumping round the corner at the top of the little cobbled hill-street, and then, progressively nearer, progressively louder, the double knock at each door, the crossings and re-crossings of the street, till finally the clumsy steps came stumbling across to the very door, and the tremendous knock came which shook the house itself.

(Miss Buell was saying, "Vast wheat-growing areas in North America and Siberia."

Deirdre had for the moment placed her left hand across the back of her neck.)

But on this particular morning, the first morning, as he lay there with his eyes closed, he had for some reason *waited* for the postman. He wanted to hear him come round the corner. And that was precisely the joke—he never did. He never came. He never had come—*round the corner*—again. For when at last the steps were heard, they had already, he was quite sure, come a little down the hill, to the first house; and even so, the steps were curiously different—they were softer, they had a new secrecy about them, they were muffled and indistinct; and while the rhythm of them was the same, it now said a new thing—it said peace, it said remoteness, it said cold, it said sleep. And he had understood the situation at once—nothing could have seemed simpler—there had been snow in the night, such as all winter he had been longing for; and it was this which had rendered the postman's first footsteps inaudible, and the later ones faint. Of course! How lovely! And even now it must be snowing—it was going to be a snowy day— the long white ragged lines were drifting and sifting across the street, across the faces of the old houses, whispering and hushing, making little triangles of white in the corners between cobblestones, seething a little when the wind blew them over the ground to a drifted corner; and so it would be all day, getting deeper and deeper and silenter and silenter.

(Miss Buell was saying, "Land of perpetual snow.")

All this time, of course (while he lay in bed), he had kept his eyes closed, listening to the nearer progress of the postman, the muffled footsteps thumping and slipping on the snow-sheathed cobbles; and all the other sounds—the double knocks, a frosty far-off voice or two, a bell ringing thinly and softly as if under a sheet of ice—had the same slightly abstracted quality, as if removed by one degree from actuality—as if everything in the world had been insulated by snow. But when at last, pleased, he opened his eyes, and turned them toward the window, to see for himself this long-desired and now so clearly imagined miracle—what he saw instead was brilliant sunlight on a roof; and when, astonished, he jumped out of bed and stared down into the street, expecting to see the cobbles obliterated by the snow, he saw nothing but the bare bright cobbles themselves.

Queer, the effect this extraordinary surprise had had upon him—all the following morning he had kept with him a sense as of snow falling about him, a secret screen of new snow between himself and the world. If he had not dreamed such a thing—and how could he have dreamed it while awake?—how else could one explain it? In any case, the delusion had been so vivid as to affect his entire behavior. He could not now remember whether it was on the first or the second morning—or was it even the third?—that his mother had drawn attention to some oddness in his manner.

"But my darling"—she had said at the breakfast table—"what has come over you? You don't seem to be listening...."

And how often that very same thing had happened since!

Miss Buell was now asking if anyone knew the difference between the North Pole and the Magnetic Pole. Deirdre was holding up her flickering brown hand, and he could see the four white dimples that marked the knuckles.

Perhaps it hadn't been either the second or the third morning—or even the fourth or fifth. How could he be sure? How could he be sure just when the delicious *progress* had become clear? Just when it had really *begun?* The intervals weren't very precise....All he now knew was, that at some point or other—perhaps the second day, perhaps the sixth—he had noticed that the presence of the snow was a little more insistent, the sound of it clearer; and, conversely, the sound of the postman's footsteps more indistinct. Not only could he not hear the steps come round the corner, he could not even hear them at the first house. It was below the first house that he heard them; and then, a few days after, it was below the second house that he heard them; and a few days later again, below the third. Gradually, gradually, the snow was becoming heavier, the sound of its seething louder, the cobblestones more and more muffled. When he found, each morning, on going to the window, after the ritual of listening, that the roofs and cobbles were as bare as ever, it made no difference. This was, after all, only what he had expected. It was even what pleased him, what rewarded him: the thing was his own, belonged to no one else. No one else knew about it, not even his mother and father. There, outside, were the bare cobbles; and here, inside, was the snow. Snow growing heavier each day, muffling the world, hiding the ugly, and deadening increasingly—above all—the steps of the postman.

"But, my darling"—she had said at the luncheon table—"what has come over you? You don't seem to listen when people speak to you. That's the third time I've asked you to pass your plate...."

How was one to explain this to Mother? Or to Father? There was, of course, nothing to be done about it: nothing. All one could do was to laugh embarrassedly, pretend to be a little ashamed, apologize, and take a sudden and somewhat disingenuous interest in what was being done or said. The cat had stayed out all night. He had a curious swelling on his left cheek—perhaps somebody had kicked him, or a stone had struck him. Mrs. Kempton was or was not coming to tea. The house was going to be housecleaned, or "turned out," on Wednesday instead of Friday. A new lamp was

provided for his evening work—perhaps it was eyestrain that accounted for this new and so peculiar vagueness of his—Mother
was looking at him with amusement as she said this, but with something else as well. A new lamp. Yes, Mother. No, Mother. Yes
Mother. School is going very well. The geometry is very interesting—particularly when it takes one to the North Pole. Why the
North Pole? Oh, well, it would be fun to be an explorer. Another
Peary or Scott or Shakleton. And then abruptly he found his interest in the talk at an end, stared at the pudding on his plate, listened, waited, and began once more—ah, how heavenly, too, the
first beginnings—to hear or feel—for could he actually hear it?—
the silent snow, the secret snow.

(Miss Buell was telling them about the search for the Northwest Passage, about Hendrik Hudson, the *Half Moon.*)

This had been, indeed, the only distressing feature of the new
experience; the fact that it so increasingly had brought him into a
kind of mute misunderstanding, or even conflict, with his father
and mother. It was as if he were trying to lead a double life. On the
one hand, he had to be Paul Hasleman, and keep up the appearance of being that person—dress, wash, and answer intelligently
when spoken to—; on the other, he had to explore this new world
which had been opened to him. Nor could there be the slightest
doubt—not the slightest—that the new world was the profounder
and more wonderful of the two. It was irresistible. It was miracu-
lous. Its beauty was simply beyond anything—beyond speech as
beyond thought—utterly incommunicable. But how then, between
the two worlds, of which he was thus constantly aware, was he to
keep a balance? One must get up, one must go to breakfast, one
must talk with Mother, go to school, do one's lessons—and, in all
this, try not to appear too much of a fool. But if all the while one
was also trying to extract the full deliciousness of another and quite
separate existence, one which could not easily (if at all) be spoken
of—how was one to manage? How was one to explain? Would it
be safe to explain? Would it be absurd? Would it merely mean that
he would get into some obscure kind of trouble?

These thoughts came and went, came and went, as softly and secretly as the snow; they were not precisely a disturbance, perhaps they were even a pleasure; he liked to have them; their presence was something almost palpable, something he could stroke with his hand, without closing his eyes, and without ceasing to see Miss Buell and the schoolroom and the globe and the freckles on Deirdre's neck; nevertheless he did in a sense cease to see, or to see the obvious external world, and substituted for this vision the vision of snow, the sound of snow, and the slow, almost soundless, approach of the postman. Yesterday, it had been only at the sixth house that the postman had become audible; the snow was much deeper now, it was falling more swiftly and heavily, the sound of its seething was more distinct, more soothing, more persistent. And this morning, it had been—as nearly as he could figure—just above the seventh house—perhaps only a step or two above; at most, he had heard two or three footsteps before the knock had sounded.... And with each such narrowing of the sphere, each nearer approach of the limit at which the postman was first audible, it was odd how sharply was increased the amount of illusion which had to be carried into the ordinary business of daily life. Each day, it was harder to get out of bed, to go to the window, to look out at the—as always—perfectly empty and snowless street. Each day it was more difficult to go through the perfunctory motions of greeting Mother and Father at breakfast, to reply to their questions, to put his books together and go to school. And at school, how extraordinarily hard to conduct with success simultaneously the public life and the life that was secret! There were times when he longed—positively ached—to tell everyone about it—to burst out with it—only to be checked almost at once by a far-off feeling as of some faint absurdity which was inherent in it—but *was* it absurd?—and more importantly by a sense of mysterious power in his very secrecy. Yes; it must be kept secret. That, more and more, became clear. At whatever cost to himself, whatever pain to others.

(Miss Buell looked straight at him, smiling, and said, "Perhaps we'll ask Paul. I'm sure Paul will come out of his daydream long enough to be able to tell us. Won't you, Paul?" He rose slowly from his chair, resting one hand on the brightly varnished desk, and deliberately stared through the snow toward the blackboard. It was an effort, but it was amusing to make it. "Yes," he said slowly, "it was what we now call the Hudson River. This he thought to be the Northwest Passage. He was disappointed." He sat down again, and as he did so Deirdre turned in her chair and gave him a shy smile, of approval and admiration.)

At whatever pain to others.

This part of it was very puzzling, very puzzling. Mother was very nice, and so was Father. Yes, that was all true enough. He wanted to be nice to them, to tell them everything—and yet, was it really wrong of him to want to have a secret place of his own?

At bed time, the night before, Mother had said, "If this goes on, my lad, we'll have to see a doctor, we will! We can't have our boy—" But what was it she had said? "Live in another world"? "Live so far away?" The word "far" had been in it, he was sure, and then Mother had taken up a magazine again and laughed a little, but with an expression which wasn't mirthful. He had felt sorry for her.

The bell rang for dismissal. The sound came to him through long curved parallels of falling snow. He saw Deirdre rise, and had himself risen almost as soon—but not quite as soon—as she.

On the walk homeward, which was timeless, it pleased him to see through the accompaniment, or counterpoint, of snow, the items of mere externality on his way. There were many kinds of brick in the sidewalks, and laid in many kinds of pattern. The garden walls, too, were various, some of wooden palings, some of plaster, some of stone. Twigs of bushes leaned over the walls: the little hard green winter-buds of lilac, on gray stems, sheathed and fat; other branches very thin and fine and black and desiccated. Dirty sparrows huddled in the bushes, as dull in color as dead fruit left in leafless trees. A single starling creaked on a weather vane. In the gutter, beside a drain, was a scrap of torn and dirty newspaper, caught in a little delta of filth; the word ECZEMA appeared in large capitals, and below it was a letter from Mrs. Amelia D. Cravath, 2100 Pine Street, Fort Worth, Texas, to the effect that after being a sufferer for years she had been cured by Caley's Ointment. In the little delta, beside the fan-shaped and deeply runneled continent of brown mud, were lost twigs, descended from their parent trees, dead matches, a rusty horse-chestnut burr, a small concentration of eggshell, a streak of yellow sawdust which had been wet, and now was dry and congealed, a brown pebble, and a broken feather. Farther on was a cement sidewalk, ruled into geometrical parallelograms, with a brass inlay at one end commemorating the contractors who had laid it, and, halfway across, an irregular and random series of dog tracks, immortalized in synthetic stone. He knew these well, and always stepped on them; to cover the little hollows with his own foot had always been a queer pleasure; today he did it once more, but perfunctorily and detachedly, all the while thinking of something else. That was a dog, a long time ago who had made a mistake and walked on the cement while it was still wet. He had probably wagged his tail, but that hadn't been recorded. Now, Paul Hasleman, aged twelve, on his way home from school, crossed the same river, which, in the meantime, had frozen into rock. Homeward through the snow, the snow falling in bright sunshine. Homeward?

Then came the gateway with the two posts surmounted by egg-shaped stones which had been cunningly balanced on their ends, as if by Columbus, and mortared in the very act of balance; a source of perpetual wonder. On the brick wall just beyond, the letter H had been stenciled, presumably for some purpose. H? H.

The elm tree, with the great gray wound in the bark, kidney-shaped, into which he always put his hand—to feel the cold but living wood. The injury, he had been sure, was due to the gnawings of a tethered horse. But now it deserved only a passing palm, a merely tolerant eye. There were more important things. Miracles. Beyond the thoughts of trees, mere elms. Beyond the thoughts of sidewalks, mere stone, mere brick, mere cement. Beyond the

thoughts even of his own shoes, which trod these sidewalks obedi-
ently, bearing a burden—far above—of elaborate mystery. He
watched them. They were not very well polished; he had neglected
them, for a very good reason: they were one of the many parts of
the increasing difficulty of the daily return to daily life, the morning struggle. To get up, having at last opened one's eyes, to go to
the window, and discover no snow, to wash, to dress, to descent the
curving stairs to breakfast.

At whatever pain to others, nevertheless, one must persevere
in severance, since the incommunicability of the experience demanded it. It was desirable, of course, to be kind to Mother and
Father, especially as they seemed to be worried, but it was also
desirable to be resolute. If they should decide—as appeared likely—
to consult the doctor, Doctor Howells, and have Paul inspected,
his heart listened to through a kind of dictaphone, his lungs, his
stomach—well, that was all right. He would go through with it.
He would give them answer for question, too—perhaps such answers as they hadn't expected? No. That would never do. For the
secret world must, at all costs, be preserved.

The birdhouse in the apple tree was empty—it was the wrong
time of year for wrens. The little round black door had lost its
pleasure. The wrens were enjoying other houses, other nests, re-
moter trees. But this, too, was a notion which he only vaguely and
grazingly entertained—as if, for the moment, he merely touched
an edge of it; there was something further on, which was already
assuming a sharper importance; something which already teased
at the corners of his eyes, teasing also at the corner of his mind. It
was funny to think that he so wanted this, so awaited it—and yet
found himself enjoying this momentary dalliance with the birdhouse, as if for a quite deliberate postponement and enhancement
of the approaching pleasure. He was aware of his delay, of his smiling and detached and now almost uncomprehending gaze at the
little birdhouse; he knew what he was going to look at next: it was
his own little cobbled hill-street, his own house, the little river at
the bottom of the hill, the grocer's shop with the cardboard man

in the window—and now, thinking of all this, he turned his head, still smiling, and looking quickly right and left through the snow-laden sunlight.

And the mist of snow, as he had foreseen, was still on it—a ghost of snow falling in the bright sunlight, softly and steadily floating and turning and pausing, soundlessly meeting the snow that covered, as with a transparent mirage, the bare bright cobbles. He loved it—he stood still and loved it. Its beauty was paralyzing—beyond all words, all experience, all dream. No fairy story he had ever read could be compared with it—none had ever given him this extraordinary combination of ethereal loveliness with a something else, unnameable, which was just faintly and deliciously terrifying. What was this thing? As he thought of it, he looked upward toward his own bedroom window which was open—and it was as if he looked straight into the room and saw himself lying half awake in his bed. There he was—at this very instant he was still perhaps actually there—more truly there than standing here at the edge of the cobbled hill-street, with one hand lifted to shade his eyes against the snow-sun. Had he indeed ever left his room, in all this time? Since that very first morning? Was the whole progress still being enacted there, was it still the same morning, and himself not yet wholly awake? And even now, had the postman not yet come round the corner?...

This idea amused him, and automatically, as he thought of it, he turned his head and looked toward the top of the hill. There was, of course, nothing there—nothing and no one. The street was empty and quiet. And all the more because of its emptiness it occurred to him to count the houses—a thing which, oddly enough, he hadn't before thought of doing. Of course, he had known there weren't many—many, that is, on his own side of the street, which were the ones that figured in the postman's progress—but nevertheless it came as something of a shock to find that there were precisely *six*, above his own house—his own house was the seventh!

Six!

Astonished, he looked at his own house—looked at the door,

on which was the number thirteen—and then realized that the whole thing was exactly and logically and absurdly what he ought to have known. Just the same, the realization gave him abruptly, and even a little frighteningly, a sense of hurry. He was being hurried—he was being rushed. For—he knit his brow—he couldn't be mistaken—it was just above the *seventh* house, his *own* house, that the postman had first been audible this very morning. But in that case—in that case—did it mean that tomorrow he would hear nothing?

But how could that be? Unless even the knocker should be muffled in the snow—frozen tight, perhaps?...But in that case.... A vague feeling of disappointment came over him; a vague sadness as if he felt himself deprived of something which he had long looked forward to, something much prized. After all this, all this beautiful progress, the slow delicious advance of the postman through the silent and secret snow, the knock creeping closer each day, and the footsteps nearer, the audible compass of the world thus daily narrowed, narrowed, narrowed, as the snow soothingly and beautifully encroached and deepened, after all this, was he to be defrauded of the one thing he had so wanted—to be able to count, as it were, the last two or three solemn footsteps, as they finally approached his own door? Was it all going to happen, at the end, so suddenly? Or indeed, had it already happened? With no slow and subtle gradations of menace, in which he could luxuriate?

He gazed upward again, toward his own window which flashed in the sun; and this time almost with a feeling that it would be better if he *were* still in bed, in that room; for in that case this must still be the first morning, and there would be six more mornings to come—or, for that matter, seven or eight or nine—how could he be sure?—or even more.

After supper, the inquisition began. He stood before the doctor, under the lamp, and submitted silently to the usual thumpings and tappings.

"Now will you please say 'Ah!?'"

"Ah!"

"Now again, please, if you don't mind."

"Ah."

"Say it slowly, and hold it if you can—"

"Ah-h-h-h-h-h—"

"Good."

How silly this all was. As if it had anything to do with his throat! Or his heart, or lungs!

Relaxing his mouth, of which the corners, after all this absurd stretching, felt uncomfortable, he avoided the doctor's eyes, and stared toward the fireplace, past his mother's feet (in gray slippers) which projected from the green chair, and his father's feet (in brown slippers) which stood neatly side by side of the hearth rug.

"Hm. There is certainly nothing wrong there..."

He felt the doctor's eyes fixed upon him, and, as if merely to be polite, returned the look, but with a feeling of justifiable evasiveness.

"Now, young man, tell me—do you feel all right?"

"Yes, sir, quite all right."

"No headaches? No dizziness?"

"No, I don't think so."

"Let me see. Let's get a book, if you don't mind—yes, thank you, that will do splendidly—and now, Paul, if you'll just read it, holding it as you would normally hold it—"

He took the book and read:

"And another praise have I to tell for this the city our mother, the gift of a great god, a glory of the land most high; the might of horses, the might of young horses, the might of the sea....For thou, son of Cronus, our lord Poseidon, hath throned herein this pride, since in these roads first thou did show forth the curb that cures the rage of steeds. And the shapely oar, apt to men's hands, hath a wondrous speed on the brine, following the hundred-footed Nereids....O land that art praised above all lands, now is it for thee to make those bright praises seen in deeds."

He stopped, tentatively, and lowered the heavy book.

"No—as I thought—there is certainly no superficial sign of eye strain."

Silence thronged the room, and he was award of the focused scrutiny of the three people who confronted him....

"We could have his eyes examined—but I believe it is something else."

"What could it be?" That was his father's voice.

"It's only this curious absent-mindedness—" This was his mother's voice.

In the presence of the doctor, they both seemed irritatingly apologetic.

"I believe it is something else. Now, Paul—I would like very much to ask you a question or two. You will answer them, won't you—you know I'm an old, old friend of yours, eh? That's right!..."

His back was thumped twice by the doctor's fat fist—then the doctor was grinning at him with false amiability, while with one fingernail he was scratching the top button of his waistcoat. Beyond the doctor's shoulder was the fire, the fingers of flame making light prestidigitation against the sooty fireback, the soft sound of their random flutter the only sound.

"I would like to know—is there anything that worries you?"

The doctor was again smiling, his eyelids low against the little black pupils, in each of which was a tiny white bead of light. Why answer him? Why answer him at all? "At whatever pain to others"— but it was all a nuisance, this necessity for resistence, this necessity for attention; it was as if one had been stood up on a brilliantly lighted stage, under a great round blaze of spotlight; as if one were merely a trained seal, or a performing dog, or a fish, dipped out of an aquarium and held up by the tail. It would serve them right if he were merely to bark or growl. And meanwhile, to miss these last few precious hours, these hours of which each minute was more beautiful than the last, more menacing! He still looked, as if from a great distance, at the beads of light in the doctor's eyes, at the fixed false smile, and then, beyond, once more at his mother's slippers, his father's slippers, the soft flutter of the fire. Even here, even amongst these hostile presences, and in this arranged light, he could see the snow, he could hear it—it was in the corners of the room, where the shadow was deepest, under the sofa, behind the half-opened door which led to the dining room. It was gentler here, softer, its seethe the quietest of whispers, as if, in deference to a drawing room, it had quite deliberately put on its "manners"; it kept itself out of sight, obliterated itself, but distinctly with an air of saying, "Ah, but just wait! Wait till we are alone together! Then I will begin to tell you something new! Something white! Something cold! Something sleepy! Something of cease and peace, and the long bright curve of space! Tell them to go away. Banish them. Refuse to speak. Leave them, go upstairs to your room, turn out the light and get into bed—I will go with you. I will be waiting for you, I will tell you a better story than Little Kay of the Skates, or the Snow Ghost—I will surround your bed, I will close the windows, pile a deep drift against the door, so that none will ever again be able to enter. Speak to them!..." It seemed as if the little hissing voice came from a slow white spiral of falling flakes in the corner by the front window—but he couldn't be sure. He felt himself smiling, then, and said to the doctor, but without looking at him, looking beyond him still—

"Oh no, I think not —"

"But are you sure, my boy?"

His father's voice came softly and coldly then—the familiar voice of silken warning.

"You needn't answer at once, Paul—remember we're trying to help you—think it over and be quite sure, won't you?"

He felt himself smiling again, at the notion of being quite sure. What a joke! As if he weren't so sure that reassurance was no longer necessary, and all this cross-examination a ridiculous farce, a grotesque parody! What could they know about it? These gross intelligences, these humdrum minds so bound to the usual, the ordinary? Impossible to tell them about it! Why, even now, even now, with the proof so abundant, so formidable, so imminent, so appallingly present here in this very room, could they believe it?—could even his mother believe it? No—it was only too plain that if anything were said about it, the merest hint given, they would be incredulous—they would laugh—they would say "Absurd!"—think things about him which weren't true....

"Why no, I'm not worried—why should I be?"

He looked then straight at the doctor's low-lidded eyes, looked from one of them to the other, from one bead of light to the other, and gave a little laugh.

The doctor seemed to be disconcerted by this. He drew back in his chair, resting a fat white hand on either knee. The smile faded slowly from his face.

"Well, Paul!" he said, and paused gravely, "I'm afraid you don't take this quite seriously enough. I think you perhaps don't quite realize—don't quite realize—" He took a deep quick breath and turned, as if helplessly, at a loss for words, to the others. But Mother and Father were both silent—no help was forthcoming.

"You must surely know, be aware, that you have not been quite yourself, of late? Don't you know that?..."

It was amusing to watch the doctor's renewed attempt at a smile, a queer disorganized look, as of confidential embarrassment.

"I feel all right, sir," he said, and again gave the little laugh.

"And we're trying to help you." The doctor's voice sharpened.

"Yes, sir, I know. But why? I'm all right. I'm just *thinking*, that's all."

His mother made a quick movement forward, resting a hand on the back of the doctor's chair.

"Thinking?" She said. "But my dear, about what?"

This was a direct challenge—and would have to be directly met. But before he met it, he looked again into the corner by the door, as if for reassurance. He smiled again at what he saw, at what he heard. The little spiral was still there, still softly whirling, like the ghost of a white kitten chasing the ghost of a white tail, and making as it did so the faintest of whispers. It was all right! If only he could remain firm, everything was going to be all right.

"Oh, about anything, about nothing—*you* know the way you do!"

"You mean—daydreaming?"

"Oh, no—thinking!"

"But thinking about *what?*"

"Anything."

He laughed a third time—but this time, happening to glance toward his mother's face, he was appalled at the effect his laughter seemed to have upon her. Her mouth had opened in an expression of horror....This was too bad! Unfortunate! He had known it would cause pain, of course—but he hadn't expected it to be quite so bad as this. Perhaps—perhaps if he just gave them a tiny gleaming hint—?

"About the snow," he said.

"What on earth?"This was his father's voice. The brown slippers came a step nearer on the hearth rug.

"But my dear, what do you mean?" This was his mother's voice. The doctor merely stared.

"Just *snow*, that's all. I like to think about it."

"Tell us about it, my boy."

"But that's all it is. There's nothing to tell. *You* know what snow is?"

This he said almost angrily, for he felt that they were trying to corner him. He turned sideways so as no longer to face the doctor, and the better to see the inch of blackness between the window-sill and the lowered curtain—the cold inch of beckoning and delicious night. At once he felt better, more assured.

"Mother—can I go to bed, now, please, I've got a headache."

"But I thought you said—"

"It just came now. It's all these questions—! Can I, mother?"

"You can go as soon as the doctor has finished."

"Don't you think this thing ought to be gone into thoroughly, and *now?* This was Father's voice. The brown slippers again came a step nearer, the voice was the well-known "punishment" voice, resonant and cruel.

"Oh, what's the use, Norman—"

Quite suddenly, everyone was silent. And without precisely facing them, nevertheless he was aware that all three of them were watching him with an extraordinary intensity—staring hard at him—as if he had done something monstrous, or was himself some kind of monster. He could hear the soft irregular flutter of the flames; the cluck-click-cluck-click of the clock; far and faint, two sudden spurts of laughter from the kitchen, as quickly cut off as begun; a murmur of water in the pipes; and then, the silence seemed to deepen, to spread out, to become world-long and world-wide, to become timeless and shapeless, and to center inevitably and rightly, with a slow and sleepy but enormous concentration of all power, on the beginning of a new sound. What this new sound was going to be, he knew perfectly well. It might begin with a hiss, but it would end with a roar—there was no time to lose—he must escape. It mustn't happen here—

Without another word, he turned and ran up the stairs.

Not a moment too soon. The darkness was coming in long white waves. A prolonged sibilance filled the night—a great seamless seethe of wild influence went abruptly across it—a cold low humming shook the windows. He shut the door and flung off his clothes in the dark. The bare black floor was like a little raft tossed in waves of snow, almost overwhelmed, washed under whitely, up again, smothered in curled billows of feather. The snow was laughing; it spoke from all sides at once; it pressed closer to him as he ran and jumped exulting into his bed.

"Listen to us!" it said. "Listen! We have come to tell you the story we told you about. You remember? Lie down. Shut your eyes, now—you will no longer see much—in this white darkness who could see, or want to see? We will take the place of everything....Listen—"

A beautiful varying dance of snow began at the front of the room, came forward and then retreated, flattened out toward the floor, then rose fountain-like to the ceiling, swayed, recruited itself from a new stream of flakes which poured laughing in through the humming window, advanced again, lifted long white arms. It said peace, it said remoteness, it said cold—it said…

But then a gash of horrible light fell brutally across the room from the opening door—the snow drew back hissing—something alien had come into the room—something hostile. This thing rushed at him, clutched at him, shook him—and he was not merely horrified, he was filled with such a loathing as he had never known. What was this? This cruel disturbance? This act of anger and hate? It was as if he had to reach up a hand toward another world for any understanding of it—an effort of which he was only barely capable. But of that other world he still remembered just enough to know the exorcizing words. They tore themselves from his other life suddenly–

"Mother! Mother! Go away! I Hate you!"

And with that effort, everything was solved, everything became all right. The seamless hiss advanced once more, the long white wavering lines rose and fell like enormous whispering sea-waves, the whisper becoming louder, the laughter more numerous.

"Listen!" it said. "We'll tell you the last, the most beautiful and secret story—shut your eyes—it is a very small story—a story that gets smaller and smaller—it comes inward instead of opening like a flower—it is a flower becoming a seed—a little cold seed—do you hear? We are leaning closer to you—"

The hiss was not becoming a roar—the whole world was a vast moving screen of snow—but even now it said peace, it said re-moteness, it said cold, it said sleep.

Conrad Aiken's *Silent Snow, Secret Snow,* the tale of a boy's de-scent into mental illness[2], is perhaps the most psychologically as-tute story ever written. It is a perfect example of a brilliant writer working with psychiatric material.

Paul Hasleman was twelve years old when he had a delusion

"of paralyzing beauty," in which he heard the approaching postman's steps sound "curiously different," softer, muffled and indistinct, as though it had snowed during the night. All the following morning he kept the sense of the snow falling about him, as if there was "a secret screen of new snow between himself and the world."

Paul was at the threshold of adolescence, the age of psychosexual maturation when physical changes and the pressure of strange and terrifying impulses must be coped with. One of the urges is that of emerging sexuality, another is rage; both accompanied by a dread of being unable to handle the surging emotions. Freud said that if the boy of three had the strength of a man, he would sleep with his mother and kill his father. Adolescence is a harrowing time for youngsters, who experience the urges of the three-year-old, along with the strength of a man. Having a loving father is a reality that helps the growing boy put his infantile fears to rest. We don't know much about Mr. Hasleman, except that in his son's mind he had a "well-known 'punishment' voice, resonant and cruel." He would not have appreciated Paul's incestuous desires nor his wish to do away with him. Paul certainly felt ambivalent about his father, needing, fearing, and hating him at the same time.

Paul escaped his conflict by burying himself in a fantasy of a snowbound world, "a fortress, a wall behind which he could retreat into heavenly seclusion. (It) said peace, it said remoteness, it said cold, it said sleep." It also said "death." The snow was a barricade which protected him from his wishes and his punitive father. The wall grew heavier every day, "hiding the ugly and deadening increasingly...the steps of the postman." So engrossed was Paul in his fantasy that he lost all interest in the ordinary details of living, and briefly came to life in class only when he spoke of the North Pole.

In analysis we speak of "the return of the repressed," in which warded off feelings return in another form. Paul's pathology intimates that there were many periods in his life when he was happier than at age twelve. In all likelihood, his infancy was one in which he experienced bliss at the breast of his mother. The whiteness of the snow suggests that Paul yearned to return to that beautiful period, and perhaps to regress to the womb itself. Paul wanted desperately to be able to count the footsteps of the postman as they approached his door. (How he must have longed for an "approachable" father!) Yet his great fear was that the postman would disappear and he would never hear him again. This fear was based on a wish to get rid of his father, his "rival," and indeed was a return of the repressed.

Deep, deep into his psychosis Paul retreated, with the snow telling him a "secret story—a story that gets "smaller and smaller—it comes inward instead of opening like a flower—it is a flower becoming a seed—a little cold seed." Until Paul, frozen into his icy womb fantasy, no longer existed, and "everything was solved, everything became all right."

The prognosis for Paul's future is unknown. In some cases of Schizoid Disorder of Childhood, the individual goes on to develop increased socialization in adolescence. In other instances, there is increased withdrawal and detachment in adolescence which develops in adulthood into Schizoid Personality Disorder or Schizophrenia. In my opinion, Paul's illness is likely to take the latter course.

11

HOW TO WIN

ROSELLEN BROWN

All they need at school is permission on a little green card that says *Keep this child at bay. Muffle him, tie his hands, his arms to his ankles, anything at all. Distance, distance. Dose him.* And they gave themselves permission. They never even mentioned a doctor, and their own certified bureaucrat in tweed (does he keep a badge in his pocket like the cops?) drops by the school twice a year for half a day. But I insisted on a doctor. And did and did, had to, because Howard keeps repeating vaguely that he is "within the normal range of boyish activity."

"But I live with it, all day every day."

"It? Live with *it?*"

Well, Howard can be as holy as he likes, I am his mother and I will not say "him." Him is the part I know, Christopher my first child and first son, the boy who was a helpless warm mound once in a blue nightie tied at the bottom to keep his toes in. (God, Margaret, you are dramatic and sentimental and sloppy. How about being realistic for a change?) "It" is what races around my room at night, a bat, pulling down the curtain cornice, knocking over the lamps, tearing the petals off the flowers and stomping them, real or fake, to a powder.

Watch Christopher take a room some time; that's the word for it, like an army subduing a deserted plain. He stands in the door-way always for one extra split-split second, straining his shoulders down as though he's hitching himself to some machine, getting into harness. He has no hips, and round little six-year-old shoulders that look frail but are made of welded steel that have no give when you grab them. Then what does he see ahead of him? I'm no good at guessing. The room is an animal asleep, trusting the air, its last mistake. (See, I am sympathetic to the animal.) He leaps on it and leaves it disemboweled, then turns his dark eyes to me where I stand—when I stand, usually I'm dervishing around trying to stop the bloodshed—and they ask me Where did it go? What happened? Who killed this thing, it was just breathing. I wanted to *play* with it. Christopher. When you're not here to look at me I have to laugh at your absurd powers. You are incontinent, you leak energy. As for me, I gave birth to someone else's child.

There is a brochure inside the brown bottle that the doctor assigned us, very gay, full-color, busy with children riding their bicycles right through patches of daffodils, sleeping square in the middle of their pillows, doing their homework with a hazy expression to be attributed to concentration, not medication. *Non-addictive! No significant side effects!* Dosage should decrease by or around puberty. Counter-indications epilepsy, heart and circulatory complications, severe myopia and related eye problems. See *Journal of pediatric Medicine*, iii 136, F'71; *Pharmacology Bulletin*, v. 798, 18, pp. 19-26, D'72. *Caution: Do not allow children access to pills! Special feature: U-lok-it cap! Remember, teach your child the etiquette of the medicine cabinet!*

I know how he dreams of me. I know because I dream his dreams. He runs to hide in me. Battered by the stick of the old dark he comes fast, hiccoughing in terror. By the time I am up, holding him, it has hobbled off, it must be, into his memory. I've pulled on a robe, I spread my arms—do they looked winged or webbed?—to pull him out of himself, hide him, swear the witch is nowhere near. He doesn't go to his father. But he won't look at my face.

It was you! He looks up at me finally and says nothing but I see him thinking. So: *I* was the witch, with a club behind my bent back. I the hundred-stalked flower with webbed branches. I with the flayed face held in my two hands like a bloody towel. Then how can I help him?

I whisper to him, wordless; just a music. He answers, "Mama." It is a faint knocking, through layers of dirt, through flowers.

His sister, Jody, will dream those dreams, and all the children who will follow her. I suppose she will, like chicken pox every child can expect them: there's a three o'clock in the dark night of children's souls too, let's not be too arrogant taking our prerogatives. But if she does, she'll dream them alone, no accomplices. I won't meet her halfway, give her my own last fillip, myself in shreds.

I've been keeping a sort of log: a day in the life. For no purpose, since my sense of futility runs deeper than any data can testify to. Still it cools me off.

He is playing with Jacqueline. They are in the Rosenbergs' yard. C. is on his way to the sandbox which belongs to Jackie's baby brother, Brian, so I see trouble ahead. I will not interfere. No, *intervene* is the word they use. Interfere is not as objective, it's the mess that parents make, as opposed to the one the doctors make. As he goes down the long narrow yard at a good clip C. pulls up two peonies, knocks over Brian's big blonde blocky wooden horse (for which he had to stop and plant his feet very deliberately, it's that well-balanced, i.e., expensive). Kicks over short picket fence around tulips, finally gets to sandbox, walks up to Jackie whose back is to him and pushes her hard. She falls against fence and goes crying to her mother with a splinter. She doesn't even bother to retaliate, knowing him too well? Then he leans down into the sand. Turns to me again, that innocent face. It is not conniving, or falsely naive. I swear it is not. He isn't that kind of clever. Nor is he

a gruff bully boy who likes to fly from trees and conquer turf: he
has a small peaked face, a little French, I think, in need of one of
those common Gallic caps with the peak on the front; a narrow
forehead on which his dark hair lies flat like a salon haircut. Anything but a bully, this helpless child of mine—he has a weird natural elegance that terrifies me, as though it is true, what I feel, that
he was intended to be someone else...Now he seems to be saying,
Well, take all this stuff away if you don't want me to touch it. Get
me out of this goddamn museum. Who says I'm not provoked?
That's what you say to each other.

Why is *he* not glass? He will break us all without so much as
chipping.

The worst thing I can think. I am dozing in the sun, Christopher is in kindergarten, Jody is napping, and I am guiltily trying to
coax a little color into my late-fall pallor. It's a depressingly bleary
sun up there. But I sleep a little, waking in fits and snatches when
Migdalia next door lets her kid have it, and his whine sails across
the yards, and when the bus shakes the earth all the way under the
gas mains and water pipes to China. The worst thing is crawling
through my head like a stream of red ants: What if he and I, Howie
and I, had been somewhere else way back that night we smiled
and nodded and made Christopher? If the night had been bone-
cracking cold? If we were courting some aloneness, back to back?
But it was summer, we were married three months, and the bottom sheet was spread like a picnic cloth. If there's an astrologer's
clock, that's what we heard announcing to us the time was propitious; but I rehearse the time again. We lived off Riverside Drive
that year and the next, I will float a thundercloud across the river
from the Palisades and just as Howie turns to me I will have the
most extraordinary burst of rain, sludgy and cold, explode through
the open windows everywhere and finish us for the evening. The
rugs are soaked, our books are corrugated with dampness, we snap
at each other, Howie breaks a beer glass and blames me. We unmake him...another night we will make a different child. Don't

the genes shift daily in their milky medium like lottery tickets in their fishbowl? I unmake Christopher's skin and bone: egg in the water, blind, a single sperm thrusts out of its soft side, retreating. Arrow swimming backwards, tail drags the heavy head away from life. All the probability in the universe cheers. He is unjoined. I wake in a clammy sweat. The sun, such as it was, is caught behind the smokestacks at the far end of Pacific Street. I feel dirty, as though I've sinned in my sleep, and there's that fine perpetual silt on my arms and legs and face, the Con Ed sunburn. I go in and start making lunch for Christopher, who will survive me.

Log: He is sitting at the kitchen table trying to string kidney beans on a needle and thread. They do it in kindergarten. I forgot to ask why. Jody wakes upstairs, way at the back of the house with her door closed, and C. says quietly, without looking up from his string, "Ma, she's up." It's like hearing something happening, I don't know, a mile away. He has the instincts of an Indian guide, except when I stand right next to him to talk. Then it blows right by. And when she's up. He seems to make a very special effort to be gentle with his little sister. I can see him forcibly subdue himself, tuck his hands inside his pockets or push them into the loops of his pants so that he loses no honor in restraint. But every now and then it gets the better of him. He walked by her just a minute ago and did just what he does to anything that's not nailed down or bigger than he is: gave her a casual but precise push. The way the bathmat slips into the tub without protest, the glass bowl gets smashed, its pieces settling with a resigned tinkle. I am, of course, the one who's resigned: I hear them ring against each other before they hit the ground, in the silence that envelops the shove.

This time Jody chose to lie back on the rug—fortunately it wasn't cement, I am grateful for small favors—and watch him. An amazing, endearing thing for a two year old. I think she has all the control that was meant for the two of them, and this is fair to neither. Eyes wide open, untearful, Jody the antidote, was thinking something about her brother. She cannot say what.

When his dosage has been up a while he begins to cringe before her. It is unpredictable and unimaginable but true and I bear
witness to it here. As I was writing the above he ran in and hid
behind my chair. Along came J., who had just righted herself after
the attack on her; she was pulling her corn popper, vaguely humming. For C., an imagined assault? Provoked? Real? Wished-for?

Howard, on his way out of the breakfast chaos, bears his briefcase like a shield, holds it in front of him for lack of space while he
winds his way around the table in our little alcove, planting firm
kisses on our foreheads. On his way out the door he can be expected to say something cheerful and blind to encourage me
through the next unpredictable half hour before I walk Christopher up the block to school. This morning, unlocking the front
gate I caught him pondering, "Well, what are other kids like? I
mean we've never had any others so how do we know where they
fall on the spectrum?"

"We know," I said. "What about Jody?"

"Oh," he said, waving her away like a fly. "I mean boys."

"We also know because we're not knots on logs, some of us,
that's how we know. What was it he did to your shaver this morning?"

Smashed it to smithereens is what he did, and left cobweb cracks
in the mirror he threw it at.

To which his father shrugged and turned to pull the gate shut fast.

Why did we have Jody? People dare to ask, astonished, though
it's none of their business. They mean, and expect us to forgive
them, how could we take such a martyr's chance. I tell them that
when C. was born I was ready for a large family. You can't be a
secretary forever, no matter how many smash titles your boss edits.
Nor an administrative assistant, not the hands I've got. I like to be
boss, thank you, in my own house. It's a routine by now, canned as
an Alka-Seltzer ad.

But I'll tell you. For a long time I guarded very tensely against
having another baby. C. was hurting me too much, already he

was. Howard would rap with his fist on my nightgowned side, demanding admission. For a while I played virgin. I mean, I didn't try, I wasn't playing. He just couldn't make any headway. I've heard it called dys-something; also crossbones, to get right down to what it's like. (Dys-something put me right in there with my son, doesn't it? I'll bet there's some drug, some muscle relaxant that bones you and just lays you out on the knife like a chicken to be stuffed and trussed...) Even though it wasn't his fault I'll never forgive Howard for using his fists on me, even as gently and facetiously as he did. Finally I guess he got tired of trying to disarm me one night at a time, of bringing wine to bed or dancing with me obscenely like a kid at a petting party or otherwise trying to distract me while he stole up on me. So that's when he convinced me to have another baby. I guess it seemed easier. "We'll make Christopher our one exceptional child while we surround him with ordinary ones. We'll grow a goddamn garden around him, he'll be outnumbered."

Well—I bought it. We could make this child matter less. It was an old and extravagant solution. Black flowers in his brain, what blight would the next one have. I insisted he *promise* me. He lied, ah, he lied with his hand between my legs, he swore the next would be just as beautiful but timid—"Downright phlegmatic, how's that?"—and would teach Christopher to be human. So I sighed, desperate to believe, and unlocked my thighs, gone rusty and stiff. But I'll tell you, right as he turned out, by luck, to be, I think I never trusted him again, one of my two deceitful boys, because whatever abandon I once had is gone, sure as my waist is gone. I feel it now and Howard is punished for it. Starting right then, making Jody, I have dealt myself out in careful proportions, like an unreliable cook bent only on her batter.

Meanwhile I lose one lamp, half the ivory on the piano keys, and all my sewing patterns to my son in a single day. On the same day I lose my temper, lose it so irretrievably that I am tempted to pop one of Christopher's little red pills myself and go quietly. Who's the most frightening, the skimpy six-year-old flying around on the tail of his bird of prey, or his indispensable right hand mama smashing the canned goods into the closet with a sound generally reserved for the shooting range? All the worse, off his habit for a few days, his eyes clear, his own, he is trying to be sweet, he smiles wanly whenever some catastrophe overtakes him, like an actor with no conviction. But someone else controls his muscles. He is not riding it now but lives in the beak of something huge and dark that dangles him just out of my reach.

Our brains are all circuitry; not very imaginative, I tend to see it blue and red and yellow like the wires in phones, easier to sort impulses that way. I want to see inside Christopher's head, I stare viciously though I try to do it when he's involved with something else. (He never is, he would feel me a hundred light years behind him.) I vow never to *study* him again, it's futile anyway, his forehead's not a one-way mirror. Promises, always my promises: they are glass. I knew when they shatter—no, when he shatters them, throwing something of value—there will be edges to draw blood, edges everywhere. He says, "What are you *looking* at all the time? Bad Christopher the dragon?" He looks wilted, pathetic. seen-through. But I haven't seen a thing.

"Chrissie." I put my arms around him. He doesn't want to bruise the air he breaths, maybe we're all jumbled up in his sight. He doesn't read yet, I know that's why. It's all upside down or somehow mixed together—cubist sight, is there such a thing? He sees my face and the top of my head, say, at the same time. Or everything looms at him, quivering like a fun-house mirror, swollen, then slowly disappears down to a point. He has to subdue it before it overtakes him? How would we ever know? Why, if he saw just what we see—the cool and calm of all the things of the world all sorted out like the laundry. (Oh, Margaret, come off it!)why would he look so bewildered most of the time like a terrier being dragged around by its collar, his small face thrust forward into his own perpetual messes?

He comes to me just for a second, pulling on his tan windbreaker, already breathing fast to run away somewhere, and while

I hold him tight a minute, therapeutic hug for both of us, he pinches my arm until the purple capillaries dance with pain.

"Let me take him with me when I go to D.C. next week." Howard.

I stare at him. "You've got to be kidding."

"No, why would I kid about it? We'll manage, we can go see some buildings after my conference is out, go to the Smithsonian. He'd love the giant pendulum." His eyes are already there in the cool of the great vaulted room where everything echoes and everything can break. I am fascinated by his casualness. "What would he do all day while you're in your meeting? Friend. My intrepid friend."

"Oh, we'd manage something. He'd keep busy. Paper and pencil..."

"*Howie*." Am I crazy? Is he? Do we live in the same house?

He comes and takes both my hands. There is that slightly conniving look my husband gets that makes me forget, goddamit, why I married him. He is all too reasonable and gentle a man most of the time, but this look is way in the back of his eyes behind a pillar, peeking out. I feel surrounded. "You can't take him." I wrench my hands away.

"Maggie—" and he tries to take them again, bungler, as though they're contested property.

"I forbid it. Insanity. You'll end up crushing him to death to get a little peace! I know."

He smiles with unbearable patience. "I know how to handle my son."

But I walk out of the room, thin-lipped, taking a bowl of fruit to the children who are raging around, both of them, in front of the grade-A educational television that's raging back.

The next week Howie goes to Washington and we all go to the airport to see him off. I don't know what Howard told him but while Jody sleeps Christopher cries noisily in the back of the car and flings himself around so wildly, like a caged bear, that I have to stop the car on the highway shoulder and buckle him into his seat belt. "You will walk home," I threaten, calm because I can see the battle plan. He's got a little of his father in him; that should make me feel better.

He hisses at me and goes on crying, forcing the tears and walloping the back of my seat with his feet the whole way home.

Log: The long, long walk to school. A block and a half. Most of the kids in kindergarten with Christopher walk past our house alone, solidly bearing straight west with the bland eight o'clock sun at their backs. They concentrate, they have been told not to cross heavy traffic alone, not to speak to strangers, not to dawdle. All the major wisdom of motherhood pinned to their jackets like a permission slip. Little orders turning into habits and hardening slowly to super-ego: an amber that holds commands forever. Christopher lacks it the way some children are born without a crucial body chemical. Therefore, I walk him to school every day, rain or shine, awake or asleep.

Jody's in her stroller slouching. She'd rather be home. So would I. It's beginning to get chilly out, edgy, and that means the neighborhood's been stripped of summer and fall, as surely as if a man came by one day confiscating color. What little there is, you wouldn't think it could matter. Blame the mayor. The windowboxes are crowded with brown stringy corpses, like tall crabgrass. Our noble pint-sized trees have shrunk back into themselves, they lose five years in winter. Fontaine, always improving his property, has painted his new brick wall *silver* over the weekend—it has a sepulchral gleam in the vague sunlight, twinkling as placidly as a woman who's come in sequins to a business meeting, *believing* in herself. Bless him. Next door to him the Rosenbergs have bought subtle aged wood shutters, they look like some dissected Vermont barn door, and a big rustic barrel that will stand achingly empty all winter, weighted with a hundred pounds of dirt to exhaust the barrel burglars. I wonder what my illusions look like through the front window.

Christopher's off and running. "Not in the street!" I get so tired of my voice, especially because I know he doesn't hear it. "Stay on the curb, Christopher." There's enough damage to be done there. He is swinging on that new couple's gate, straining the hinges, trying to fan up a good wind; then, when I look up from attending to Jody's dropped and splintered cracker, he's gone—clapping together two garbage can lids across the street. Always under an old lady's window, though with no particular joy—his job, it's there to be done. Jody is left with her stroller braked against a tree for safe keeping while I retrieve him. No one ever told me I'd grow up to be a shepherdess, and bad at it too—undone by a single sheep.

We are somehow at the corner, at least I can demand he hold my hand and drag us across the street where the crossing guard stands and winks at me daily, as dependably as a blinking light. She is a good lady, Mrs. Cortes, from a couple of blocks down in the projects, with many more matching daughters, one son, Anibal, on the sixth grade honor roll and another on Riker's Island, a junkie. She is waving cars and people in waves, demonstrating a "community involvement" to placate the gods who are seeing to Anibal's future, I know it. I recognize something deep behind her lively eyes, sunk there, a certain desperate casualness while the world has its way with her children. Another shepherdess without a chance. I give her my little salute.

By now, my feet heavy with the monotony of this trip, we are on the long school block. The barbed wire of the playground breaks for the entrance halfway down. This street, unlived on, is an unrelenting tangle—no one ever sees the generous souls who bequeath their dead cars to the children, but there are dozens, in various stages of decay; they must make regular deliveries. Christopher's castles; creative playthings, and broken already so he never gets blamed. For some reason he picks the third one. He's already in there, across a moat of broken windshield glass, reaching for the steering wheel. The back seat's burned out, the better to jump on. All the chrome as been cannibalized by the adults—everything that twists or lifts off, leaving a carcass of flung bones, its tin flesh dangling.

"Christopher, you are late and I. Am. Not. Waiting." But he will not come that way. My son demands the laying-on of hands. Before I can maneuver my way in, feeling middle-aged and worrying about my skirt, hiked up over my rear, he is tussling not with one boy but with two. They fight over nothing—just lock hands and wrestle as a kind of greeting. "I break the muh-fuh's head," one announces matter-of-factly—second grader maybe. Christopher doesn't fight for stakes like that, though. Whoever wants his head can have it, he's fighting to get his hands on something, keep them warm. I am reaching over the jagged door, which is split in two and full of rain water. The school bell rings, that raspy grinding, and the two boys, with a whoop, leap over the downed windshield and are gone. Christopher is grater-scraped along one cheek but we have arrived more or less in one piece.

I decide I'd better come in with him and see to it his cheek is washed off. He is, of course, long gone by the time I park the stroller and take the baby out. He never bothers to say good-bye. Maybe six year olds don't.

I pull open the heavy door to P. S. 193. It comes reluctantly, like it's in many parts. These doors are not for children. But then, neither is the school...It's a fairly new building but the 1939 World's Fair architecture has just about caught up with the lobby—those heavy streamlined effects. A ship, that's what it looks like; a dated ocean liner, or the lobby of Rockefeller Center, one humble corner of it. What do the kids see, I wonder? Not grandeur.

There's a big lit-up case to the left that shows off sparse student pieties, untouchable as seven-layer cakes at the bakery. *This Land Is Your Land, This Land Is My Land.* Every figure in the pictures, brown, black, dead-white (blank), mustard yellow, tulip red and olive green (who's that?) is connected more or less at the wrist, like uncut paper dolls (HANDS ACROSS THE SEA). The whole world's afraid to drop hands, the hell with summit talks, SALT talks, we're on the buddy system. Well, *they* go up and down the halls irrevocably linked so, their lips sealed, the key thrown over their endless shoulder, only the teacher nattering on and on about discipline and respect, wearing heels that must sound like SS boots, though they are intended merely to mean business. Christopher tells me only that his teachers are noisy and hurt his ears; he does not bother to specify how.

And what he sees when he puts his thin shoulder to the door at 8:30 and heaves? He probably catches that glaring unnecessary shine on the floor, an invitation, and takes it. That worried crease between big eyes, his face looks back at him out of deep water. Deeper when he's drugged. So he careens around without ice-skates, knocks against other kids hard, thumps into closed doors, nearly cracks open *This Land Is Your Land.* He is the wiseacre who dances to hold the door for his class, then when the last dark pigtail is through skips off in the wrong direction, leaps the steps to the gym or the auditorium or whatever lives down there in de-serted silence most of the morning, the galley of this ship. I don't blame him, of course I don't, but that isn't the point, is it? I am deprived of these fashionable rebellious points. We only, madam, allow those in control to be out of control. As it were. If you follow. Your son, madam, is not rebelling. He is unable. Is beyond. Is utterly. Is unthinkable. Catch him before we do.

We are certainly late, the lines are all gone, the kids settling into their rooms, their noise dwindling like a cut-back motor. Jody and I just stand for a minute or two tuning in. Her head is heavy on my shoulder. Already there's a steady monitor traffic, the offi-cious kids scurrying to do their teachers' bidding like tailless mice. I was one of them for years and years, God, faceless and obliging: official blackboard eraser (which meant a few cool solitary min-utes just before three each day, down in the basement storeroom clapping two erasers together, hard, till they smoked with the day's vanished lessons). I would hardly have stopped my frantic do-gooding to give the time of day (off the clocks that jerked forward with a click every new minute) to the likes of Christopher. I'd have given him a wide berth, I can see myself going the other way if I saw him coming toward me in the narrow hall.

This hall, just like the ones I grew up in except for the "modernistic" shower tile that reaches halfway up, has a muted darkened feeling, an underwater thrum. Even the tile is like the Queens Midtown Tunnel, deserted. I will not be particularly welcome in Christopher's kindergarten room, there is that beleaguered proprietary feeling that any parent is a spy or come to complain. (I, in my own category, have been forbidden to complain, at least tacitly, having been told that my son really needs one whole teacher to himself, if not for his sake, then for the safety of the equipment and "the consumables," of which he is not one.)

Christopher has disappeared into his class which—I see it through the little porthole—is neat and earnest and not so terribly different from a third-grade room, say, with its alphabets and exhortations to patriotism and virtue above eye level. They are allowed to paint in one color at a time. A few, I see, have graduated to two; they must be disciplined, promising children in their securely tied smocks. One spring they will hatch into monitors. Christopher is undoubtedly banned from the painting corner. (Classroom economy? Margaret, your kitchen, your bedroom, your bathroom this morning. Searching for the glass mines hidden between the tiles.) Mrs. Seabury is inspecting hands, the children turn them, patty-cake, and step back when she finishes her scrutiny, which is as grave as a doctor's. Oh, Christopher! She has sent him and another little boy to the sink to scrub; to throw water, that is, and stick their fingers in the spout in order to shower the children in the back of the room. I am not going in there to identify myself.

Mrs. Seabury is the kind of teacher who, with all her brown and black kids on one side of the room (this morning in the back, getting showered), talks about discrimination and means big from little, forward from backward, ass from elbow. Now I see she has made Christopher an honorary black child, or maybe one of your more rambunctious Puerto Ricans. They are all massed back there for the special inattention of the aide, who is one of my least favorite people: she is very young and wears a maxi skirt that the kids keep stepping on when she bends down. (Therefore, she bends down as little as possible.) The Future Felons of America and their den mother. I'm caught somewhere between my first flash of anger and then shame at what I suppose, wearily, is arrogance. What am I angry at? That he had attained pariah-hood with them, overcoming his impeccable WASP heritage in a single leap of adrenaline? Jesus. they are the "unruly characters" he's supposed to be afraid of: latchkey babies, battered boys and abused girls, or loved but hungry, scouted by rats while they sleep. Products of this-and-that converging, social, political, economic, each little head impaled on a point of the grid. Christopher? My warm, healthy, nursed and coddled, vitamin-enriched boy, born on Blue Cross, swaddled in his grandparents' gifts from Lord & Taylor. What in the hell is our excuse? My pill-popping baby, so sad, so reduced and taken from himself when he's on, so indescribable, air-borne, when he's off. This week he's off; I am sneaking him a favor.

I see him now flapping around in a sort of ragged circle with the other unimaginables, under the passive eye of that aide. Crows? Buzzards? Not pigeons, anyway. They make their own rowdy music. Then Christopher clenches his whole body, I see it coming, and stops short slamming half a dozen kids together, solid rear-end collisions. It looks like the New Jersey Turnpike, everybody whiplashed, tumbling down. No reason, no why's, there is never anything to explain. Was the room taking off, spinning him dizzy? Was he fending something off, or trying to catch hold? The others turn to him, shout so loud I can hear them out here where I'm locked, underwater—and they all pile on. Oh, can they pile! It's a sport in itself. Feet and hands and dark faces deepening a shade. The aide gets out of the way, picking her skirt out of the rubble of children at her feet.

One heavy dark boy with no wrists finally breaks through the victor. His foot is on Christopher's neck. The little pale face jerks up stiffly, like an executed man's. I turn away. When I make myself turn back the crowd is unraveling as Mrs. Seabury approaches. Faces all around are taking on that half-stricken, half-delighted "uh-oh" look. I was always good at that, one of the leaders of censure and shock. It felt good.

But Christopher sinks down, quiet. She reaches down roughly and yanks his fresh white collar. Good boy, he doesn't look up at her. But something is broken. The mainspring, the defiant arch of his back that I would recognize, his, mine. I find I am weeping, soundless as everything around me. I feel it suddenly like blood on my cheeks. This teacher, this stranger and her cohorts have him by his pale limp neck. They are teaching him how to lose; or me how to win. My son is down for the count, breathing comfortably, accommodating, only his fingers twitching fiercely at his sides like gill slits puffing, while I stand outside, a baby asleep on my shoulder. I am the traitor, he sees me through my one-way mirror, and he is right. I am the witch. Every day they walk on his neck, I see that now, but he will never tell me about it. I weep but cannot move.

How to Win, by Rosellen Brown, is a harrowing yet moving tale of an almost totally undisciplined child. Six-year-old Christopher disembowels and bloodies up a room before his poor mother knows what hit it. Christopher doesn't know what hit it (or him) either. He races around her bedroom at night, "a bat, pulling down the curtain cornice, knocking over the lamps, tearing the petals off the flowers and stomping them, real or fake, to a powder." She feels like she "gave birth to someone else's child." In school, he is considered a hopeless case, and is massed together "for the special inattention of the aide" with incorrigible black and Puerto Rican children, "the Future Felons of America."

According to DSM 111 Christopher's behavior matches the criteria for "Intermittent Explosive Disorder," in which "several discrete episodes of loss of control of aggressive impulses that result in serious assault or destruction of property" occur. The afflicted person may suddenly start to hit strangers and throw furniture. The behavior is often a surprise to those about him, and often is even to the individual himself, who sometimes describes it as resulting from "a compelling force beyond his or her control." At such times, Margaret, the boy's mother, calls him an "it" and not a "him." She says he lacks a super-ego "the way some children are born without a crucial body chemical."

Scientists have recently identified cases in which injuries to the brain in infancy prevented people from learning normal rules of social and moral behavior in childhood and adolescence. The results fit in with earlier research of people with other kinds of brain damage that suggest brain injury can alter moral judgments.

Despite an almost certain organic understructure to Christopher's pathology, one must look for possible psychological factors that might complicate the picture. Although no one can be certain whether it is cause or effect, there seems to be a symbiotic relationship between Christopher and his mother. He dreams her dreams and she dreams his. "Maybe we're all jumbled up in his sight," she says. He runs to his mother for comfort, never his father. When he wants to take Christopher away for the weekend, she forbids it, saying he will crush the son to death "to get a little peace." Since "the father cuts the cord" in healthy families, it is possible that by holding on to her son so tightly, Margaret is keeping him from a relationship that could help him develop more normally. When she holds him tight for a "therapeutic hug," he pinches her arm "until the purple capillaries dance with pain." This is very telling behavior. Many symbiotic people use aggression to rescue themselves from what they consider a devouring relationship.

Margaret wonders from whence comes this "warm, healthy, nursed and coddled, vitamin-enriched boy, born on Blue Cross, swaddled in his grandparents' gifts from Lord and Taylor." She would not like to hear that Christopher could also be acting out her own repressed aggression, she who speaks with contempt of "the officious kids scurrying to do their teachers' bidding like tailless mice. I was one of them for years and years, God, faceless and obliging."

12

THE TEST

ANGELICA GIBBS

O n the afternoon Marian took her second driver's test, Mrs. Ericson went with her. "It's probably better to have some one a little older with you," Mrs. Ericson said as Marian slipped into the driver's seat beside her. "Perhaps the last time your cousin Bill made you nervous, talking too much on the way."

"Yes, Ma'am," Marian said in her soft unaccented voice. "They probably do like it better if a white person shows up with you."

"Oh, I don't think it's *that*," Mrs. Ericson began, and subsided after a glance at the girl's set profile. Marian drove the car slowly through the shady suburban streets. It was one of the first hot days in June, and when they reached the boulevard they found it crowded with cars headed for the beaches.

"Do you want me to drive?" Mrs. Ericson asked. "I'll be glad to if you're feeling jumpy." Marian shook her head. Mrs. Ericson watched her dark, competent hands and wondered for the thousandth time how the house had ever managed to get along without her, or how she had lived through those earlier years when her household had been presided over by a series of slatternly white girls who had considered housework demeaning and the care of children an added insult. "You drive beautifully, Marian," she said.

The Test, by Angelica Gibbs. Originally printed in *The New Yorker Magazine*, June 15, 1940.

"Now, don't think of the last time. Anybody would slide on a steep hill on a wet day like that."

"It takes four mistakes to flunk you," Marian said. "I don't remember doing all the things the inspector marked down on my blank."

"People say that they only want you to slip them a little something," Mrs. Ericson said doubtfully.

"No," Marian said. "That would only make it worse, Mrs. Ericson, I know."

The car turned right, at a traffic signal, into a side road and slid up to the curb at the rear of a short line of parked cars. The inspectors had not arrived yet.

"You have the papers," Mrs. Ericson asked. Marian took them out of her bag: her learner's permit, the car registration, and her birth certificate. They settled down to the dreary business of waiting.

"It will be marvelous to have someone dependable to drive the children to school every day," Mrs. Ericson said.

Marian looked up from the list of driving requirements she had been studying. "It'll make things simpler at the house, won't it?" she said.

"Oh, Marian," Mrs. Ericson exclaimed, "if I could only pay you half of what you are worth!"

"Now, Mrs. Ericson," Marian said firmly. They looked at each other and smiled with affection.

Two cars with official insignia on their doors stopped across the street. The inspectors leaped out, very brisk and military in their neat uniforms. Marian's hands tightened on the wheel. "There's the one who flunked me last time," she whispered, pointing to a stocky, self-important man who had begun to shout directions at the driver at the head of the line. "Oh, Mrs. Ericson."

"Now, Marian," Mrs. Ericson said. They smiled at each other again, rather weakly.

The inspector who finally reached their car was not the stocky one but a genial, middle-aged man who grinned broadly as he thumbed over their papers. Mrs. Ericson started to get out of the car. "Don't you want to come along?" the inspector asked. "Mandy and I don't mind company."

Mrs. Ericson was bewildered for a moment. "No," she said, and stepped to the curb. "I might make Marian self-conscious. She's a fine driver, Inspector."

"Sure thing," the inspector said, winking at Mrs. Ericson. He slid into the seat beside Marian. "Turn right at the corner, Mandy-Lou."

From the curb, Mrs. Ericson watched the car move smoothly up the street.

The inspector made notations in a small black book. "Age?" he inquired presently, as they drove along.

"Twenty-seven."

He looked at Marian out of the corner of his eye. "Old enough to have quite a flock of pickaninnies, eh?"

Marian did not answer.

"Left at this corner," the inspector said, "and park between that truck and the green Buick."

The two cars were very close together, but Marian squeezed in between them without too much maneuvering. "Driven before, Mandy-Lou?" the inspector asked.

"Yes, sir. I had a license for three years in Pennsylvania."

"Why do you want to drive a car?"

"My employer needs me to take her children to and from school."

"Sure you don't want to sneak out nights to meet some young blood?" the inspector asked. He laughed as Marian shook her head.

"Let's see you take a left at the corner and then turn around in the middle of the next block," the inspector said. He began to whistle "Swanee River." "Make you homesick?" he asked.

Marian put out her hand, swung around neatly in the street, and headed back in the direction from which they had come.

"No, sir," she said. "I was born in Scranton, Pennsylvania."

The inspector feigned astonishment. "You-all ain't Southern?" he said. "Well, dog my cats if I didn't think you-all came from down yondah."

"No, sir," Marian said.

"Turn onto Main Street and let's see how you-all does in heavier traffic."

They followed a line of cars along Main Street for several blocks until they came in sight of a concrete bridge which arched high over the railroad tracks.

"Read that sign at the end of the bridge," the inspector said.

"You-all sho can read fine," the inspector exclaimed. "Where d'you learn to do that, Mandy?"

"I got my college degree last year," Marian said. Her voice was not quite steady.

As the car crept up the slope of the bridge the inspector burst out laughing. He laughed so hard he could hardly give his next direction. "Stop here," he said, wiping his eyes, "then start 'er up again. Mandy got her degree, did she? Dog my cats!"

Marian pulled up beside the curb. She put the car in neutral, pulled on the emergency, waited a moment, and then put the car into gear again. Her face was set. As she released the brake her foot slipped off the clutch pedal and the engine stalled.

"Now, Mistress Mandy," the inspector said, "remember your degree."

"*Damn* you!" Marian cried. She started the car with a jerk.

The inspector lost his joviality in an instant. "Return to the starting point, please," he said, and made four very black crosses at random in the squares on Marian's application blank.

Mrs. Ericson was waiting at the curb where they had left her. As Marian stopped the car, the inspector jumped out and brushed past her, his face purple. "What happened?" Mrs. Ericson asked, looked after him with alarm.

Marian stared down at the wheel and her lip trembled.

"Oh, Marian, *again?*" Mrs. Ericson said.

Marian nodded. "In a sort of different way," she said, and slid over to the right-hand side of the car.

~~~~~

While any black person in the United States will recognize the appalling truth in *The Test*, it is less familiar to many people of different races. The story is included in *Tales of Psychology: Stories to Make You Wise* because I believe it is one of those rare serendipitous phenomena with the power to change the world. As an upper middle-class college student, I dutifully paid lip service to the principle of equality of the races. But like Marion's well-meaning employer, Mrs. Ericson, I understood the horror of race relations in the United States with my head rather than my heart. Reading Angelica Gibbs's *The Test* changed that for me forever. I experienced Marion's catastrophic experience as if it were my own. From that moment on, I have been truly "color blind."

The story is a simple description of a highly competent black woman's repeated attempts to get a driver's license in the deep south, and how she was failed yet again because she got angry with the instructor's cruelly expressed prejudice. Although the story was written in 1940, it is a moving testimonial to the racial situation in the United States as it still exists today.

The story, which opened *my* eyes, should be required reading for every white child in the United States.

13

IN THE REGION OF ICE

JOYCE CAROL OATES

Sister Irene was a tall, deft woman in her early thirties. What one could see of her face made a striking impression—serious, hard gray eyes, a long slender nose, a face waxen with thought. Seen at the right time, from the right angle, she was almost handsome. In her past teaching positions she had drawn a little upon the fact of her being young and brilliant and also a nun, but she was beginning to grow out of that.

This was a new university and an entirely new world. She had heard—of course it was true—that the Jesuit administration of this school had hired her at the last moment to save money and to head off the appointment of a man of dubious religious commitment. She had prayed for the necessary energy to get her through this first semester. She had no trouble with teaching itself; once she stood before a classroom she felt herself capable of anything. It was the world immediately outside the classroom that confused and alarmed her, though she let none of this show—the cynicism of her colleagues, the indifference of many of the students, and,

---

above all, the looks she got that told her nothing much would be expected of her because she was a nun. This took energy, strength. At times she had the idea that she was on trial and that the excuses she made to herself about her discomfort were only the common excuses made by guilty people. But in front of a class she had no time to worry about herself or the conflicts in her mind. She became, once and for all, a figure existing only for the benefit of others, an instrument by which facts were communicated.

About two weeks after the semester began, Sister Irene noticed a new student in her class. He was slight and fair-haired, and his face was blank, but not blank by accident, blank on purpose, suppressed and restricted into a dumbness that looked hysterical. She was prepared for him before he raised his hand, and when she saw his arm jerk, as if he had at last lost control of it, she nodded to him without hesitation.

"Sister, how can this be reconciled with Shakespeare's vision in *Hamlet?* How can these opposing views be in the same mind?"

Students glanced at him, mildly surprised. He did not belong in the class, and this was mysterious, but his manner was urgent and blind.

"There is no need to reconcile opposing views," Sister Irene said, leaning forward against the podium. "In one play Shakespeare suggests one vision, in another play another; the plays are not simultaneous creations, and even if they were, we never demand a logical—"

"We must demand a logical consistency," the young man said. "The idea of education is itself predicated upon consistency, order, sanity—"

He had interrupted her, and she hardened her face against him—for his sake, not her own, since she did not really care. But he noticed nothing. "Please see me after class," she said.

After class the young man hurried up to her.

"Sister Irene, I hope you didn't mind my visiting today. I'd heard some things, interesting things," he said. He stared at her, and something in her face allowed him to smile. "I...could we talk in your office? Do you have time?"

They walked down to her office. Sister Irene sat at her desk, and the young man sat facing her; for a moment they were self-conscious and silent.

"Well, I suppose you know—I'm a Jew," he said.

Sister Irene stared at him. "Yes?" she said.

"What am I doing at a Catholic university, huh?" He grinned. "That's what you want to know."

She made a vague movement of her hand to show that she had no thoughts on this, nothing at all, but he seemed not to catch it. He was sitting on the edge of the straight-backed chair. She saw that he was young but did not really look young. There were harsh lines on either side of his mouth, as if he had misused that youthful mouth somehow. His skin was almost as pale as hers, his eyes were dark and not quite in focus. Her looked at her and through her and around her, as his voice surrounded them both. His voice was a little shrill at times.

"Listen, I did the right thing today—visiting your class! God, what a lucky accident it was; some jerk mentioned you, said you were a good teacher—I thought, what a laugh! These people know about good teachers here? But yes, listen, yes, I'm not kidding—you are good. I mean that."

Sister Irene frowned. "I don't quite understand what all this meant."

He smiled and waved aside her formality, as if he knew better. "Listen, I got my B.A. at Columbia, then I came back here to this crappy city. I mean, I did it on purpose, I wanted to come back. I wanted to. I have my reasons for doing things. I'm on a three-thousand-dollar fellowship," he said, and waited for that to impress her. "You know, I could have gone almost anywhere with that fellowship, and I came back home here—my home's in the city—and enrolled here. This was the last year. This is my second year. I'm working on a thesis, I mean I was, my master's thesis—but the hell with that. What I want to ask you is this: Can I enroll in your class, is it too late? We have to get special permission if we're late."

Sister Irene felt something nudging her, some uneasiness in him that was pleading with her not to be offended by his abrupt, familiar manner. He seemed to be promising another self, a better self, as if his fair, childish almost cherubic face were doing tricks to distract her from what his words said.

"Are you in English studies?" she asked.

"I was in history. Listen," he said, and his mouth did something odd, drawing itself down into a smile that made the lines about it deepen like knives, "listen, they kicked me out."

He sat back, watching her. He crossed his legs. He took out a package of cigarettes and offered her one. Sister Irene shook her head, staring at his hands. They were small and stubby and might have belonged to a ten-year-old, and the nails were a strange near-violet color. It took him a while to extract a cigarette.

"Yeah, kicked me out. What do you think of that?"

"I don't understand."

"My master's thesis was coming along beautifully, and then this bastard—I mean, excuse me, this professor, I won't pollute your office with his name—he started making criticisms, he said some things were unacceptable, he—" The boy leaned forward and hunched his narrow shoulders in a parody of secrecy. "We had an argument. I told him some frank things, things only a broad-minded person could hear about himself. That takes courage, right? He didn't have it! He kicked me out of the master's program, so now I'm coming into English. Literature is greater than history; European history is one big pile of garbage. Sky-high. Filth and rotting corpses, right? Aristotle says that poetry is higher than history; he's right; in your class today I suddenly realized that this is my field, Shakespeare, only Shakespeare is—"

Sister Irene guessed that he was going to say that only Shakespeare was equal to him, and she caught the moment of recognition and hesitation, the half-raised arm, the keen, frowning forehead, the narrowed eyes; then he thought better of it and didn't end the sentence. "The students in your class are mainly negligible, I can tell you that. You're new here, and I've been here a year—I would have finished my studies last year but my father got sick, he was hospitalized, I couldn't take exams and it was a mess—but I'll make it through English in one year or drop dead. I can do it, I can do anything. I'll take six courses at once—" He broke off, breathless. Sister Irene tried to smile. "All right then, it's settled? You'll let me in? Have I missed anything so far?"

He had no idea of the rudeness of his question. Sister Irene, feeling suddenly exhausted, said, "I'll give you a syllabus of the course."

"Fine! Wonderful!"

He got to his feet eagerly. He looked through the schedule, muttering to himself, making favorable noises. It struck Sister Irene that she was making a mistake to let him in. There were these moments when one had to make an intelligent decision....But she was sympathetic with him, yes. She was sympathetic with something about him.

She found out his name the next day: Allen Weinstein.

After this she came to her Shakespeare class with a sense of excitement. It became clear to her at once that Weinstein was the most intelligent student in the class. Until he had enrolled, she had not understood what was lacking, a mind that could appreciate her own. Within a week, his jagged, protean mind had alienated the other students, and though he sat in the center of the class, he seemed totally alone, encased by a miniature world of his own. When he spoke of the "frenetic humanism of the High Renaissance," Sister Irene dreaded the raised eyebrows and mocking smiles of the other students, who no longer bothered to look at Weinstein. She wanted to defend him, but she never did, because there was something rude and dismal about his knowledge; he used it like a weapon, talking passionately of Nietzsche and Goethe and Freud until Sister Irene would be forced to close discussion.

In meditation, alone, she often thought of him. When she tried to talk about him to a young nun, Sister Carlotta, everything sounded gross. "But no, he's an excellent student," she insisted. "I'm very grateful to have him in class. It's just that...he thinks ideas are real." Sister Carlotta, who loved literature also, had been forced to teach grade-school arithmetic for the last four years. That might have been why she said, a little sharply, "You don't think ideas are real?"

Sister Irene acquiesced with a smile, but of course she did not think so; only reality is real.

When Weinstein did not show up for class on the day the first paper was due, Sister Irene's heart sank, and the sensation was somehow a familiar one. She began her lecture and kept waiting for the door to open and for him to hurry noisily back to his seat, grinning an apology toward her—but nothing happened. If she had been deceived by him, she made herself think angrily, it was as a teacher and not as a woman. He had promised her nothing.

Weinstein appeared the next day near the steps of the liberal arts building. She heard someone running behind her, a breathless exclamation: "Sister Irene!" She turned and saw him, panting and grinning in embarrassment. He wore a dark-blue suit with a necktie, and he looked, despite his childish face, like a little old man; there was something oddly precarious and fragile about him. "Sister Irene, I owe you an apology, right?" He raised his eyebrows and smiled a sad, forlorn, yet irritatingly conspiratorial smile. "The first paper—not in on time, and I know what your rules are...You won't accept late papers, I know—that's good discipline, I'll do that when I teach, too. But, unavoidably, I was unable to come to school yesterday. There are many—many —" he gulped for breath, and Sister Irene had the startling sense of seeing the real Weinstein stare out at her, a terrified prisoner behind the confident voice. "There are many complications in family life. Perhaps you are unaware—I mean —."

She did not like him, but she felt this sympathy, something tugging and nagging at her the way her parents had competed for her love so many years before. They had been whining, weak people, and out of their wet need for affection, the girl she had been (her name was Yvonne) had emerged stronger than either of them, contemptuous of tears because she had seen so many. But Weinstein was different; he was not simply weak—perhaps he was not weak at all—but his strength was confused and hysterical. She felt her customary rigidity as a teacher begin to falter. "You may turn your paper in today if you have it," she said, frowning.

Weinstein's mouth jerked into an incredulous grin. "Wonderful! Marvelous! He said. "You are very understanding, Sister Irene, I must say....I didn't expect, really..." He was fumbling in a shabby old briefcase for he paper. Sister Irene waited. She was prepared for another of his excuses, certain that he did not have the paper when he suddenly straightened up and handed her something. "Here! I took the liberty of writing thirty pages instead of just fifteen," he said. He was obviously quite excited; his cheeks were mottled pink and white. "You may disagree violently with my interpretation—I expect you to, in fact I'm counting on it—but let me warn you, I have the exact proof, right here in the play itself!" He was thumping at a book, his voice growing louder and shriller. Sister Irene, startled, wanted to put her hand over his mouth and soothe him.

"Look," he said breathlessly, "may I talk with you? I have a class now I hate, I loathe, I can't bear to sit through. Can I talk with you instead?"

Because she was nervous, she stared at the title page of the paper: "Erotic Melodies in *Romeo and Juliet*" by Allen Weinstein, Jr.

"All right?" he said. "Can we walk around here? Is it all right? I've been anxious to talk with you about some things you said in class."

She was reluctant, but he seemed not to notice. They walked slowly along the shaded campus paths. Weinstein did all the talking, of course, and Sister Irene recognized nothing in his cascade of words that she had mentioned in class. "The humanist must be committed to the totality of life," he said passionately. "This is the failing one finds everywhere in the academic world! I found it in

New York and I found it here and I'm no ingenue, I don't go around with my mouth hanging open—I'm experienced, look, I've been to Europe, I've lived in Rome! I went everywhere in Europe except Germany, I don't talk about Germany...Sister Irene, think of the significant men in the last century, the men who've changed the world! Jews, right? Marx, Freud, Einstein! Not that I believe Marx, Marx is a madman...and Freud, no, my sympathies are with spiritual humanism. I believe that the Jewish race is the exclusive...the exclusive, what's the word, the exclusive means by which humanism will be extended...Humanism begins by excluding the Jew, and now," he said with a high, surprised laugh, "the Jew will perfect it. After the Nazis, only the Jew is authorized to understand humanism, its limitations and its possibilities. So, I say that the humanist is committed to life in its totality and not just to his profession! The religious person is totally religious, he is his religion! What else? I recognize in you a humanist and a religious person—."

But he did not seem to be talking to her or even looking at her.

"Here, read this," he said. "I wrote it last night." It was a long free-verse poem, typed on a typewriter whose ribbon was worn out.

"There's this trouble with my father, a wonderful man, a lovely man, but his health—his strength is fading, do you see? What must it be to him to see his son growing up? I mean, I'm a man now, he's getting old, weak, his health is bad—it's hell, right? I sympathize with him. I'd do anything for him, I'd cut open my veins, anything for a father—right? That's why I wasn't in school yesterday," he said, and his voice dropped for the last sentence, as if he had been dragged back to earth by a fact.

Sister Irene tried to read the poem, then pretended to read it. A jumble of words dealing with "life" and "death" and "darkness" and "love." "What do you think?" Weinstein said nervously, trying to read it over her shoulder and crowding against her.

"It's very...passionate," Sister Irene said.

This was the right comment; he took the poem back from her in silence, his face flushed with excitement. "I haven't shown anyone else that poem." He looked at her with his dark, intense eyes, and Sister Irene felt them focus upon her. She was terrified at what he was trying to do—he was trying to force her into a human relationship.

"Thank you for your paper," she said, turning away.

When he came the next day, ten minutes late, he was haughty and disdainful. He had nothing to say and sat with his arms folded. Sister Irene took back with her to the convent a feeling of betrayal and confusion. She had been hurt. It was absurd, and yet—She spent too much time thinking about him, as if he were somehow a kind of crystallization of her own loneliness; but she had no right to think so much of him. She did not want to think of him or of her loneliness. But Weinstein did so much more than think of his predicament: he embodied it, he acted it out, and that was perhaps why he fascinated her. It was as if he were doing a dance for her, a dance of shame and agony and delight, and so long as he did it, she was safe. She felt embarrassment for him, but also anxiety; she wanted to protect him. When the dean of the graduate school questioned her about Weinstein's work, she insisted that he was an "excellent" student, though she knew the dean had not wanted to hear that.

She prayed for guidance, she spent hours on her devotions, she was closer to her vocation than she had been for some years. Life at the convent became tinged with unreality, a misty distortion that took its tone from the glowering skies of the city at night, identical smokestacks ranged against the clouds and giving to the sky the excrement of the populated and successful earth. This city was not her city, this world was not her world. She felt no pride in knowing this, it was a fact. The little convent was not like an island in the center of this noisy world, but rather a kind of hole or crevice the world did not bother with, something of no interest. The convent's rhythm of life had nothing to do with the world's rhythm, it did not violate or alarm it in any way. Sister Irene tried to draw together the fragments of her life and synthesize them somehow in her vocation as a nun. She was a nun, she was recognized as a nun, and had given herself happily to that life, she had a name, a place, she had dedicated her superior intelligence to the church, she worked without pay and without expecting gratitude, she had given up pride, she did not think of herself but only of her work and her vocation, she did not think of anything external to these, she saturated herself daily in the knowledge that she was involved in the mystery of Christianity.

A daily terror attended this knowledge, however, for she sensed herself being drawn by that student, that Jewish boy, into a relationship she was not ready for. She wanted to cry out in fear that she was being forced into the role of a Christian, and what did that mean? What could her studies tell her? What could the other nuns tell her? She was alone, no one could help; he was making her into a Christian, and to her that was a mystery, a thing of terror, something others slipped on the way they slipped on their clothes, casually and thoughtlessly, but to her a magnificent and terrifying wonder.

For days she carried Weinstein's paper, marked A, around with her; he did not come to class. One day she checked with the graduate office and was told that Weinstein had called in to say his father was ill and that he would not be able to attend classes for a while. "He's strange, I remember him," the secretary said. "He missed all his exams last spring and made a lot of trouble. He was in and out of here every day."

So there was no more of Weinstein for a while, and Sister Irene stopped expecting him to hurry into class. Then, one morning, she found a letter from him in her mailbox.

He had printed it in black ink, very carefully, as if he had not trusted handwriting. The return address was in bold letters that, like his voice, tried to grab onto her: Birchcrest Manor. Somewhere north of the city. "Dear Sister Irene," the block letters said, "I am doing well here and have time for reading and relaxing. The Manor is delightful. My doctor here is an excellent intelligent man who has time for me, unlike my former doctor. If you have time, you might drop in on my father, who worries about me too much,

I think, and explain to him what my condition is. He doesn't seem to understand. I feel about this new life the way that boy, what's his name, in *Measure for Measure*, feels about the prospects of a different life; you remember what he says to his sister when she visits him in prison, how he is looking forward to an escape into another world. Perhaps you could *explain* this to my father and he would stop worrying. The letter ended with the father's name and address, in letters that were just a little too big. Sister Irene, walking slowly down the corridor as she read the letter, felt her eyes cloud over with tears. She was cold with fear, it was something she had never experienced before. She knew what Weinstein was trying to tell her, and the desperation of his attempt made it all the more pathetic; he did not deserve this, why did God allow him to suffer so?

She read through Claudio's speech to his sister in *Measure for Measure*:

> Ay, but to die, and go we know not where;
> To lie in cold obstruction and to rot;
> This sensible warm motion to become
> A kneaded clod; and the delighted spirit
> To bathe in fiery floods, or to reside
> In thrilling region of thick-ribbed ice,
> To be imprison'd in the viewless winds
> And blown with restless violence round about
> The pendent world; or to be worse than worst
> Of those that lawless and incertain thought
> Imagines howling! 'Tis too horrible!
> The weariest and most loathed worldly life
> That age, ache, penury, and imprisonment
> Can lay on nature is a paradise
> To what we fear of death.

Sister Irene called the father's number that day. "Allen Weinstein residence, who may I say is calling? A woman said, bored. "May I speak to Mr. Weinstein? It's urgent—about his son," Sister Irene said. There was a pause at the other end. "You want to talk to his mother, maybe?" the woman said. "His mother? Yes, his mother, then. Please. It's very important."

She talked with the strange, unsuspected woman, a disembodied voice that suggested absolutely no face, and insisted upon going over that afternoon. The woman was nervous, but Sister Irene, who was a university professor, after all, knew enough to hide her own nervousness. She kept waiting for the woman to say, "Yes, Allen has mentioned you..." but nothing happened.

She persuaded Sister Carlotta to ride over with her. This urgency of hers was something they were all amazed by. They hadn't suspected that the set of her gray eyes could change to this blurred, distracted alarm, this sense of mission that seemed to have come to her from nowhere. Sister Irene drove across the city in the late afternoon traffic, with the high whining noises from residential streets where trees were being sawed down in pieces. She understood now the secret, sweet wildness that Christ must have felt, giving himself for man, dying for the billions of men who would never know of him and never understand the sacrifice. For the first time she approached the realization of that great act. In her troubled mind, the city traffic was jumbled and yet oddly coherent, an image of the world that was always out of joint with what was happening in it, its inner history struggling with its external spectacle. This sacrifice of Christ's, so mysterious and legendary now, almost lost in time—it was that by which Christ transcended both God and man at one moment, more than man because of his fate to do what no other man could do, and more than God because no god could suffer as he did. She felt a flicker of something close to madness.

She drove nervously, uncertainly, afraid of missing the street and afraid of finding it too, for while one part of her rushed forward to confront these people who had betrayed their son, another part of her would have liked nothing so much as to be waiting for the summons to dinner, safe in her room.... When she found the street and turned onto it, she was in a state of breathless excitement. Here lawns were bright green and marred with only a few leaves, magically clean, and the houses were enormous and pompous, a mixture of styles: ranch houses, colonial houses, French country houses, white-bricked wonders with curving glass and clumps of birch trees somehow encircled by white concrete. Sister Irene stared as if she had blundered into another world. This was a kind of heaven, and she was too shabby for it.

The Weinstein house was the strangest one of all: it looked like a small Alpine lodge, with an inverted-V-shaped front entrance. Sister Irene drove up the black-topped driveway and let the car slow to a stop; she told Sister Carlotta she would not be long.

At the door she was met by Weinstein's mother, a small, nervous woman with hands like her son's. "Come in, come in," the woman said. She had once been beautiful, that was clear, but now in missing beauty she was not handsome or even attractive but looked ruined and perplexed, the misshapen swelling of her white-blond professionally set hair like a cap lifting up from her surprised face. "He'll be right in. Allen?" she called, "our visitor is here." They went into the living room. There was a grand piano at one end and an organ at the other. In between were scatterings of brilliant modern furniture in conversational groups, and several puffed-up white rugs on the polished floor. Sister Irene could not stop shivering.

"Professor, it's so strange, but let me say when the phone rang I had a feeling—I had a feeling," the woman said, with damp eyes. Sister Irene sat, and the woman hovered about her. "Should I call you Professor? We don't...you know...we don't understand the technicalities that go with—Allen—my son, wanted to go here to the Catholic school; I told my husband why not? Why fight? It's the thing these days, they do anything they want for knowledge. And he had to come home, you know. He couldn't take care of himself in New York, that was the beginning of the trouble.... Should I call you Professor?"

"You can call me Sister Irene."

"Sister Irene?" The woman said, touching her throat in awe, as if something intimate and unexpected had happened.

Then Weinstein's father appeared, hurrying. He took long,

impatient strides. Sister Irene stared at him and in that instant doubted everything—he was in his fifties, a tall sharply handsome man, heavy but not fat, holding his shoulders back with what looked like an effort, but holding them back just the same. He wore a dark suit and his face was flushed, as if he had run a long distance.

"Now," he said, coming to Sister Irene and with a precise wave of his hand motioning his wife off, "now, let's straighten this out. A lot of confusion over that kid, eh?" He pulled a chair over, scraping it across a rug and pulling one corner over, so that its brown underside was exposed. "I came home early just for this, Libby phoned me. Sister, you got a letter from him, right?"

The wife looked at Sister Irene over her husband's head as if trying somehow to coach her, knowing that this man was so loud and impatient that no one could remember anything in his presence.

"A letter—yes—today—."

"He says what in it? You got the letter, eh? Can I see it?"

She gave it to him and wanted to explain, but he silenced her with a flick of his hand. He read through the letter so quickly that Sister Irene thought perhaps he was trying to impress her with his skill at reading. "So?" he said, raising his eyes, smiling, "so what is this? He's happy out there, he says. He doesn't communicate with us any more, but he writes to you and says he's happy—what's that? I mean, what the hell is that?"

"But he isn't happy. He wants to come home," Sister Irene said. It was so important that she make him understand that she could not trust her voice; goaded by this man, it must suddenly turn shrill, as his son's did. "Someone must read their letters before they're mailed, so he tried to tell me something by making an allusion to—"

"What?"

"—an allusion to a play, so that I would know. He may be thinking suicide, he must be very unhappy—."

She ran out of breath. Weinstein's mother had begun to cry, but the father was shaking is head jerkily back and forth. "Forgive me, Sister, but it's a lot of crap, he needs the hospital, he needs help—right? It costs me fifty a day out there, and they've got the best place in the state. I figure it's worth it. He needs help, that kid, what do I care if he's unhappy? He's unbalanced!"

He said angrily. "You want us to get him out again? We argued with the judge for two hours to get him in, an acquaintance of mine. Look, he can't control himself—he was smashing things here, he was hysterical. They need help, lady, and you do something about it fast! You do something! We made up our minds to do something and we did it! This letter—what the hell is this letter? He never talked like that to us!"

"But he means the opposite of what he says—"

"Then he's crazy! I'm the first to admit it." He was perspiring, and his face had darkened. "I've got no pride left this late. He's a little bastard, you want to know? He calls me names, he's filthy, got a filthy mouth—that's being smart, huh? They give him a big scholarship for his filthy mouth? I went to college, too, and I got out and knew something, and I for Christ's sake did something with it; my wife is an intelligent woman, a learned woman, would you guess she does book reviews for the little newspaper out here? Intelligent isn't crazy—crazy isn't intelligent. Maybe for you at the school he writes nice papers and gets an A, but out here, around the house, he can't control himself, and we got him committed!"

"But—"

"We're fixing him up, don't worry about it!" He turned to his wife. "Libby, get out of here, I mean it. I'm sorry, but get out of here, you're making a fool of yourself, go stand in the kitchen or something, you and the goddamn maid can cry on each other's shoulders. That one in the kitchen is nuts, too, they're all nuts. Sister," he said, his voice lowering, "I thank you immensely for coming out here. This is wonderful, your interest in my son. And I see he admires you—that letter there. But what about that letter? If he did want to get out, which I don't admit—he was willing to be committed, in the end he said okay himself—if he wanted out I wouldn't do it. Why? So what if he wants to come back? The next day he wants something else, what then? He's a sick kid, and I'm the first to admit it."

Sister Irene felt that sickness spread to her. She stood. The room was so big it seemed it must be a public place; there had been nothing personal or private about their conversation. Weinstein's mother was standing by the fireplace, sobbing. The father jumped to his feet and wiped his forehead in a gesture that was meant to help Sister Irene on her way out. "God, what a day," he said, his eyes snatching at hers for understanding, "you know— one of those days all day long? Sister, I thank you a lot. There should be more people in the world who care about others, like you. I mean that."

On the way back to the convent, the man's words returned to her, and she could not get control of them; she could not even feel anger. She had been pressed down, forced back, what could she do? Weinstein might have been watching her somehow from a barred window, and he surely would have understood. The strange idea she had had on the way over, something about understanding Christ, came back to her now and sickened her. But the sickness was small. It could be contained.

About a month after her visit to his father, Weinstein himself showed up. He was dressed in a suit as before, even the necktie was the same. He came right into her office as if he had been pushed and could not stop.

"Sister," he said, and shook her hand. He must have seen fear in her because he smiled ironically. "Look, I'm released. I'm let out of the nut house. Can I sit down?"

He sat. Sister Irene was breathing quickly, as if in the presence of an enemy who does not know he is an enemy.

"So, they finally let me out. I heard what you did. You talked with him, that was all I wanted. You're the only one who gave a damn. Because you're a humanist and a religious person, you respect...the individual. "Listen," he said, whispering, "it was hell out there! Hell Birchcrest Manor! All fixed up with fancy chairs and *Life* magazines lying around—and what do they do to you?

They locked me up, they gave me shock treatments, how do you like that, it's discredited by everybody now—they're crazy out there themselves, sadists. They locked me up, they gave me hypodermic shots, they didn't treat me like a human being! Do you know what that is," Weinstein demanded savagely, "not to be treated like a human being? They made me an animal—for fifty dollars a day! Dirty filthy swine! Now I'm an outpatient because I stopped swearing at them. I found someone's bobby pin and it stopped me—the screaming went inside and not out—so they gave me good reports, those sick bastards. Now I'm an outpatient and I can walk along the street and breathe in the same filthy exhaust from the buses like all you normal people! Christ," he said, and threw himself back against the chair.

Sister Irene stared at him. She wanted to take his hand, to make some gesture that would close the aching distance between them. "Mr. Weinstein—"

"Call me Allen!" he said sharply.

"I'm very sorry—I'm terribly sorry—"

"My own parents committed me, but of course they didn't know what it was like. It was hell," he said thickly, "and there isn't any hell except what other people do to you. The psychiatrist out there, the main shrink, he hates Jews too, some of us were positive of that, and he's got a bigger nose than I do, a real beak." He made a noise of disgust. "A dirty bastard, a sick, dirty, pathetic bastard—all of them. Anyway, I'm getting out of here, and I came to ask you a favor."

"What do you mean?"

"I'm getting out. I'm leaving. I'm going up to Canada and lose myself. I'll get a job, I'll forget everything, I'll kill myself maybe— what's the difference? Look, can you lend me some money?"

"Money?"

"Just a little! I have to get to the border, I'm going to take a bus."

"But I don't have any money—"

"No money?" He stared at her. "You mean—you don't have any? Sure you have some!"

She stared at him as if he had asked her to do something obscene. Everything was splotched and uncertain before her eyes.

"You must...you must go back," she said, "you're making a—"

"I'll pay it back. Look, I'll pay it back, can you go to where you live or something and get it? I'm in a hurry. My friends are sons of bitches; one of them pretended he didn't see me yesterday—I stood right in the middle of the sidewalk and yelled at him, I called him some appropriate names! So he didn't see me, huh? You're the only one who understands me, you understand me like a poet, you—"

"I can't help you, I'm sorry—"

He looked to one side of her and flashed his gaze back, as if he could control it. He seemed to be trying to clear his vision.

"You have the soul of a poet," he whispered, "you're the only one. Everybody else is rotten! Can't you lend me some money, ten dollars maybe? I have three thousand in the bank, and I can't touch it. They take everything away from me, they make me into an animal...You know I'm not an animal, don't you? Don't you?"

"Of course," Sister Irene whispered.

"You could get money. Help me. Give me your hand or something, touch me, help me, please...." He reached for her hand and she drew back. He stared at her and his face seemed about to crumble, like a child's. "I want something from you, but I don't know what—I want something!" he cried. "Something real! I want you to look at me like I was a human being, is that too much to ask? I have a brain, I'm alive, I'm suffering—what does that mean? Does that mean nothing? I want something real and not this phony Christian love garbage—it's all in the books, it isn't personal—I want something real—look...."

He tried to take her hand again, and this time she jerked away. She got to her feet. "Mr. Weinstein," she said, "please—"

"You! You nun!" he said scornfully, his mouth twisted into a mock grin. "You nun! There's nothing under that ugly outfit, right? And you're not particularly smart even though you think you are; my father has more brains in his foot than you—"

He got to his feet and kicked the chair.

"You bitch!" he cried.

She shrank back against her desk as if she thought he might hit her, but he only ran out of the office.

Weinstein: the name was to become disembodied from the figure, as time went on. The semester passed, the autumn drizzle turned into snow, Sister Irene rode to school in the morning and left in the afternoon, four days a week, anonymous in her black winter cloak, quiet and stunned. University teaching was an anonymous task, each day dissociated from the rest, with no necessary sense of unity among the teachers. They came and went separately and might for a year just miss a colleague who left his office five minutes before they arrived, and it did not matter.

She heard of Weinstein's death, his suicide by drowning, from the English Department secretary, a handsome white-haired woman who kept a transistor radio on her desk. Sister Irene was not surprised; she had been thinking of him as dead for months. "They identified him by some special television way they have now," the secretary said. "They're shipping the body back. It was up in Quebec...."

Sister Irene could feel a part of herself drifting off, lured by the plains of white snow to the north, the quiet, the emptiness, the sweep of the Great Lakes up to the silence of Canada. But she called that part of herself back. She could only be one person in her lifetime. That was the ugly truth, she thought, that she could not really regret Weinstein's suffering and death; she had only one life and had already given it to someone else. He had come too late to her. Fifteen years ago, perhaps, but not now.

She was only one person, she thought, walking down the corridor in a dream. Was she safe in this single person, or was she trapped? She had only one identity. She could make only one choice. What she had done or hadn't done was the result of that choice, and how was she guilty? If she could have felt guilt, she thought, she might at least have been able to feel something.

A reading group I belong to has met monthly for many years to discuss short stories brought in by the members. At the end of each discussion, we vote on the merits of the story, grading it from 0 to 10. In all the years the group has met, only one story was ever given an unanimous 10. That story was *In the Region of Ice*, by Joyce Carol Oates.

Although the story ostensibly is about Allen Weinstein, a mad young graduate student who has a great need for some response from his professor, Sister Irene, it really is about an interaction on the deepest level between two hurt souls, the wildly needy student and the emotionally closed off teacher. A woman who tried to "saturate herself in the mystery of Christianity," her humanity essentially was frozen.

Sister Irene felt that Allen was pressuring her to love him, as her weak and whining parents had done many years before. Because of her contempt for them, she resisted their pull by freezing all her feelings and living purely on an intellectual level.

"Help me," Allen said. "Give me your hand or something, touch me, help me—please...I want something from you, but I don't know what...I want something real and not this phony Christian love garbage." Although the nun felt the urge to reach out and touch and soothe him, to defend him from hostile classmates, she refused him because "She was terrified at what he was trying to do— he was trying to force her into a human relationship...a relationship she was not ready for." She told herself it was too late, that maybe fifteen years ago she could have done it, but not now. She was unaware that she needed the relationship as much as Allen did, in order to become a whole human being. Had she been able to respond to him on an emotional level, she could have reopened the emotional box she had put herself in many years before, and she too might have been "cured."

Oates' portrait of Allen's parents in a few sparse lines is equally insightful. His mother spoke with "a disembodied voice that suggested absolutely no face." She was bullied by her husband, a hateful, controlling man who refused to listen to Sister Irene when she told him his son was suicidal, just as he never heard what his son was trying to tell him. As a patient in analysis seeks to go back in time to relive the trauma of his or her upbringing and reexperience it with a different ending, so Allen needed to return to his childhood and live it over again with the Sister as he should have done the first time round. His desperation came from sensing that he never would be well until he received what he had never had. It is not unusual that he sought these qualities in a person no more able to give them to him than his parents were. This is known in psychoanalysis as the Repetition Compulsion.

When Sister Irene hears that Allen had drowned himself, she thinks that if only she could feel guilt, at least she would be able to feel something.

14

THE DEATH OF JUSTINA

JOHN CHEEVER

S o help me God, it gets more and more preposterous, it corresponds less and less to what I remember and what I expect, as if the force of life were centrifugal and threw one further and further away from one's purest memories and ambitions, and I can barely recall the old house where I was raised, where in midwinter Parma violets bloomed in a cold frame near the kitchen door and down the long corridor, past the seven views of Rome—up two steps and down three—one entered the library where all the books were in order, the lamps were bright, where there was a fire and a dozen bottles of good bourbon, locked in a cabinet with a veneer of tortoise shell whose silver key my father wore on his watch chain. Just let me give you one example and if you don't believe me look honestly into your own past and see if you can't find a comparable experience. On Saturday, the doctor told me to stop smoking and drinking and I did. I won't go into the commonplace symptoms of withdrawal, but I would like to point out that, standing at my window in the evening, watching the brilliant after light and the spread of darkness, I felt, through the lack of these humble stimulants, the force of some primitive memory

---

in which the coming of night with its stars and its moon was apoca-
lyptic. I thought suddenly of the neglected graves of my three brothers on the mountainside and that death is a loneliness much crueler
than any loneliness hinted at in life. The soul (I thought) does not
leave the body, but lingers with it through every degrading stage of
decomposition and neglect, through heat, through cold, through
the long winter nights when no one comes with a wreath or a
plant and no one says a prayer. This unpleasant premonition was
followed by anxiety. We were going out for dinner and I thought
that the oil burner would explode in our absence and burn the
house. The cook would get drunk and attack my daughter with a
carving knife, or my wife and I would be killed in a collision on
the main highway, leaving our children bewildered orphans with
nothing in life to look forward to but sadness. I was able to ob-
serve, along with these foolish and terrifying anxieties, a definite
impairment to my discretionary poles. I felt as if I were being lowered by ropes into the atmosphere of my childhood. I told my
wife—when she passed through the living room—that I had
stopped smoking and drinking but she didn't seem to care and
who would reward me for my privations? Who cared about the
bitter taste in my mouth and that my head seemed to be leaving
my shoulders? It seemed to me that men had honored one another with medals, statuary and cups for much less and that abstinence is a social matter. When I abstain from sin it is more often a
fear of scandal than a private resolve to improve on the purity of
my heart, but here was a call for abstinence without the worldly
enforcement of society, and death is not the threat that scandal is.
When it was time for us to go out I was so light-headed that I had
to ask my wife to drive the car. On Sunday I sneaked seven cigarettes in various hiding places and drank two martinis in the downstairs coat closet. At breakfast on Monday my English muffin stared
up at me from the plate. I mean I *saw* a face there in the rough,
toasted surface. The moment of recognition was fleeting, but it
was deep, and I wondered who it had been. Was it a friend, an
aunt, a sailor, a ski instructor, a bartender or a conductor on a

train? The smile faded off the muffin, but it had been there for a second—the sense of a person, a life, a pure force of gentleness and censure, and I am convinced that the muffin had contained the presence of some spirit. As you can see, I was nervous.

On Monday my wife's old cousin, Justina, came to visit her. Justina was a lively guest, although she must have been crowding eighty. On Tuesday my wife gave her a lunch party. The last guest left at three and a few minutes later, Cousin Justina, sitting on the livingroom sofa with a glass of brandy, breathed her last. My wife called me at the office and I said that I would be right out. I was clearing my desk when my boss, MacPherson, came in.

"Spare me a minute," he asked. "I've been bird-dogging all over the place, trying to track you down. Pierson had to leave early and I want you to write the last Elixircol commercial."

"Oh, I can't, Mac," I said. "My wife just called. Cousin Justina is dead."

"You write that commercial," he said. His smile was satanic. "Pierson had to leave early because his grandfather fell off a step-ladder."

Now I don't like fictional accounts of office life. It seems to me that if you're going to write fiction you should write about mountainclimbing and tempests at sea and I will go over my predicament with MacPherson briefly, aggravated as it was by his refusal to respect and honor the death of dear old Justina. It was like MacPherson. It was a good example of the way I've been treated. He is, I might say, a tall, splendidly groomed man of about sixty who changes his shirt three times a day, romances his secretary every afternoon between two and two-thirty, and makes the habit of continuously chewing gum seem hygienic and elegant. I write his speeches for him and it has not been a happy arrangement for me. If the speeches are successful, MacPherson takes all the credit. I can see that his presence, his tailor and his fine voice are all a part of the performance, but it makes me angry never to be given credit for what was said. On the other hand, if the speeches are unsuccessful—if his presence and his voice can't carry the hour—

his threatening and sarcastic manner is surgical and I am obliged to contain myself in the role of a man who can do no good in spite of the piles of congratulatory mail that my eloquence sometimes brings in. I must pretend, I must, like an actor, study and improve on my pretension, to have nothing to do with his triumphs and I must bow my head gracefully in shame when we have both failed. I am forced to appear grateful for injuries, to lie, to smile falsely and to play out a role as asinine and as unrelated to the facts as a minor prince in an operetta, but if I speak the truth it will be my wife and children who will pay in hardships for my outspokenness. Now he refused to respect or even to admit the solemn fact of a death in our family and if I couldn't rebel it seemed as if I could at least hint at it.

The commercial he wanted me to write was for a tonic called Elixircol and was to be spoken on television by an actress who was neither young nor beautiful, but who had an appearance of ready abandon and who was anyhow the mistress of one of the sponsor's uncles. *Are you growing old?* I wrote. *Are you falling out of love with your image in the looking glass? Does your face in the morning seem racked and seamed with alcoholic and sexual excesses and does the rest of you appear to be a greyish-pink lump, covered all over with brindle hair? Walking in the autumn woods, do you feel that subtle distance has come between you and the smell of wood smoke? Have you drafted your obituary? Are you easily winded? Do you wear a girdle? Is your sense of smell fading, is your interest in gardening waning, is your fear of height increasing and are your sexual drives as ravening and intense as ever and does your wife look more and more to you like a stranger with sunken cheeks who has wandered into your bedroom by mistake? If this or any of this is true you need Elixircol, the true juice of youth. The small economy size* (business with bottle) *costs seventy-five dollars and the giant family bottle comes at two hundred and fifty. It's a lot of scratch, God knows, but these are inflationary times and who can put a price on youth? If you don't have the cash, borrow it from your neighborhood loan shark or hold up the local bank. The odds are three to one that with*

a ten-cent water pistol and a slip of paper you can shake ten thou-
sand out of any fainthearted teller. Everybody's doing it. (Music up
and out.)

I sent this into MacPherson via Ralphie, the messenger boy,
and I took the 4:16 home, traveling through a landscape of utter
desolation.

Now my journey is a digression and has no real connection to
Justina's death, but what followed could only have happened in
my country and in my time and since I was an American traveling
across an American landscape, the trip may be part of the sum.
There are some Americans who, although their fathers emigrated
from the old world three centuries ago, never seem to have quite
completed the voyage, and I am one of these. I stand, figuratively,
with one wet foot on Plymouth Rock, looking with some delicacy,
not into a formidable and challenging wilderness but onto a half-
finished civilization embracing glass towers, oil derricks, suburban continents and abandoned movie houses and wondering why,
in this most prosperous, equitable and accomplished world—where
even the cleaning women practice the Chopin preludes in their
spare time—everyone should seem to be so disappointed?

At Proxmire Manor I was the only passenger to get off the random, meandering and profitless local that carried its shabby lights
off into the dusk like some game-legged watchman or beadle,
making his appointed rounds. I went around to the front of the
station to wait for my wife and to enjoy the traveler's fine sense of
crises. Above me on the hill was my home and the homes of my
friends, all lighted and smelling of fragrant wood smoke like the
temples in a sacred grove, dedicated to monogamy, feckless childhood and domestic bliss, but so like a dream that I felt the lack of
viscera with much more than poignance—the absence of that inner dynamism we respond to in some European landscapes. In
short, I was disappointed. It was my country, my beloved country
and there have been mornings when I could have kissed the earth
that covers its many provinces and state. There was a hint of bliss—
romantic and domestic bliss. I seemed to hear the jingle bells of

the sleigh that would carry me to grandmother's house, although in fact grandmother spent the last years of her life working as a hostess on an ocean liner and was lost in the tragic sinking of the S.S. *Lorelei* and I was responding to a memory that I had not experienced. But the hill of light rose like an answer to some primitive dream of homecoming. On one of the highest lawns I saw the remains of a snow man who still smoked a pipe and wore a scarf and cap, but whose form was wasting away and whose anthracite eyes stared out at the view with terrifying bitterness. I sensed some disappointing greenness of spirit in the scene, although I knew in my bones, no less, how like yesterday it was that my father left the old world to found a new; and I thought of the forces that had brought stamina to the image: the cruel towns of Calabria with their cruel princes, the badlands northwest of Dublin, ghettos, despots, whorehouses, bread lines, the graves of children. Intolerable hunger, corruption, persecution and despair had generated these faint and mellow lights and wasn't it all a part of the great migration that is the life of man?

My wife's cheeks were wet with tears when I kissed her. She was distressed, of course, and really quite sad. She had been attached to Justina. She drove me home where Justina was still sitting on the sofa. I would like to spare you the unpleasant details, but I will say that both her mouth and her eyes were wide open. I went into the pantry to telephone Dr. Hunter. His line was busy. I poured myself a drink—the first since Sunday—and lighted a cigarette. When I called the doctor again he answered and I told him what had happened. "Well, I'm awfully sorry to hear about it, Moses," he said. "I can't get over until after six and there isn't much that I can do. This sort of thing has come up before and I'll tell you all I know. You see you live in a B zone—two acre lots, no commercial enterprises, and so forth. A couple of years ago some stranger bought the old Plewett mansion and it turned out that he was planning to operate it as a funeral home. We didn't have any zoning provision at the time that would protect us and one was rushed through the village council at midnight and they overdid it. It seems that you not only can't have a funeral home in zone B—you can't bury anything there and you can't die there. Of course it's absurd, but we all make mistakes, don't we?"

"Now there are two things you can do. I've had to deal with this before. You can take the old lady and put her into the car and drive her over to Chestnut Street where zone C begins. The boundary is just beyond the traffic light by the high school. As soon as you get her over to zone C, it's all right. You can just say she died in the car. You can do that or if this seems distasteful you can call the mayor and ask him to make an exception to the zoning laws. But I can't write you out a death certificate until you get her out of that neighborhood and of course no undertaker will touch her until you get a death certificate."

"I don't understand," I said, and I didn't, but then the possibility that there was some truth in what he had just told me broke against me or over me like a wave, exciting mostly indignation. "I've never heard of such a lot of damned foolishness in my life," I said. "Do you mean to tell me that I can't die in one neighborhood and that I can't fall in love in another and that I can't eat...."

"Listen. Calm down, Moses. I'm not telling you anything but the facts and I have a lot of patients waiting. I don't have the time to listen to you fulminate. If you want to move her, call me as soon as you get her over to the traffic light. Otherwise, I'd advise you to get in touch with the mayor or someone on the village council." He cut the connection. I was outraged, but this did not change the fact that Justina was still sitting on the sofa. I poured a fresh drink and lit another cigarette.

Justina seemed to be waiting for me and to be changing from an inert into a demanding figure. I tried to imagine carrying her out to the station wagon, but I couldn't complete the task in my imagination and I was sure that I couldn't complete it in fact. I then called the mayor, but this position in our village is mostly honorary and as I might have known he was in his New York law office and was not expected home until seven. I could cover her, I thought; that would be a decent thing to do, and I went up the back steps to the linen closet and got a sheet. It was getting dark when I came back into the living room, but this was no merciful twilight. Dusk seems to be playing directly into her hands and she had gained power and stature with the dark. I covered her with the sheet and turned on a lamp at the other end of the room, but the rectitude of the place with its old furniture, flowers, paintings, etc. was demolished by her monumental shape. The next thing to worry about was the children who would be home in a few minutes. Their knowledge of death, excepting their dreams and intuitions of which I knew nothing, is zero and the bold figure in the parlor was bound to be traumatic. When I heard them coming up the walk I went out and told them what had happened and sent them up to their rooms. At seven I drove over to the mayor's.

He had not come home, but he was expected at any minute and I talked with his wife. She gave me a drink. By this time I was chainsmoking. When the mayor came in we went into a little office or library where he took up a position behind a desk, putting me in the low chair of a supplicant.

"Of course I sympathize with you, Moses," he said, settling back in his chair. "It's an awful thing to have happened, but the trouble is that we can't give you a zoning exception without a majority vote of the village council and all the members of the council happen to be out of town. Pete's in California and Jack's in Paris and Larry won't be back from Stowe until the end of the week."

I was sarcastic. "Then I suppose Cousin Justina will have to gracefully decompose in my parlor until Jack comes back from Paris."

"Oh, no," he said, "oh, *no*. Jack won't be back from Paris for another month, but I think you might wait until Larry comes from Stowe. Then we'd have a majority, assuming of course that they would agree to your appeal."

"For Christ's sake," I snarled.

"Yes, yes," he said, "it is difficult, but after all you must realize that this is the world you live in and the importance of zoning can't be overestimated. Why, if a single member of the council could give out zoning exceptions I could give you permission right now to open a saloon in your garage, put up neon lights, hire an orchestra and destroy the neighborhood and all the human and commercial values we've worked so hard to protect."

"I don't want to open a saloon in my garage," I howled. "I don't want to hire an orchestra. I just want to bury Justina."

"I know, Moses, I know," he said. "I understand that. But it's just that it happened in the wrong zone and if I make an exception for you I'll have to make an exception for everyone, and this kind of morbidity, when it gets out of hand, can be very depressing. People don't like to live in a neighborhood where this sort of thing goes on all the time."

"Listen to me," I said. "You give me an exception and you give it to me now or I'm going home and dig a hole in my garden and bury Justina myself."

"But you can't do that, Moses. You can't bury anything in zone B. You can't even bury a cat."

"You're mistaken" I said. "I can and I will. I can't function as a doctor and I can't function as an undertaker, but I can dig a hole in the ground and if you don't give me my exception, that's what I'm going to do."

I got out of the low chair before I finished speaking and started for the door.

"Come back, Moses, come back," he said. "Please come back. Look. I'll give you an exception if you'll promise not to tell anyone. It's breaking the law, it's a forgery, but I'll do it if you promise to keep it a secret."

I promised to keep it a secret, he gave me the documents and I used his telephone to make the arrangements. Justina was removed a few minutes after I got home, but that night I had the strangest dream.

I dreamed that I was in a crowded supermarket. It must have been night because the windows were dark. The ceiling was paved with fluorescent light—brilliant, cheerful, but, considering our prehistoric memories, a harsh link in the chain of light that binds us to the past. Music was playing and there must have been at least a thousand shoppers pushing their wagons among the long corridors of comestibles and victuals. Now is there—or isn't there—something about the posture we assume when we push a wagon that unsexes us? Can it be done with gallantry? I bring this up because the multitude of shoppers seemed that evening, as they pushed their wagons, penitential and unsexed. There were all kinds, this being my beloved country. There were Italians. Finns, Jews, Negroes, Shropshiremen, Cubans—anyone who had heeded the voice of liberty—and they were dressed with that sumptuary abandon that European caricaturists record with such bitter disgust. Yes, there were grandmothers in shorts, big-butted women in knitted pants, and men wearing such an assortment of clothing that it looked as if they had dressed hurriedly in a burning building. But this, as I say, is my own country and in my opinion the caricaturist who vilifies the old lady in shorts, vilifies himself. I am a native and I was wearing buckskin jump boots, chino pants cut so tight that my sexual organs were discernible and a rayon acetate pajama top printed with representations of the *Nina*, the *Pinta* and the *Santa Maria* in full sail. The scene was strange—the strangeness of a dream where we see familiar objects in an unfamiliar light, but as I looked more closely I saw that there were some irregularities. Nothing was labeled. Nothing was identified or known. The cans and boxes were all bare. The frozen food bins were full of brown parcels, but they were such odd shapes that you couldn't tell if they contained a frozen turkey or a Chinese dinner. All the goods at the vegetable and the bakery counters were concealed in brown bags and even the books for sale had no titles. In spite of the fact that the contents of nothing was known, my companions of the dream—my thousands of bizarrely dressed compatriots—were deliberating gravely over these mysterious containers as if the choices they made were critical. Like any dreamer, I was omniscient—I was with them and I was withdrawn—and stepping above the scene for a minute I noticed the men at the check-out counters.

They were brutes. Now sometimes in a crowd, in a bar or a street, you will see a face so full-blown in its obdurate resistance to the appeals of love, reason and decency—so lewd, so brutish and un-regenerate—that you turn away. Men like these were stationed at the only way out and as the shoppers approached them they tore their packages open—I still couldn't see what they contained—but in every case the customer, at the sight of what he had chose, showed all the symptoms of the deepest guilt; that force that brings us to our knees. Once their choice had been opened, to their shame they were pushed—in some cases kicked—toward the door in groups to be taken away in some conveyance that I couldn't see. As I watched, thousands and thousands pushed their wagons through the market, made their careful and mysterious choices and were reviled and taken away. What could be the meaning of this?

We buried Justina in the rain the next afternoon. The dead are not, as God knows, a minority, but in Proxmire Manor their unexalted kingdom is on the outskirts, rather like a dump, where they are transported furtively as knaves and scoundrels and where they lie in an atmosphere of perfect neglect. Justina's life had been exemplary, but by ending it she seemed to have disgraced us all. The priest was a friend and a cheerful sight, but the undertaker and his helpers, hiding behind their limousines, were not, and aren't they at the root of most of our troubles with their claim that death is a violet-flavored kiss? How can a people who do not mean to understand death hope to understand love and who will sound the alarm?

I went from the cemetery back to my office.

The commercial was on my desk and MacPherson had writ-ten across it in large letters in grease pencil: "Very funny, you bro-ken-down bore. Do again."

I was tired but unrepentant and didn't seem able to force my-self into a practical posture of usefulness and obedience. I did an-other commercial.

Don't lose your loved ones because of excessive radioactivity. Don't be a wallflower at the dance because of strontium 90 in your bones. Don't be a victim of fallout. When the tart on 36ᵗʰ Street gives you the big eye, does your body stride off in one direction and your imagination in another? Does your mind follow her up the stairs and taste her wares in revolting detail while your flesh goes off to Brooks Brothers or the foreign exchange desk of the Chase Manhattan Bank? Haven't you noticed the size of the ferns, the lushness of the grass, the bitterness of the string beans and the brilliant markings on the new breeds of butterflies? You have been inhaling lethal atomic waste for the last twenty-five years and only Elixircol can save you.

I gave this copy to Ralphie and waited perhaps ten minutes, when it was returned, marked again with grease pencil. "Do," he wrote, "or you'll be dead."

I felt very tired. I returned to the typewriter, put another piece of paper into the machine and wrote: *The Lord is my Shepherd, therefore can I lack nothing. He shall feed me in a green pasture and lead me forth beside the waters of comfort. He shall convert my soul and bring me forth in the paths of righteousness for His name's sake. Yea, though I walk through the valley of the shadow of death I will fear no evil for thou art with me; thy rod and thy staff comfort me. Thou shalt prepare a tale for me in the presence of them that trouble me; thou hast anointed my head with oil and my cup shall be full. Surely thy loving kindness and thy mercy shall follow me all the days of my life and I will dwell in the house of the Lord forever.* I gave this to Ralphie and went home.

In *The Death of Justina*, John Cheever has delineated the character of an alcoholic smoker and the psychology of drinking and smoking as astutely as any psychiatrist's case history. The story begins with the protagonist paying a visit to his doctor on Saturday.

The doctor orders him to stop drinking and smoking. On the first evening of sobriety, he found himself mournfully picturing the neglected graves of his three brothers. In the wake of these thoughts were unearthed fears that his house would burn down, his daughter attacked by the cook with a carving knife, and that he and his wife would be killed in an automobile accident, leaving behind bewildered and sad orphan children. He felt as if he were "being lowered by ropes into the atmosphere of (his)...childhood," when ordinarily he could barely remember the house where he was raised. He felt so lightheaded he had to ask his wife to drive the car, and snuck seven cigarettes in various hiding places and drank two martinis in the downstairs coat closet.

By the end of the first page, Cheever has clearly indicated that his hero uses liquor and cigarettes to ward off grief, despair, and panic, and that without these crutches he abruptly sinks into depression and a heightened state of anxiety. He "travels through a landscape of utter desolation," as repressed memories of his childhood return to haunt him, and he recognizes for the first time the terrors of aging.

On Monday his wife's cousin, Justina, comes to visit, and on Tuesday she dies in his home. He tries to get the doctor on the phone to issue a death certificate, but the line is busy. He pours himself the first drink and lights up his first cigarette since Sunday. When the doctor says he cannot be of help because Justina died in a B zone where no commercial enterprises are allowed, the protagonist pours himself a fresh drink and lights up another cigarette. By this time he is chain smoking. In a vain effort to get around the zoning law, he consults with the mayor, whose wife pours him another drink.

The hero dreams he is shopping in a dark and crowded supermarket where nothing is labeled, nothing is identified or known. Frozen foods are wrapped in brown parcels, so that no one can tell if they contain Chinese food or a frozen turkey (an allusion to problems of national identity?) Even the books have no names. The men at the checkout counter are brutes, and tear open the customers' packages. On having their choices exposed, all the customers show the deepest guilt, and, filled with shame, are kicked or pushed toward the door.

The affect in this dream must be how the hero (and Cheever?) felt about himself and his life. He is a man with severe identity problems. Even though his father had emigrated from the old world three centuries ago, the hero never feels quite at home in the United States. When he pushes a shopping wagon, he feels "unsexed"' suggesting that he also is confused about his sexual identity. I see him as a homosexual trapped in a loveless marriage (his wife was not interested in whether he drank or not, that he had a bitter taste in his mouth, or that his head seemed to be leaving his shoulders). What he genuinely wanted sexually was usually repressed and disguised. When homosexual impulses broke through, perhaps in one-night sexual stands when he was drunk, he was filled with guilt and shame, as portrayed in the dream when the lewd and brutal "check-out man" exposed his "choice" in front of other "customers." The "check-out man" may well refer to the aging protagonist's fears of Judgment Day. From this dream one can intimate that Cheever himself never came to terms with his own sexual preferences. (And indeed, his biography by his daughter Susan Cheever supports this assumption.) At Justina's funeral, in a burst of insight, the "hero" becomes further aware of his terror of death, and realizes that people who do not understand it cannot hope to understand love. The story ends with his version of the 23rd Psalm. At readings of this story, one of Cheever's favorites for that purpose, he always ended with the 23rd Psalm itself, which suggests that he himself was a possible convert to Alcoholics Anonymous, where he learned to look to God for comfort.

15

PAUL'S CASE

WILLA CATHER

I t was Paul's afternoon to appear before the faculty of the Pittsburgh High School to account for his various misdemeanors.
He had been suspended a week ago, and his father had called
at the principal's office and confessed his perplexity about his son.
Paul entered the faculty room suave and smiling. His clothes were
a trifle outgrown, and the tan velvet of the collar of his open overcoat was frayed and worn; but for all that there was something of
the dandy about him, and he wore an opal pin in his neatly knot-
ted black four-in-hand, and a red carnation in his buttonhole. The
latter adornment the faculty somehow felt was not properly significant of the contrite spirit befitting a boy under the ban of
suspension.

Paul was tall for his age and very thin, with high, cramped
shoulders and a narrow chest. His eyes were remarkable for a certain hysterical brilliancy, and he continually used them in a conscious, theatrical sort of way, peculiarly offensive in a boy. The
pupils were abnormally large, as though he were addicted to bella-
donna, but there was a glassy glitter about them which that drug
does not produce.

When questioned by the principal as to why he was there, Paul
stated, politely enough, that he wanted to come back to school.

Paul's Case, by Willa Cather, from THE TROLL GARDEN, 1905.

This was a lie, but Paul was quite accustomed to lying; found it, indeed, indispensable for overcoming friction. His teachers were asked to state their respective charges against him, which they did with such a rancour and aggrievedness as evinced that this was not a usual case. Disorder and impertinence were among the offenses named, yet each of his instructors felt that it was scarcely possible to put into words the real cause of the trouble, which lay in a sort of hysterically defiant manner of the boy's; in the contempt which they all knew he felt for them, and which he seemingly made not the least effort to conceal. Once, when he had been making a synopsis of a paragraph at the blackboard, his English teacher had stepped to his side and attempted to guide his hand. Paul had started back with a shudder and thrust his hands violently behind him. The astonished woman could scarcely have been more hurt and embarrassed had he struck at her. The insult was so involuntary and definitely personal as to be unforgettable. In one way and another, he had made all his teachers, men and women alike, conscious of the same feeling of physical aversion. In one class he habitually sat with his hand shading his eyes; in another he always looked out of the window during the recitation; in another he made a running commentary on the lecture, with humorous intent.

His teachers felt this afternoon that his whole attitude was symbolized by his shrug and his flippantly red carnation flower, and they fell upon him without mercy, his English teacher leading the pack. He stood through it smiling, his pale lips parted over his white teeth. (His lips were continually twitching, and he had a habit of raising his eyebrows that was contemptuous and irritating to the last degree.) Older boys than Paul had broken down and shed tears under that ordeal, but his set smile did not once desert him, and his only sign of discomfort was the nervous trembling of the fingers that toyed with the buttons of his overcoat, and an occasional jerking of the other hand which held his hat. Paul was always smiling, always glancing about him, seeming to feel that people might be watching him and trying to detect something. This conscious expression, since it was as far as possible from boyish mirthfulness, was usually attributed to insolence or "smartness."

As the inquisition proceeded, one of his instructors repeated an impertinent remark of the boy's, and the principal asked him whether he thought that a courteous speech to make to a woman. Paul shrugged his shoulders slightly and his eyebrows twitched.

"I don't know," he replied. "I didn't mean to be polite or impolite, either. I guess it's sort of a way I have, of saying things regardless."

The principal asked him whether he didn't think that a way it would be well to get rid of. Paul grinned and said he guessed so. When he was told that he could go, he bowed gracefully and went out. His bow was like a repetition of the scandalous red carnation,

His teachers were in despair, and his drawing master voiced the feeling of them all when he declared there was something about the boy which none of them understood. He added: "I don't really believe that smile of his comes altogether from insolence, there's something sort of haunted about it. The boy is not strong, for one thing. There is something wrong about the fellow."

The drawing master had come to realize that, in looking at Paul, one saw only his white teeth and the forced animation of his eyes. One warm afternoon the boy had gone to sleep at his drawing board, and his master had noted with amazement what a white, blue-veined face it was; drawn and wrinkled like an old man's about the eyes, the lips twitching even in his sleep.

His teachers left the building dissatisfied and unhappy; humiliated to have felt so vindictive toward a mere boy, to have uttered this feeling in cutting terms, and to have set each other on, as it were, in the gruesome game of intemperate reproach. One of them remembered having seen a miserable street cat set at bay by a ring of tormentors.

As for Paul, he ran down the hill whistling the Soldiers' Chorus from "Faust," looking behind him now and then to see whether some of his teachers were not there to witness his light-heartedness. As it was not late in the afternoon and Paul was on duty that evening as usher at Carnegie Hall, he decided that he would not go home to supper.

When he reached the concert hall, the doors were not yet open. It was chilly outside, and he decided to go up into the picture gallery—always deserted at this hour—where there were some of Rafael's gay studies of Paris streets and an airy blue Venetian scene or two that always exhilarated him. He was delighted to find no one in the gallery but the old guard, who sat in the corner, a newspaper on his knee, a black patch over one eye and the other closed. Paul possessed himself of the place and walked confidently up and down, whistling under his breath. After a while he sat down before a blue Rico and lost himself. When he bethought him to look at his watch, it was after seven o'clock, and he rose with a start and ran downstairs, making a face at Augustus Caesar, peering out from the cast room, and an evil gesture at the Venus of Milo as he passed her on the stairway.

When Paul reached the ushers' dressing room, half a dozen boys were there already, and he began excitedly to tumble into his uniform. It was one of the few that at all approached fitting, and Paul thought it very becoming—though he knew the tight, straight coat accentuated his narrow chest, about which he was exceedingly sensitive. He was always excited while he dressed, twanging all over to the tuning of the strings and the preliminary flourishes of the horns in the music room; but tonight he seemed quite beside himself, and he teased and plagued the boys until, telling him that he was crazy, they put him down on the floor and sat on him.

Somewhat calmed by his suppression, Paul dashed out to the front of the house to seat the early comers. He was a model usher. Gracious and smiling he ran up and down the aisles. Nothing was too much trouble for him; he carried messages and brought programmes as though it were his greatest pleasure in life, and all the people in his section thought him a charming boy, feeling that he remembered and admired them. As the house filled, he grew more and more vivacious and animated, and the colour came to his cheeks and lips. It was very much as though this were a great reception and Paul were the host. Just as the musicians came out to take their places, his English teacher arrived with checks for the seats which a prominent manufacturer had taken for the season. She betrayed some embarrassment when she handed Paul the tickets, and a hauteur which subsequently made her feel very foolish. Paul was startled for a moment, and had the feeling of wanting to put her out; what business had she here among all these fine people and gay colours? He looked her over and decided that she was not appropriately dressed and must be a fool to sit downstairs in such togs. The tickets had probably been sent her out of kindness, he reflected, as he put down a seat for her, and she had about as much right to sit there as he had.

When the symphony began, Paul sank into one of the rear seats with a long sigh of relief, and lost himself as he had done before the Rico. It was not that symphonies, as such, meant anything in particular to Paul, but the first sight of the instruments seemed to free some hilarious spirit within him; something that struggled there like the Genius in the bottle found by the Arab fisherman. He felt a sudden zest for life; the lights danced before his eyes and the concert hall blazed into unimaginable splendour. When the soprano soloist came on, Paul forgot even the nastiness of his teacher's being there, and gave himself up to the peculiar intoxication such personages always had for him. The soloist chanced to be a German woman, by no means in her first youth, and the mother of many children; but she wore a satin gown and a tiara, and she had that indefinable air of achievement, that world-shine upon her, which always blinded Paul to any possible defects.

After a concert was over, Paul was often irritable and wretched until he got to sleep—and tonight he was even more than usually restless. He had the feeling of not being able to let down; of its being impossible to give up this delicious excitement which was the only thing that could be called living at all. During the last number he withdrew and, after hastily changing his clothes in the dressing room, slipped out to the side door where the singer's carriage stood. Here he began pacing rapidly up and down the walk, waiting to see her come out.

Over yonder the Schenley, in its vacant stretch, loomed big and square through the fine rain, the windows of its twelve stories glowing like those of a lighted cardboard house under a Christmas tree. All the actors and singers of any importance stayed there when they were in Pittsburgh, and a number of the big manufacturers of the place lived there in the winter. Paul had often hung about the hotel, watching the people go in and out, longing to enter and leave schoolmasters and dull care behind him forever.

At last the singer came out, accompanied by the conductor, who helped her into her carriage and closed the door with a cordial *auf wiedersehen*—which set Paul to wondering whether she were not an old sweetheart of his. Paul followed the carriage over to the hotel, walking so rapidly as not to be far from the entrance when the singer alighted and disappeared behind the swinging glass doors which were opened by a Negro in a tall hat and a long coat. In the moment that the door was ajar, it seemed to Paul that he, too, entered. He seemed to feel himself go after her up the steps, into the warm lighted building, into an exotic, a tropical world of shiny, glistening surfaces and basking ease. He reflected upon the mysterious dishes that were brought into the dining room, the green bottles in buckets of ice, as he had seen them in the supper-party pictures of the Sunday supplement. A quick gust of wind brought the rain down with sudden vehemence, and Paul was startled to find that he was still outside in the slush of the gravel driveway; that his boots were letting in the water and his scanty overcoat was clinging wet about him; that the lights in front of the concert hall were out, and that the rain was driving in sheets between him and the orange glow of the windows above him. There it was, what he wanted—tangibly before him, like the fairy world of a Christmas pantomime; as the rain beat in his face, Paul wondered whether he were destined always to shiver in the black night outside, looking up at it.

He turned and walked reluctantly toward the car tracks. The end had to come sometime, his father in his night clothes at the top of the stairs, explanations that did not explain, hastily improvised fictions that were forever tripping him up, his upstairs room and its horrible yellow wallpaper, the creaking bureau with the greasy plush collar-box, and over his painted wooden bed the pictures of George Washington and John Calvin, and the framed motto, "Feed my Lambs," which had been worked in red worsted by his mother, whom Paul could not remember.

Half an hour later, Paul alighted from the Negley Avenue car and went slowly down one of the side streets off the main thoroughfare. It was a highly respectable street, where all the houses were exactly alike, and where business men of moderate means begot and reared large families of children, all of whom went to Sabbath School and learned the shorter catechism, and were interested in arithmetic; all of whom were as exactly alike as their homes, and of a piece with the monotony in which they lived. Paul never went up Cordelia Street without a shudder of loathing. His home was next the house of the Cumberland minister. He approached it tonight with the nerveless sense of defeat, the hopeless feeling of sinking back forever into ugliness and commonness that he had always had when he came home. The moment he turned into Cordelia Street he felt the waters close above his head. After each of these orgies of living, he experienced all the physical depression which follows a debauch; the loathing of respectable beds, of common food, of a house permeated by kitchen odours, a shuddering repulsion for the flavourless, colourless mass of everyday existence; a morbid desire for cool things and soft lights and fresh flowers.

The nearer he approached the house, the more absolutely unequal Paul felt to the sight of it all: his ugly sleeping chamber; the old bathroom with the grimy zinc tub, the cracked mirror, the dripping spigots; his father, at the top of the stairs, his hairy legs sticking out from his nightshirt, his feet thrust into carpet slippers. He was so much later than usual that there would certainly be enquiries and reproaches. Paul stopped short before the door. He felt that he could not be accosted by his father tonight; that he could not toss again on that miserable bed. He would not go in.

He would tell his father that he had no car fare, and it was raining so hard he had gone home with one of the boys and stayed all night.

Meanwhile, he was wet and cold. He went around to the back of the house and tried one of the basement windows, found it open, raised it cautiously, and scrambled down the cellar wall to the floor. There he stood, holding his breath, terrified by the noise he had made; but the floor above him was silent, and there was no creak on the stairs. He found a soap box, and carried it over to the soft ring of light that streamed from the furnace door, and sat down. He was horribly afraid of rats, so he did not try to sleep, but sat looking distrustfully at the dark, still terrified lest he might have awakened his father.

In such reactions, after one of the experiences which made days and nights out of the dreary blanks of the calendar, when his senses were deadened, Paul's head was always singularly clear. Suppose his father had heard him getting in at the window and had come down and shot him for a burglar? Then, again, suppose his father had come down, pistol in hand, and he had cried out in time to save himself, and his father had been horrified to think how nearly he had killed him? Then again, suppose a day should come when his father would remember that night, and wish there had been no warning cry to stay his hand? With this last supposition, Paul entertained himself until daybreak.

The following Sunday was fine; the sodden November chill was broken by the last flash of autumnal summer. In the morning Paul had to go to church and Sabbath school, as always. On seasonable Sunday afternoons the burghers of Cordelia Street usually sat out on their front "stoops," and talked to their neighbors on the next stoop, or called to those across the street in neighborly fashion. The men sat placidly on gay cushions placed upon the steps that led down to the sidewalk, while the women, in their Sunday "waists," sat in rockers on the cramped porches, pretending to be greatly at their ease. The children played in the street; there were so many of them that the place resembled the recreations grounds of a kindergarten. The men on the steps, all in their shirt-sleeves, their vests unbuttoned, sat with their legs well apart, their stomachs comfortably protruding, and talked of the prices of things, or told anecdotes of the sagacity of their various chiefs and overlords. They occasionally looked over the multitude of squabbling children, listened affectionately to their high-pitched, nasal voices, smiling to see their own proclivities reproduced in their offspring, and interspersed their legends of the iron kings with remarks about their sons' progress at school, their grades in arithmetic, and the amounts they had saved in their toy banks.

On this last Sunday of November, Paul sat all the afternoon on the lowest step of his "stoop," staring into the street, while his sisters, in their rockers, were talking to the minister's daughters next door about how many shirtwaists they had made in the last week, and how many waffles someone had eaten in the last church supper. When the weather was warm, and his father was in a particularly jovial frame of mind, the girls made lemonade, which was always brought out in a red-glass pitcher, ornamented with forget-me-nots in blue enamel. This the girls thought very fine, and the neighbors joked about the suspicious colour of the pitcher.

Today Paul's father, on the top step, was talking to a young man who shifted a restless baby, from knee to knee. He happened to be the young man who was daily held up to Paul as a model, and after whom it was his father's dearest hope that he would pattern. This young man was of a ruddy complexion, with a compressed, red mouth, and faded, nearsighted eyes, over which he wore thick spectacles, with gold bows that curved about his ears. He was clerk to one of the magnates of a great steel corporation, and was looked upon in Cordelia Street as a young man with a future. There was a story that, some five years ago—he was now barely twenty-six—he had been a trifle "dissipated," but in order to curb his appetites and save the loss of time and strength that a sowing of wild oats might have entailed, he had taken his chief's advice, oft reiterated to his employees, and at twenty-one had married the first woman whom he could persuade to share his fortunes. She happened to be an angular schoolmistress, much older than he, who also wore thick glasses, and who had now borne him four children, all nearsighted like herself.

The young man was relating how his chief, now cruising in the Mediterranean, kept in touch with all the details of the business, arranging his office hours on his yacht just as though he were at home, and "knocking off work enough to keep two stenographers busy." His father told, in turn, the plan his corporation was considering, of putting in an electric railway plant at Cairo. Paul snapped his teeth; he had an awful apprehension that they might spoil it all before he got there. Yet he rather liked to hear these legends of the iron kings, that were told and retold on Sundays and holidays: these stories of palaces in Venice, yachts on the Mediterranean, and high play at Monte Carlo appealed to his fancy, and he was interested in the triumphs of cash-boys who had become famous, though he had no mind for the cash-boy stage.

After supper was over, and he had helped to dry the dishes, Paul nervously asked his father whether he could go to George's to get some help in his geometry, and still more nervously asked for car fare. This latter request he had to repeat, as his father, on principle, did not like to hear requests for money, whether much or little. He asked Paul whether he could not go to some boy who lived nearer, and told him that he ought not leave his school work until Sunday; but he gave him the dime. He was not a poor man, but he had a worthy ambition to come up in the world. His only reason for allowing Paul to usher was that he thought a boy ought to be earning a little.

Paul bounded upstairs, scrubbed the greasy odour of the dishwater from his hands with the ill-smelling soap he hated, and then shook over his fingers a few drops of violet water from the bottle he kept hidden in his drawer. He left the house with his geometry conspicuously under his arm, and the moment he got out of Cordelia Street and boarded a downtown car, he shook off the lethargy of two deadening days, and began to live again.

The leading juvenile of the permanent stock company which played at one of the downtown theatres was an acquaintance of

Paul's, and the boy had been invited to drop in at the Sunday night rehearsals whenever he could. For more than a year Paul had spent every available moment loitering about Charley Edward's dressing room. He had won a place among Edward's following not only because the young actor, who could not afford to employ a dresser, often found him useful, but because he recognized in Paul something akin to what churchmen term "vocation."

It was at the theatre and at Carnegie Hall that Paul really lived; the rest was but a sleep and a forgetting. This was Paul's fairy tale, and it had for him all the allurement of a secret love. The moment he inhaled the gassy, painty, dusty odour behind the scenes, he breathed like a prisoner set free, and felt within him the possibility of doing or saying splendid, brilliant things. The moment the cracked orchestra beat out the overture from "Martha," or jerked at the serenade from "Rigoletto,"all stupid and ugly things slid from him, and his senses were deliciously, yet delicately fired.

Perhaps it was because, in Paul's world, the natural nearly always wore the guise of ugliness, that a certain element of artificiality seemed to him necessary in beauty. Perhaps it was because his experience of life elsewhere was so full of Sabbath-School picnics, petty economies, wholesome advice as to how to succeed in life, and the unescapable odours of cooking, that he found this existence so alluring, these smartly clad men and women so attractive, that he was so moved by these starry apple orchards that bloomed perennially under the limelight. It would be difficult to put it strongly enough how convincingly the stage entrance of that theatre was for Paul the actual portal of Romance. Certainly none of the company ever suspected it, least of all Charley Edwards. It was very like the old stories that used to float about London of fabulously rich Jews, who had subterranean halls, with palms, and fountains, and soft lamps and richly appareled women who never saw the disenchanting light of London day. So in the midst of that smoke-palled city, enamoured of figures and grimy toil, Paul had his secret temple, his wishing carpet, his bit of blue-and-white Mediterranean shore bathed in perpetual sunshine.

Several of Paul's teachers had a theory that his imagination had been perverted by garish fiction; but the truth was he scarcely ever read at all. The books at home were not such as would either tempt or corrupt a youthful mind, and as for reading the novels that some of his friends urged upon him — well, he got what he wanted much more quickly from music; any sort of music, from an orchestra to a barrel organ. He needed only the spark, the indescribable thrill that made his imagination master of his senses, and he could make plots and pictures enough of his own. It was equally true that he was not stage struck — not, at any rate, in the usual acceptation of that expression. He had no desire to become an actor, any more than he had to become a musician. He felt no necessity to do any of these things; what he wanted was to see, to be in the atmosphere, float on the wave of it, to be carried out, blue league after league, away from everything.

After a night behind the scenes, Paul found the schoolroom more than ever repulsive; the bare floors and naked walls; the prosy men who never wore frock coats, or violets in their buttonholes; the women with their dull gowns, shrill voices and pitiful seriousness about prepositions that govern the dative. He could not bear to have the other pupils think, for a moment, that he took these people seriously; he must convey to them that he considered it all trivial, and was there only by way of a joke, anyway. He had autographed pictures of all the members of the stock company which he showed his classmates, telling them the most incredible stories of his familiarity with these people, his acquaintance with the soloists who came to Carnegie Hall, his suppers with them and the flowers he sent them. When these stories lost their effect and the audience grew listless, he would bid all the boys goodbye, announcing that he was going to travel for a while; going to Naples, to California, to Egypt. Then, next Monday, he would slip back, conscious and nervously smiling; his sister was ill, and he would have to defer his voyage until spring.

Matters went steadily worse with Paul at school. In the itch to let his instructors know how heartily he despised them, and how thoroughly he was appreciated elsewhere, he mentioned once or twice that he had no time to fool with theorems; adding—with a twitch of the eyebrows and a touch of that nervous bravado which so perplexed them—that he was helping the people down at the stock company; they were old friends of his.

The upshot of the matter was that the principal went to Paul's father, and Paul was taken out of school and put to work. The manager at Carnegie Hall was told to get another usher in his stead; the doorkeeper at the theatre was warned not to admit him to the house; and Charley Edwards remorsefully promised the boy's father not to see him again.

The members of the stock company were vastly amused when some of Paul's stories reached them—especially the women. They were hard-working women, most of them supporting indolent husbands or brothers, and they laughed rather bitterly at having stirred the boy to such fervid and florid inventions. They agreed with the faculty and with his father, that Paul's was a bad case.

The east-bound train was ploughing through a January snow-storm; the dull dawn was beginning to show grey when the engine whistled a mile out of Newark. Paul started up from the seat where he had lain curled in uneasy slumber, rubbed the breath-misted window glass with his hand, and peered out. The snow was whirling in curling eddies above the white bottom lands, and the drifts lay already deep in the fields and along the fences, while here and there the tall dead grass and dried weed stalks protruded black above it. Lights shone from the scattered houses, and a gang of labourers who stood beside the track waved their lanterns.

Paul had slept very little, and he felt grimy and uncomfortable. He had made the all-night journey in a day coach because he was afraid if he took a Pullman he might be seen by some Pittsburgh business man who had noticed him in Denny and Carson's office. When the whistle woke him, he clutched quickly at his breast pocket, glancing about him with an uncertain smile. But the little, clay-spattered Italians were still sleeping, the slatternly women across the aisle were in open-mouthed oblivion, and even the crumby, crying babies were for the time stilled. Paul settled back to struggle with his impatience as best he could.

When he arrived at the Jersey City station, he hurried through his breakfast, manifestly ill at ease and keeping a sharp eye about him. After he reached the Twenty-third Street station, he consulted a cabman, and had himself driven to a men's furnishing establishment which was just opening for the day. He spent upward of two hours there, buying with endless reconsidering and great care. His new street suit he put on in the fitting room; the frock coat and dress clothes he had bundled into the cab with his new shirts. Then he drove to a hatter's and a shoe house. His next errand was at Tiffany's, where he selected silver-mounted brushes and a scarf pin. He would not wait to have his silver marked, he said. Lastly, he stopped at a trunk shop on Broadway, and had his purchases packed into various traveling bags.

It was a little after one o'clock when he drove up to the Waldorf, and after settling with the cabman, went into the office. He registered from Washington, said his mother and father had been abroad, and that he had come down to await the arrival of their steamer. He told his story plausibly and had no trouble, since he offered to pay for them in advance, in engaging his rooms; a sleeping room, sitting room, and bath.

Not once, but a hundred times Paul had planned this entry into New York. He had gone over every detail of it with Charley Edwards, and in his scrapbook at home there were pages of description about New York hotels, cut from the Sunday papers.

When he was shown to his sitting room on the eighth floor, he saw at a glance that everything was as it should be; there was but one detail in his mental picture that the place did not realize, so he rang for the bellboy and sent him down for flowers. He moved about nervously until the boy returned, putting away his new linen and fingering it delightedly as he did so. When the flowers came, he put them hastily into water, and then tumbled into a hot bath. Presently he came out of his white bathroom, resplendent in his new silk underwear, and playing with the tassels of his red robe. The snow was whirling so fiercely outside his windows that he could scarcely see across the street; but within the air was deliciously soft and fragrant. He put the violets and jonquils on the tabouret beside the couch, and threw himself down with a long sigh, covering himself with Roman blanket. He was thoroughly tired; he had been in such haste, he had stood up to such a strain, covered so much ground in the last twenty-four hours, that he wanted to think how it had all come about. Lulled by the sound of the wind, the warm air, and the cool fragrance of the flowers, he sank into deep, drowsy retrospection.

It had been wonderfully simple; when they had shut him out of the theatre and concert hall, when they had taken away his bone, the whole thing was virtually determined. The rest was a mere matter of opportunity. The only thing that at all surprised him was his own courage—for he realized well enough that he had always been tormented by fear, a sort of apprehensive dread which, of late years, as the meshes of the lies he had told closed about him, had been pulling the muscles of his body tighter and tighter. Until now he could not remember a time when he had not been dreading something. Even when he was a little boy, it was always there—behind him, or before, or on either side. There had always been the shadowed corner, the dark place into which he dared not look, but from which something seemed always to be watching him—and Paul had done things that were not pretty to watch, he knew.

But now he had a curious sense of relief, as though he had at last thrown down the gauntlet to the thing in the corner.

Yet it was but a day since he had been sulking in the traces, but yesterday afternoon that he had been sent to the bank with Denny and Carson's deposit as usual—but this time he was instructed to leave the book to be balanced. There was above two thousand dollars in checks, and nearly a thousand in the bank notes which he had taken from the book and quietly transferred to his pocket.

At the bank he had made out a new deposit slip. His nerves had been steady enough to permit of his returning to the office, where he had finished his work and asked for a full day's holiday tomorrow, Saturday, giving a perfectly reasonable pretext. The bank book, he knew, would not be returned before Monday or Tuesday, and his father would be out of town for the next week. From the time he slipped the bank notes into his pocket until he boarded the night train for New York, he had not known a moment's hesitation. It was not the first time Paul had steered through treacherous waters.

How astonishingly easy it had all been; here he was, the thing done; and this time there would be no awakening, no figure at the top of the stairs. He watched the snow flakes whirling by his window until he fell asleep.

When he awoke, it was three o'clock in the afternoon. He bounded up with a start; one of his precious days gone already! He spent nearly an hour dressing, watching every stage of his toilet carefully in the mirror. Everything was quite perfect; he was exactly the kind of boy he had always wanted to be.

When he went downstairs, Paul took a carriage and drove up Fifth Avenue toward the park. The snow had somewhat abated; carriages and tradesmen's wagons were hurrying soundlessly to and fro in the winter twilight; boys in woollen mufflers were shoveling off the doorsteps, the Avenue stages made fine spots of colour against the white street. Here and there on the corners whole flower gardens blooming behind glass windows, against which the snowflakes stuck and melted; violets, roses, carnations, lilies-of-the-valley — somehow vastly more lovely and alluring that they blossomed thus unnaturally in the snow. The park itself was a wonderful stage winter piece.

When he returned, the pause of the twilight had ceased, and the tune of the streets had changed. The snow was falling faster, lights streamed from the hotels that reared their many stories fearlessly up into the storm, defying the raging Atlantic winds. A long, black stream of carriages poured down the Avenue, intersected here and there by other streams, tending horizontally. There were a score of cabs about the entrance of his hotel, and his driver had to wait. Boys in livery were running in and out of the awning stretched across the sidewalk, up and down the red velvet carpet laid from the door to the street. Above, about, within it all, was the rumble and roar, the hurry and toss of thousands of human beings as hot for pleasure as himself, and on every side of him towered the glaring affirmation of the omnipotence of wealth.

The boy set his teeth and drew his shoulders together in a spasm of realization; the plot of all dramas, the text of all romances, the nerve stuff of all sensations was whirling about him like the snow-flakes. He burnt like a fagot in a tempest.

When Paul came down to dinner, the music of the orchestra floated up the elevator shaft to greet him. As he stepped into the thronged corridor, he sank back into one of the chairs against the wall to get his breath. The lights, the chatter, the perfumes, the bewildering medley of colour—he had, for a moment, the feeling of not being able to stand it. But only for a moment; these were his own people, he told himself. He went slowly about the corridors through the writing rooms, smoking rooms, reception rooms, as though he were exploring the chambers of an enchanted palace, built and peopled for him alone.

When he reached the dining room he sat down at a table near a window. The flowers, the white linen, the many-coloured wine glasses, the gay toilettes of the women, the low popping of corks, the undulating repetitions of the "Blue Danube" from the orches-tra, all flooded Paul's dream with bewildering radiance. When the roseate tinge of his champagne was added—that cold, precious, bubbling stuff that creamed and foamed in his glass—Paul won-dered that there were honest men in the world at all. This was what all the world was fighting for, he reflected; this was what all the struggle was about. He doubted the reality of his past. Had he ever known a place called Cordelia Street, a place where fagged-looking business men boarded the early car? Mere rivets in a ma-chine they seemed to Paul—sickening men, with combings of children's hair always hanging to their coats, and the smell of cook-ing in their clothes. Cordelia Street—ah, that belonged to another time and country! Had he not always been thus, had he not sat here night after night, from as far back as he could remember, looking pensively over just such shimmering textures, and slowly twirling the stem of a glass like this one between his thumb and middle finger? He rather thought he had.

He was not in the least abashed or lonely. He had no special desire to meet or to know any of these people; all he demanded was the right to look on and conjecture, to watch the pageant. The mere stage properties were all he contended for. Nor was he lonely later on in the evening, in his loge at the opera. He was entirely rid of his nervous misgivings, of his forced aggressiveness, of the imperative desire to show himself different from his surroundings. He felt now that his surroundings explained him. Nobody questioned the purple; he had only to wear it passively. He had only to glance down at t his dress coat to reassure himself that here it would be impossible for anyone to humiliate him.

He found it hard to leave his beautiful sitting room to go to bed that night, and sat long watching the raging storm from his turret window. When he went to sleep, it was with the lights turned on in his bedroom; partly because of his old timidity, and partly so that, if he should wake in the night, there would be no wretched moment of doubt, no horrible suspicion of yellow wallpaper, or of Washington and Calvin above his bed.

On Sunday morning the city was practically snowbound. Paul breakfasted late, and in the afternoon he fell in with a wild San Francisco boy, a freshman at Yale, who said he had run down for a "little flyer" over Sunday. The young man offered to show Paul the night side of the town, and the two boys went off together after dinner, not returning to the hotel until seven o'clock the next morning. They had started out in the confiding warmth of a champagne friendship, but their parting in the elevator was singularly cool. The freshman pulled himself together to make his train, and Paul went to bed. He awoke at two o'clock in the afternoon, very thirsty and dizzy, and rang for ice water, coffee, and the Pittsburgh papers.

On the part of the hotel management, Paul excited no suspicion. There was this to be said for him, that he wore his spoils with dignity and in no way made himself conspicuous. His chief greediness lay in his ears and eyes, and his excesses were not offensive ones. His dearest pleasures were the grey winter twilights in his sitting room; his quiet enjoyment of his flowers, his clothes, his wide divan, his cigarette, and his sense of power. He could not remember a time when he had felt so at peace with himself. The mere release from the necessity of petty lying, lying every day and every day, restored his self-respect. He had never lied for pleasure, even at school, but to make himself noticed and admired, to assert his difference from other Cordelia Street boys; and he felt a good deal more manly, more honest, even, now that he had no need for boastful pretensions, now that he could, as his actor friends used to say, "dress the part." It was characteristic that remorse did not occur to him. His golden days went by without a shadow, and he made each as perfect as he could.

On the eighth day after his arrival in New York, he found the whole affair exploited in the Pittsburgh papers, exploited with a wealth of detail which indicated that local news of a sensational nature was at a low ebb. The firm of Denny and Carson announced that the boy's father had refunded the full amount of his theft, and that they had no intention of prosecuting. The Cumberland minister had been interviewed, and expressed his hope of yet reclaiming the motherless lad, and Paul's Sabbath-School teacher declared that she would spare no effort to that end. The rumour had reached Pittsburgh that the boy had been seen in a New York hotel, and his father had gone East to find him and bring him home.

Paul had just come in to dress for dinner; he sank into a chair, weak in the knees, and clasped his head in his hands. It was to be worse than jail, even; the tepid waters of Cordelia Street were to close over him finally and forever. The grey monotony stretched before him in hopeless, unrelieved years — Sabbath-School, Young People's Meeting, the yellow-papered room, the damp dishtowels; it all rushed back upon him with sickening vividness. He had the old feeling that the orchestra had suddenly stopped, the sinking sensation that the play was over. The sweat broke out on his face, and he sprang to his feet, looked about him with his white, conscious smile, and winked at himself in the mirror. With something of the childish belief in miracles with which he had so often gone to class, all his lessons unlearned, Paul dressed and dashed whistling down the corridor to the elevator.

He had no sooner entered the dining room and caught the measure of the music than his remembrance was lightened by his old elastic power of claiming the moment, mounting with it, and finding it all-sufficient. The glare and glitter about him, the mere scenic accessories had again, and for the last time, their old potency. He would show himself that he was game, he would finish the thing splendidly. He doubted, more than ever, the existence of Cordelia Street, and for the first time he drank his wine recklessly. Was he not, after all, one of these fortunate beings? Was he not still himself, and in his own place? He drummed a nervous accompaniment to the music and looked about him, telling himself over and over that it had paid.

He reflected drowsily, to the swell of the violin and the chill sweetness of his wine, that he might have done it more wisely. He might have caught an outbound steamer and been well out of their clutches before now. But the other side of the world had seemed too far away and too uncertain then; he could not have waited for it; his need had been too sharp. If he had to choose over again, he would do the same thing tomorrow. He looked affectionately about the dining room, now gilded with a soft mist. Ah, it had paid indeed!

Paul was awakened next morning by a painful throbbing in his head and feet. He had thrown himself across the bed without undressing, and had slept with his shoes on. His limbs and hands were lead-heavy, and his tongue and throat were parched. There came upon him one of those fateful attacks of clear-headedness that never occurred except when he was physically exhausted and his nerves hung loose. He lay still and closed his eyes and let the tide of realities wash over him.

His father was in New York; "stopping at some joint or other," he told himself. The memory of successive summers on the front stoop fell upon him like a weight of black water. He had not a hundred dollars left; and he knew now, more than ever, that money was everything, the wall that stood between all he loathed and all he wanted. The thing was winding itself up; he had thought of that on his first glorious day in New York, and had even provided a way to snap the thread. It lay on his dressing table now; he had got it out last night when he came blindly up from dinner—but the shiny metal hurt his eyes, and he disliked the look of it, anyway.

He rose and moved about with a painful effort, succumbing now and again to attacks of nausea. It was the old depression exaggerated; all the world had become Cordelia Street. Yet somehow he was not afraid of anything, was absolutely calm; perhaps because he had looked into the dark corner at last, and knew. It was bad enough, what he saw there; but somehow not so bad as his long fear of it had been. He saw everything clearly now. He had a feeling that he had made the best of it, that he had lived the sort of life he was meant to live, and for half an hour he sat staring at the revolver. But he told himself that was not the way, so he went downstairs and took a cab to the ferry.

When Paul arrived at Newark, he got off the train and took another cab, directing the driver to follow the Pennsylvania tracks out of town. The snow lay heavy on the roadways and had drifted deep in the open fields. Only here and there the dead grass or dried weed stalks projected, singularly black, above it.

Once well into the country, Paul dismissed the carriage and walked, floundering along the tracks, his mind a medley of irrelevant things. He seemed to hold in his brain an actual picture of everything he had seen that morning. He remembered every feature of both his drivers, the toothless old woman from whom he had got his ticket, and all of the fellow passengers on the ferry. His mind, unable to cope with vital matters near at hand, worked feverishly and deftly at sorting and grouping these images. They made for him a part of the ugliness of the world, of the ache in his head, and the bitter burning on his tongue. He stopped and put a handful of snow into his mouth as he walked, but that, too, seemed hot. When he reached a little hillside, where the tracks ran through a cut some twenty feet below him, he stopped and sat down.

The carnations in his coat were drooping with the cold, he noticed; their red glory over. It occurred to him that all the flowers he had seen in the snow windows that first night must have gone the same way, long before this. It was only one splendid breath they had, in spite of their brave mockery at the winter outside the glass. It was a losing game in the end, it seemed, this revolt against the homilies by which the world is run. Paul took one of the blossoms carefully from his coat and scooped a little hole in the snow, where he covered it up. Then he dozed awhile, from his weak condition, seeming insensible to the cold.

The sound of an approaching train woke him up and he started to his feet, remembering only his resolution, and afraid lest he should be too late. He stood watching the approaching locomotive, his teeth chattering, his lips drawn away from them in a frightened smile; once or twice he glanced nervously sidewise, as though he were being watched. When the right moment came, he jumped. As he fell, the folly of his haste occurred to him with merciless clearness, the vastness of what he had left undone. There flashed through his brain, clearer than ever before, the blue of Adriatic water, the yellow of Algerian sands.

He felt something strike his chest—his body was being thrown swiftly through the air, on and on, immeasurably far and fast, while his limbs gently relaxed. Then, because the picture-making mechanism was crushed, the disturbing visions flashed into black, and Paul dropped back into the immense design of things.

Paul's Case, by Willa Cather, is a story that has saved lives. It tells of how the discrepancy between an adolescent boy's dreams and his reality led to depression, and ultimately to suicide. Paul was a motherless young man who despaired of "his ugly sleeping chamber, the old bathroom with the grimy zinc tub, the cracked mirror, the dripping spigots; his father, at the top of the stirs, his hairy legs sticking out from his nightshirt, his feet thrust into carpet slippers." He loathed the "flavorless, colorless mass of everyday existence." Paul's continuing dream was to feel part of the elegant world of art and society, of "a delicious excitement which was the only thing that could be called living."

Paul brought himself whatever joy was in his life by ushering at Carnegie Hall, listening to music, going to art museums, and attending performances of a local stock company. After such an evening, he found the schoolroom more repulsive than ever. To show his disdain for his teachers, he told them he had no time for theorems because he was helping out the people down at the stock company. When the principal complained to Paul's father, the boy was forbidden to usher at the opera or attend the theatre. He was taken out of school and put to work at Denny and Carson's office.

Then, for a little while anyway, Paul made his fantasy come true. He stole $2,000 from a bank deposit he was supposed to make for the office, and took a train to New York. There he was elegantly outfitted with new clothes, and silver handled brushes and a scarf pin from Tiffany's. At the Waldorf, he lied his way into the suite of his dreams. After ordering flowers, he was resplendent in his new silk underwear, as he played with the tassels of his red robe. All was as it should be in Paul's life. "Everything was quite perfect; he was exactly the kind of boy he had always wanted to be."

Paul didn't really want to know or meet any of the people who surrounded him in the elegant dining room. "The mere stage properties were all he contended for." As his actor friends had said, he only wanted to "dress the part." Paul had something in common with "as if" personalities who don't have genuine feelings for an identification, but imitate persons who do.³ In that respect, he was like a transvestite who spends all his time and energy getting and caring for his feminine clothing, and is satisfied merely to parade in and be seen in the female finery.

The boom fell when Paul got the Pittsburgh newspapers and read that his theft had been discovered and his father, who had repaid the debt, was coming to New York to bring him home. "It was worse than jail, even," he thought; "the tepid waters of Cordelia Street were to close over him finally and forever." In addition, he had less than $100 left, and knew that money was all that stood between everything he loathed and everything he wanted.

When Paul realized that his dream was coming to an end and that he had no option but to return to his dreary former life, he decided to kill himself. Planning his demise as carefully as he did his brief interlude of joy, the boy took himself out to the countryside and waited for a train to come. At the right moment, he jumped.

Then came the utterly magnificent ending of the story, one I vividly recall 50 years after I first read it. "*As he fell, the folly of his haste occurred to him, with merciless clearness, the vastness of what he had left undone. There flashed through his brain, clearer than ever before, the blue of Adriatic water, the yellow of Algerian sands....*Then, because the picture-making mechanism was crushed, the disturbing visions flashed into black, and Paul dropped back into the immense design of things."

As a psychoanalyst, I frequently recommended Paul's story to suicidal patients. It helped save lives. In my opinion, doctors and therapists alike should prescribe *Paul's Case* to every depressed and/or potentially suicidal patient.

16

THE OTHER WOMAN

SHERWOOD ANDERSON

I am in love with my wife," he said—a superficial remark, as I had not questioned his attachment to the woman he had married. We walked for ten minutes and then he said it again. I turned to look at him. He began to talk and told me the tale I am now about to set down.

The thing he had on his mind happened during what must have been the most eventful week of his life. He was to be married on Friday afternoon. On Friday of the week before he got a telegram announcing his appointment to a government position. Something else happened that made him very proud and glad. In secret he was in the habit of writing verses and during the year before several of them had been printed in poetry magazines. One of the societies that give prizes for what they think the best poems published during the year put his name at the head of their list. The story of his triumph was printed in the newspapers of his home city, and one of them also printed his picture.

As might have been expected, he was excited and in a rather highly strung nervous state all during that week. Almost every evening he went to call on his fianceé, the daughter of a judge. When he got there the house was filled with people and many

---

letters, telegrams and packages were being received. He stood a little to one side and men and women kept coming to speak with him. They congratulated him upon his success in getting the government position and on his achievement as a poet. Everyone seemed to be praising him, and when he went home to bed he could not sleep. On Wednesday evening he went to the theatre and it seemed to him that people all over the house recognized him. Everyone nodded and smiled. After the first act five or six men and two women left their seats to gather about him. A little group was formed. Strangers sitting along the same row of sets stretched their necks and looked. He had never received so much attention before, and now a fever of expectancy took possession of him.

As he explained when he told me of his experience, it was for him an altogether abnormal time. He felt like one floating in air. When he got into bed after seeing so many people and hearing so many words of praise his head whirled round and round. When he closed his eyes a crowd of people invaded his room. It seemed as though the minds of all the people of his city were centered on himself. The most absurd fancies took possession of him. He imagined himself riding in a carriage through the streets of a city. Windows were thrown open and people ran out at the doors of houses. "There he is! That's him!" they shouted, and at the words a glad cry arose. The carriage drove into a street blocked with people. A hundred thousand pairs of eyes looked up at him. "There you are! What a fellow you have managed to make of yourself!" the eyes seemed to be saying.

My friend could not explain whether the excitement of the people was due to the fact that he had written a new poem or whether, in his new government position he had performed some notable act. The apartment where he lived at that time was on a street perched along the top of a cliff far out at the edge of the city and from his bedroom window he could look down over trees and factory roofs to a river. As he could not sleep and as the fancies that kept crowding in upon him only made him more excited, he got out of bed and tried to think.

As would be natural under such circumstances, he tried to control his thoughts, but when he sat by the window and was wide awake a most unexpected and humiliating thing happened. The night was clear and fine. There was a moon. He wanted to dream of the woman who was to be his wife, think out lines for noble poems or make plans that would affect his career. Much to his surprise his mind refused to do anything of the sort.

At a corner of the street where he lived there was a small cigar store and newspaper stand run by a fat man of forty and his wife, a small active woman with bright grey eyes. In the morning he stopped there to buy a paper before going down to the city. Sometimes he saw only the fat man, but often the man had disappeared and the woman waited on him. She was, as he assured me at least twenty times in telling me his tale, a very ordinary person with nothing special or notable about her, but for some reason he could not explain being in her presence stirred him profoundly. During that week in the midst of his distraction she was the only person he knew who stood out clear and distinct in his mind. When he wanted so much to think noble thoughts, he could think only of her. Before he knew what was happening his imagination had taken hold of the notion of having a love affair with the woman.

"I could not understand myself," he declared, in telling me the story. "At night, when the city was quiet and when I should have been asleep, I thought about her all the time. After two or three days of that sort of thing the consciousness of her got into my daytime thoughts. I was terribly muddled. When I went to see the woman who is now my wife I found that my love for her was in no way affected by my vagrant thoughts. There was but one woman in the world I wanted to live with me and to be my comrade in undertaking to improve my own character and my position in the world, but for the moment, you see, I wanted this other woman to be in my arms. She had worked her way into my being. On all sides people were saying I was a big man who would do big things, and there I was. That evening when I went to the theatre I walked home because I knew I would be unable to sleep, and to satisfy the annoying impulse in myself I went and stood on the sidewalk before the tobacco shop. It was a two story building, and I knew the woman lived upstairs with her husband. For a long time I stood in the darkness with my body pressed against the wall of the building and then I thought of the two of them up there, no doubt in bed together. That made me furious.

"Then I grew more furious at myself. I went home and got into bed shaken with anger. There are certain books of verse and some prose writings that have always moved me deeply, and so I put several books on a table by my bed.

"The voices in the book were like the voices of the dead. I did not hear them. The words printed on the lines would not penetrate into my consciousness. I tried to think of the woman I loved, but her figure had also become something far away, something with which I for the moment seemed to have nothing to do. I rolled and tumbled about in the bed. It was a miserable experience.

"On Thursday morning I went into the store. There stood the woman alone. I think she knew how I felt. Perhaps she had been thinking of me as I had been thinking of her. A doubtful hesitating smile played about the corners of her mouth. She had on a dress made of cheap cloth, and there was a tear on the shoulder. She must have been ten years older than myself. When I tried to put my pennies on the glass counter behind which she stood my hand trembled so that the pennies made a sharp rattling noise. When I spoke the voice that came out of my throat did not sound like anything that had ever belonged to me. It barely arose above a thick whisper. "I want you," I said. "I want you very much. Can't you run away from your husband? Come to me at my apartment at seven tonight."

"The woman did come to my apartment at seven. That morning she did not say anything at all. For a moment perhaps we stood looking at each other. I had forgotten everything in the world but her. Then she nodded her head and I went away. Now that I think of it I cannot remember a word I ever heard her say. She came to my apartment at seven and it was dark. You must understand this was in the month of October. I had not lighted a light and I had sent my servant away.

"During that day I was no good at all. Several men came to see me at my office, but I got all muddled up in trying to talk with them. They attributed my rattle-headedness to my approaching marriage and went away laughing.

"It was on that morning, just the day before my marriage, that I got a long and very beautiful letter from my fianceé. During the night before she also had been unable to sleep and had got out of bed to write the letter. Everything she said in it was very sharp and real, but she herself, as a living thing, seemed to have receded into the distance. It seemed to me that she was like a bird, flying far away in distant skies, and I was like a perplexed bare-footed boy standing in the dusty road before a farm house and looking at her receding figure. I wonder if you will understand what I mean?

"In regard to the letter. In it she, the awakening woman, poured out her heart. She of course knew nothing of life, but she was a woman. She lay, I suppose, in her bed feeling nervous and wrought up as I had been doing. She realized that a great change was about to take place in her life and was glad and afraid too. There she lay thinking of it all. Then she got out of bed and began talking to me on the bit of paper. She told me how afraid she was and how glad too. Like most young women she had heard things whispered. In the letter she was very sweet and fine. 'For a long time, after we are married, we will forget that we are a man and a woman,' she wrote. 'We will be human beings. You must remember that I am ignorant and often I will be very stupid. You must love me and be very patient and kind. When I know more, when after a long time you have taught me the way of life, I will try to repay you. I will love you tenderly and passionately. The possibility of that is in me, or I would not want to marry at all. I am afraid but I am also happy. O, I am so glad our marriage time is near at hand.'

"Now that you see clearly enough into what a mess I had got. In my office, after I read my fianceé's letter, I became at once very resolute and strong. I remember that I got out of my chair and walked about, proud of the fact that I was to be the husband of so noble a woman. Right away I felt concerning her as I had been feeling about myself before I found out what a weak thing I was. To be sure I took a strong resolution that I would not be weak. At nine that evening I had planned to run in to see my fianceé. 'I'm all right now,' I said to myself. 'The beauty of her character has saved me from myself. I will go home now and send the other woman away.'" In the morning I had telephoned to my servant and told him that I did not want him to be at the apartment that evening and I now picked up the telephone to tell him to stay at home.

"Then a thought came to me. 'I will not want him there in any event,' I told myself. 'What will he think when he sees a woman coming to my place on the evening before the day I am supposed to be married?' I put the telephone down and prepared to go home. 'If I want my servant out of the apartment it is because I do not want him to hear me talk with the woman. I cannot be rude to her. I will have to make some kind of an explanation,' I said to myself.

"The woman came at seven o'clock, and, as you may have guessed, I let her in and forgot the resolution I had made. It is likely I never had any intention of doing anything else. There was a bell on my door, but she did not ring, but knocked very softly. It seems to me that everything she did that evening was soft and quiet but very determined and quick. Do I make myself clear? When she came I was standing just within the door, where I had been standing and waiting for a half hour. My hands were trembling as they had trembled in the morning when her eyes looked at me and when I tried to put the pennies on the counter in the store. When I opened the door she stepped quickly in and I took her into my arms. We stood together in the darkness. My hands no longer trembled. I felt very happy and strong.

"Although I have tried to make everything clear I have not told you what the woman I married is like. I have emphasized, you see, the other woman. I make the blind statement that I love my wife, and to a man of your shrewdness that means nothing at all. To tell the truth, had I not started to speak of this matter I would feel more comfortable. It is inevitable that I give you the impression that I am in love with the tobacconist's wife. That's not true. To be sure I was very conscious of her all during the week before my marriage, but after she had come to me at my apartment she went entirely out of my mind.

"Am I telling the truth? I am trying very hard to tell what happened to me. I am saying that I have not since that evening thought of the woman who came to my apartment. Now, to tell the facts of the case, that is not true. On that evening I went to my fiancée at nine, as she had asked me to do in her letter. In a kind of way I cannot explain the other woman went with me. This is what I mean—you see I had been thinking if anything happened between me and the tobacconist's wife I would not be able to go through with my marriage. 'It is one thing or the other with me,' I had said to myself.

"As a matter of fact I went to see my beloved on that evening filled with a new faith in the outcome of our life together. I am afraid I muddle this matter in trying to tell it. A moment ago I said the other woman, the tobacconist's wife, went with me. I do not mean she went in fact. What I am trying to say is that something of her faith in her own desires and her courage in seeing things through went with me. Is that clear to you? When I got to my fiancée's house there was a crowd of people standing about. Some were relatives from distant places I had not seen before. She looked up quickly when I came into the room. My face must have been radiant. I never saw her so moved. She thought her letter had affected me deeply, and of course it had. Up she jumped and ran to meet me. She was like a glad child. Right before the people who turned and looked inquiringly at us, she said the thing that was in her mind. 'O, I am so happy,' she cried. 'You have understood. We will be two human beings. We will not have to be husband and wife.'

"As you may suppose, everyone laughed, but I did not laugh. The tears came into my eyes. I was so happy I wanted to shout. Perhaps you understand what I mean. In the office that day when I read the letter my fianceé had written I had said to myself, 'I will take care of the dear little woman.' There was something smug, you see, about that. In her house when she cried out in that way, and when everyone laughed, what I said to myself was something like this: 'We will take care of ourselves.' I whispered something of the sort into her ears. To tell you the truth I had come down off my perch. The spirit of the other woman did that to me. Before all the people gathered about I held my fianceé close and we kissed. They thought it very sweet of us to be so affected at the sight of each other. What they would have thought had they known the truth about me God only knows!

"Twice now I have said that after that evening I never thought of the other woman at all. That is partially true, but sometimes in the evening when I am walking alone in the street or in the park as we are walking now, and when evening comes softly and quickly as it has come tonight, the feeling of her comes sharply into my body and mind. After that one meeting, I never saw her again. On the next day I was married and I have never gone back into the street. Often, however, as I am walking along as I am doing now, a quick sharp earthy feeling takes possession of me. It is as though I were a seed in the ground and the warm rains of the spring had come. It is as though I were not a man but a tree.

"And now, you see, I am married and everything is all right. My marriage is to me a very beautiful fact. If you were to say that my marriage is not a happy one I could call you a liar and be speaking the absolute truth. I have tried to tell you about this other woman. There is a kind of relief in speaking of her. I have never done it before. I wonder why I was so silly as to be afraid that I would give you the impression I am not in love with my wife. If I did not instinctively trust your understanding I would not have spoken. As the matter stands I have a little stirred myself up. To-night I shall think of the other woman. That sometimes occurs. It will happen after I have gone to bed. My wife sleeps in the next room to mine and the door is always let open. There will be a moon tonight, and when there is a moon long streaks of light fall on her bed. I shall awake at midnight tonight. She will be lying asleep with one arm thrown over her head.

"What is it that I am talking about? A man does not speak of his wife lying in bed. What I am trying to say is that, because of this talk, I shall think of the other woman tonight. My thoughts will not take the form they did the week before I was married. I will wonder what has become of the woman. For a moment I will again feel myself holding her close. I will think that for an hour I was closer to her than I have ever been to anyone else. Then I will think of the time when I will be as close as that to my wife. She is still, you see, an awakening woman. For a moment I will close my eyes and the quick, shrewd, determined eyes of that other woman will look into mine. My head will swim and then I will quickly open my eyes and see again the dear woman with whom I have undertaken to live out my life. Then I will sleep and when I awake in the morning it will be as it was that evening when I walked out of my dark apartment after having had the most notable experience of my life. What I mean to say, you understand, is that, for me, when I awake, the other woman will be utterly gone."

Although *The Other Woman* was written by Sherwood Anderson before the heyday of psychoanalysis, it is right out of Freud's notebook. It is unlikely that this tale of the '20s would be written today, when incestuous desires are understood to be ubiquitous and our sexual mores are far more permissive. Nevertheless, a story like Oedipus Rex still delves deep into the heart of the unconscious mind, and probably always will. It is about a hero who loves his intended wife profoundly, but has an obsessional need for another woman. What becomes clear is that he displaces or transfers the lust he feels for his fianceé to the "other woman" and is not aware of his fear of having sexual relations with the "beloved woman," who is surely a mother surrogate. On a conscious level it suits him fine that his future wife writes "For a long time after we are married, we will forget that we are a man and a woman...We will be human beings...I am afraid but I am also happy."

What is pathological about the hero is that he doesn't know he is conflicted about his sexual needs. In those days, a gentleman did not have such feelings for his loved one. So he splits his emotions into two parts, those he has for "a very ordinary person with nothing special or notable about her" and the "cleaned-up" feelings for the "very sweet and fine" lady he loves. He passionately desires the first woman, but feels only "pure love" for his wife. He finally possesses the object of his desire, and as the youthful Freud noted about his consummated fantasy life with his intended, the obsession then "went entirely out of his mind."

The symptom, however, returns after he is married and sees the moonlight falling on his lovely wife who is lying chastely in bed in another room. "What is it that I am talking about?" he demands of himself. "A man does not speak of his wife lying in bed....Because of this talk I shall think of the other woman tonight....I will again feel myself holding her close....My head will swim and then I will quickly open my eyes and see again the dear woman with whom I have undertaken to live out my life." He allows himself to daydream of the time when he will possess his wife, who he feels is still "an awakening woman." At that time he feels that his obsession with "the other woman" will certainly be "cured." Although one might question how satisfactory the future love life of the couple will be...

17

TEENAGE WASTELAND

ANNE TYLER

He used to have very blond hair—almost white—cut shorter than other children's so that on his crown a little cowlick always stood up to catch the light. But this was when he was small. As he grew older, his hair grew darker, and he wore it longer—past his collar even. It hung in lank, taffy-colored ropes around his face, which was still an endearing face, fine-featured, the eyes an unusual aqua blue. But his cheeks, of course, were no longer round, and a sharp new Adam's apple jogged in his throat when he talked.

In October, they called from the private school he attended to request a conference with his parents. Daisy went alone; her husband was at work. Clutching her purse, she sat on the principal's couch and learned that Donny was noisy, lazy, and disruptive; always fooling around with his friends, and he wouldn't respond in class.

In the past, before her children were born, Daisy had been a fourth-grade teacher. It shamed her now to sit before this principal as a parent, a delinquent parent, a parent who struck Mr. Lanham, no doubt, as unseeing or uncaring. "It isn't that we're not con-

---

cerned," she said. "Both of us are. And we've done what we could, whatever we could think of. We don't let him watch TV on school nights. We don't let him talk on the phone till he's finished his homework. But he tells us he doesn't *have* any homework or he did it all in study hall. How are we to know what to believe?

From early October through November, at Mr. Lanham's suggestion, Daisy checked Donny's assignments every day. She sat next to him as he worked, trying to be encouraging, sagging inwardly as she saw the poor quality of everything he did—the sloppy mistakes in math, the illogical leaps in his English themes, the history questions left blank if they required any research.

Daisy was often late starting supper, and she couldn't give as much attention to Donny's younger sister. "You'll never guess what happened at..." Amanda would begin, and Daisy would have to tell her, "Not now, honey."

By the time her husband, Matt, came home, she'd be snappish. She would recite the day's hardships—the fuzzy instructions in English, the botched history map, the morass of unsolvable algebra equations. Matt would look surprised and confused, and Daisy would gradually wind down. There was no way, really, to convey how exhausting all this was.

In December, the school called again. This time, they wanted Matt to come as well. She and Matt had to sit on Mr. Lanham's couch like two bad children and listen to the news: Donny had improved only slightly, raising a D in history to a C, and a C in algebra to a B-minus. What was worse, he had developed new problems. He had cut classes on at least three occasions. Smoked in the furnace room. Helped Sonny Barnett break into a freshman's locker. And last week, during athletics, he and three friends had been seen off the school grounds; when they returned, the coach had smelled beer on their breath.

Daisy and Matt sat silent, shocked. Matt rubbed his forehead with his fingertips. Imagine, Daisy thought, how they must look to Mr. Lanham: an overweight housewife in a cotton dress and a too-tall, too-thin insurance agent in a baggy, frayed suit. Failures, both of them—the kind of people who are always hurrying to catch up, missing the point of things that everyone else grasps at once. She wished she'd worn nylons instead of knee socks.

It was arranged that Donny would visit a psychologist for testing. Mr. Lanham knew just the person. He would set this boy straight, he said.

When they stood to leave, Daisy held her stomach in and gave Mr. Lanham a firm, responsible handshake.

Donny said the psychologist was a jackass and the tests were really dumb; but he kept all three of his appointments, and when it was time for the follow-up conference with the psychologist and both parents, Donny combed his hair and seemed unusually sober and subdued. The psychologist said Donny had no serious emotional problems. He was merely going through a difficult period in his life. He required some academic help and a better sense of self-worth. For this reason, he was suggesting a man named Calvin Beadle, a tutor with considerable psychological training.

In the car going home, Donny said he'd be damned if he'd let them drag him to some stupid fairy tutor. His father told him to watch his language in front of his mother.

That night, Daisy lay awake pondering the term "self-worth." She had always been free with her praise. She had always told Donny he had talent, was smart, was good with his hands. She had made a big to-do over every little gift he gave her. In fact, maybe she had gone too far, although, Lord knows, she had meant every word. Was that his trouble?

She remembered when Amanda was born. Donny had acted lost and bewildered. Daisy had been alert to that, of course, but still, a new baby keeps you so busy. Had she really done all she could have? She longed—she ached—for a time machine. Given one more chance, she'd do it perfectly—hug him more, praise him more, or perhaps praise him less. Oh, who can say...

The tutor told Donny to call him Cal. All his kids did, he said. Daisy thought for a second that he meant his own children, then realized her mistake. He seemed too young, anyhow, to be a family man. He wore a heavy brown handlebar mustache. His hair was as long and stringy as Donny's, and his jeans as faded. Wire-rimmed spectacles slid down his nose. He lounged in a canvas director's chair with his fingers laced across his chest, and he casually, amiably questioned Donny, who sat upright and glaring in an armchair.

"So they're getting on your back at school," said Cal. "Making a big deal about anything you do wrong."

"Right," said Donny.

"Any idea why that would be?"

"Oh, well, you know, stuff like homework and all," Donny said.

"You don't do your homework?"

"Oh, well, I might do it sometimes but not just exactly like they want it." Donny sat forward and said, "It's like a prison there, you know? You've got to go to every class, you can never step off the school grounds."

"You cut classes sometimes?"

"Sometimes," Donny said, with a glance at his parents.

Cal didn't seem perturbed. "Well," he said, "I'll tell you what. Let's you and me try working together three nights a week. Think you could handle that? We'll see if we can show that school of yours a thing or two. Give it a month; then if you don't like it, we'll stop. If I don't like it, we'll stop. I mean, sometimes people just don't get along, right? What do you say to that?"

"Okay," Donny said. He seemed pleased.

"Make it seven o'clock till eight, Monday, Wednesday, and Friday," Cal told Matt and Daisy. They nodded. Cal shambled to his feet, gave them a little salute, and showed them to the door.

This was where he lived as well as worked, evidently. The interview had taken place in the dining room, which had been transformed into a kind of office. Passing the living room, Daisy winced at the rock music she had been hearing, without registering it, ever since she had entered the house. She looked in and saw a boy about Donny's age lying on a sofa with a book. Another boy and a girl were playing Ping-Pong in front of the fireplace. "You have several here together?" Daisy asked Cal.

"Oh, sometimes they stay on after their sessions, just to rap.

They're a pretty sociable group, all in all. Plenty of goof-offs like young Donny here."

He cuffed Donny's shoulder playfully. Donny flushed and grinned.

Climbing into the car, Daisy asked Donny, "Well, what did you think?"

But Donny had returned to his old evasive self. He jerked his chin toward the garage. "Look," he said. "He's got a basketball net."

Now on Mondays, Wednesdays, and Fridays, they had supper early—the instant Matt came home. Sometimes, they had to leave before they were really finished. Amanda would still be eating her dessert. "Bye, honey. Sorry," Daisy would tell her.

Cal's first bill sent a flutter of panic through Daisy's chest, but it was worth it, of course. Just look at Donny's face when they picked him up: alight and full of interest. The principal telephoned Daisy to tell her how Donny had improved. "Of course, it hasn't shown up in his grades yet, but several of the teachers have noticed how his attitude's changed. Yes, sir. I think we're onto something here."

At home, Donny didn't act much different. He still seemed to have a low opinion of his parents. But Daisy supposed that was unavoidable—part of being fifteen. He said his parents were too "controlling"—a word that made Daisy give him a sudden look. He said they acted like wardens. On weekends, they enforced a curfew and any time he went to a party, they always telephoned first to see if adults would be supervising. "For God's sake!" he said. "Don't you trust me?"

"It isn't a matter of trust, honey..." But there was no explaining to him.

His tutor called one afternoon. "I get the sense," he said, "that this kid's feeling...underestimated, you know? Like we ought to give him more rope."

"But see, he's still so suggestible," Daisy said. "When his friends suggest some mischief—smoking or drinking or such—why, he just finds it very hard not to go along with them."

"Mrs. Coble," the tutor said, "I think this kid is hurting. You know? Here's a serious, sensitive kid, telling you he'd like to take on some grown-up challenges, and you're giving him the message that he can't be trusted. Don't you understand how that hurts?"

"Oh," said Daisy.

"It undermines his self-esteem—don't you realize that?"

"Well, I guess you're right," said Daisy. She saw Donny suddenly from a whole new angle: his pathetically poor posture, that slouch so forlorn that his shoulders seemed about to meet his chin...oh, wasn't it awful being young? She'd had a miserable adolescence herself and had always sworn no child of hers would ever be that unhappy.

They let Donny stay out later, they didn't call ahead to see if the parties were supervised, and they were careful not to grill him about his evening. The tutor had set down so many rules! They were not allowed any questions at all about any aspect of school, nor were they to speak with his teachers. If a teacher had some complaint, she should phone Cal. Only one teacher disobeyed— the history teacher, Miss Evans. She called one morning in February. "I'm a little concerned about Donny, Mrs. Coble."

"Oh, I'm sorry, Miss Evans, but Donny's tutor handles these things now..."

"I always deal directly with the parents. You are the parent," Miss Evans said, speaking very slowly and distinctly. "Now, here is the problem. Back when you were helping Donny with his homework, his grades rose from a D to a C, but now they've slipped back, and they're closer to an F."

"They are?"

"I think you should start overseeing his homework again."

"But Donny's tutor says..."

"It's nice that Donny has a tutor, but you should still be in charge of his homework. With you, he learned it. Then he passed his tests. With the tutor, well, it seems the tutor is more of a crutch. 'Donny,' I say, 'a quiz is coming up on Friday. Hadn't you better be listening instead of talking?' 'That's okay, Miss Evans,' he says. 'I have a tutor now.' Like a talisman! I really think you ought to take over, Mrs. Coble."

"I see," said Daisy. "Well, I'll think about that. Thank you for calling."

Hanging up, she felt a rush of anger at Donny. A talisman! For a talisman, she'd given up all luxuries, all that time with her daughter, her evenings at home!

She dialed Cal's number. He sounded muzzy. "I'm sorry if I woke you," she told him, "but Donny's history teacher just called.

"She wants me to start supervising his homework again. His grades are slipping."

"Yes," said the tutor, "but you and I both know there's more to it than mere grades, don't we? I care about the *whole* child—his happiness, his self-esteem. The grades will come. Just give them time.

When she hung up, it was Miss Evans she was angry at. What a narrow woman!

It was Cal this, Cal that, Cal says this, Cal and I did that. Cal lent Donny an album by the Who. He took Donny and two other pupils to a rock concert. In March, when Donny began to talk endlessly on the phone with a girl named Miriam, Cal even let Miriam come to one of the tutoring sessions. Daisy was touched that Cal would grow so involved in Donny's life, but she was also a little hurt, because she had offered to have Miriam to dinner and Donny had refused. Now he asked them to drive her to Cal's house without a qualm.

This Miriam was an unappealing girl with blurry lipstick and masses of rough red hair. She wore a short, bulky jacket that would not have been out of place on a motorcycle. During the trip to Cal's she was silent, but coming back, she was more talkative. "What a neat guy, and what a house! All those kids hanging out, like a club. And the stereo playing rock...gosh, he's not like a grown-up at all! Married and divorced and everything, but you'd think he was our own age."

"Mr. Beadle was married?" Daisy asked.

"Yeah, to this really controlling lady. She didn't understand him a bit."

"No, I guess not," Daisy said.

Spring came, and the students who hung around at Cal's drifted out to the basketball net above the garage. Sometimes, when Daisy and Matt arrived to pick up Donny, they'd find him there with the others—spiky and excited, jittering on his toes beneath the backboard. It was staying light much longer now, and the neighboring fence cast narrow bars across the bright grass. Loud music would be spilling from Cal's windows. Once it was the Who, which Daisy recognized from the time that Donny had borrowed the album. *"Teenage Wasteland,"* she said aloud, identifying the song, and Matt gave a short, dry laugh. "It certainly is," he said. He'd misunderstood; he thought she was commenting on the scene spread before them. In fact, she might have been. The players looked like hoodlums, even her son. Why, one of Cal's students had recently been knifed in a tavern. One had been shipped off to boarding school in midterm; two had been withdrawn by their parents. On the other hand, Donny had mentioned someone who'd been studying with Cal for five years. "Five years!" said Daisy. "doesn't anyone ever stop needing him?"

Donny looked at her. Lately, whatever she said about Cal was read as criticism. "You're just feeling competitive," he said. "and controlling."

She bit her lip and said no more.

In April, the principal called to tell her that Donny had been expelled. There had been a locker check, and in Donny's locker they found five cans of beer and half a pack of cigarettes. With Donny's previous record, this offense meant expulsion.

Daisy gripped the receiver tightly and said, "Well, where is he now?"

"We've sent him home," said Mr. Lanham. "He's packed up all his belongings, and he's coming home on foot."

Daisy wondered what she would say to him. She felt him looming closer and closer, bringing this brand-new situation that no one had prepared her to handle. What other place would take him? Could they enter him in a public school? What were the rules? She stood at the living room window, waiting for him to show up. Gradually, she realized that he was taking too long. She checked the clock. She stared up the street again.

When an hour had passed, she phoned the school. Mr. Lanham's secretary answered and told her in a grave, sympathetic voice that yes, Donny Coble had most definitely gone home. Daisy called her husband. He was out of the office. She went back to the window and thought awhile, and then she called Donny's tutor.

"Donny's been expelled from school," she said, "and now I don't now where he's gone. I wonder if you've heard from him?"

There was a long silence. "Donny's with me, Mrs. Coble," he finally said.

"With you? How'd he get there?"

"He hailed a cab, and I paid the driver."

"Could I speak to him, please?"

There was another silence. "Maybe it'd be better if we had a conference," Cal said.

"I don't *want* a conference. I've been standing at the window picturing him dead or something, and now you tell me you want a—"

"Donny is very, very upset. Understandably so," said Cal. "Believe me, Mrs. Coble, this isn't what it seems. Have you asked Donny's side of the story?"

"Well, of course not, how could I? He went running off to you instead."

"Because he didn't feel he'd be listened to."

"But I haven't even—"

"Why don't you come out and talk? The three of us," said Cal, "will try to get this thing in perspective."

"Well, all right," Daisy said. But she wasn't as reluctant as she sounded. Already, she felt soothed by the calm way Cal was taking this.

Cal answered the doorbell at once. He said, "Hi, there," and led her into the dining room. Donny sat slumped in a chair, chewing the knuckle of one thumb. "Hello, Donny," Daisy said. He flicked his eyes in her direction.

"Sit here, Mrs. Coble," said Cal, placing her opposite Donny.

He himself remained standing, restlessly pacing. "So," he said.

Daisy stole a look at Donny. His lips were swollen, as if he'd been crying.

"You know," Cal told Daisy, "I kind of expected something like this. That's a very punitive school you've got him in—you realize that. And any half-decent lawyer will tell you they've violated his civil rights. Locker checks! Where's their search warrant?"

"But if the rule is—" Daisy said.

"Well, anyhow, let him tell you his side."

She looked at Donny. He said, "It wasn't my fault. I promise."

"They said your locker was full of beer."

"It was a put-up job! See, there's this guy that doesn't like me. He put all these beers in my locker and started a rumor going, so Mr. Latham ordered a locker check.

"What was the boy's name?"

"Huh?"

"Mrs. Coble, take my word, the situation is not so unusual," Cal said. "You can't imagine how vindictive kids can be sometimes."

"What was the boy's *name?*" said Daisy, "so that I can ask Mr. Lanham if that's who suggested he run a locker check."

"You don't believe me," Donny said.

"And how'd this boy get your combination in the first place?"

"Frankly," said Cal, "I wouldn't be surprised to learn the school was in on it. Any kid that marches to a different drummer, why, they'd just love an excuse to get rid of him. The school is where I lay the blame."

"Doesn't *Donny* ever get blamed?"

"Now, Mrs. Coble, you heard what he—"

"Forget it," Donny told Cal. "You can see she doesn't trust me."

Daisy drew in a breath to say that of course she trusted him— a reflex. But she knew that bold-faced, wide-eyed look of Donny's. He had worn that look when he was small, denying some petty misdeed with the evidence plain as day all around him. Still, it was hard for her to accuse him outright. She temporized and said,

"The only thing I'm sure of is that they've kicked you out of school, and now I don't know what we're going to do."

"We'll fight it," said Cal.

"We can't. Even you must see we can't."

"I could apply to Brantly," Donny said.

Cal stopped his pacing to beam down at him. "Brantly! Yes. They're really onto where a kid is coming from, at Brantly.

"Why, *I* could get you into Brantly. I work with a lot of their students."

Daisy had never heard of Brantly, but already she didn't like it. and she didn't like Cal's smile, which struck her now as feverish and avid—a smile of hunger.

On the fifteenth of April, they entered Donny in a public school, and they stopped his tutoring sessions. Donny fought both decisions bitterly. Cal, surprisingly enough, did not object. He admitted he'd made no headway with Donny and said it was because Donny was emotionally disturbed.

Donny went to his new school every morning, plodding off alone with his head down. He did his assignments, and he earned average grades, but he gathered no friends, joined no clubs. There was something exhausted and defeated about him.

The first week in June, during final exams, Donny vanished. He simply didn't come home one afternoon, and no one at school remembered seeing him. The police were reassuring, and for the first few days, they worked hard. They combed Donny's sad, messy room for clues; they visited Miriam and Cal. But then they started talking about the number of kids who ran way every year. Hundreds, just in this city. "He'll show up, if he wants to," they said. "If he doesn't, he won't."

Evidently, Donny didn't want to.

It's been three months now and still no word. Matt and Daisy still look for him in every crowd of awkward, heartbreaking teen-aged boys. Every time the phone rings, they imagine it might be Donny. Both parents have aged. Donny's sister seems to be staying away from home as much as possible.

At night, Daisy lies awake and goes over Donny's life. She is trying to figure out what went wrong, where they made their first mistake. Often, she finds herself blaming Cal, although she knows he didn't begin it. Then at other times she excuses him, for without him, Donny might have left earlier. Who really knows? In the end, she can only sigh and search for a cooler spot on the pillow. As she falls asleep, she occasionally glimpses something in the corner of her vision. It's something fleet and round, a ball—a basketball. It flies up, it sinks through the hoop, descends, lands in a yard littered with last year's leaves and striped with bars of sunlight as white as bones, bleached and parched and cleanly picked.

⁂

Teenage Wasteland, by Anne Tyler, is a typical story of an emotionally disturbed youngster with parents who didn't want to see. Tyler's portrait of the boy is so psychologically profound that it is difficult to believe it isn't a true case history.

The story is told from the perspective of Donny's caring mother, who, as often happens with such children, first became aware that her son was in trouble when she and her husband were called into the principal's office to hear that Donny was "noisy, lazy, and disruptive." Of course she was very defensive, telling how concerned both parents were, how they didn't let him look at TV on school nights, etc. On the advice of the principal, she began to go over Donny's homework with him, and was shocked at his slovenly, illogical work. Although Donny made some slight improvement, she was called in again to the office, this time with Donny's father, to be told that the boy's work was still unsatisfactory. As is characteristic of such cases, he was then taken to a psychologist, who said that Donny had no serious problems, but was simply going through a difficult period in his life. The psychologist recommended a tutor with psychological training, whom the parents contacted immediately, and with whom Donny was very taken. Nevertheless, his grades did not improve. When he was expelled from school for having cigarettes and beer in his locker, he lied to his parents that another boy had put the contraband in his locker. The parents sat there shocked. Daisy had a fleeting insight that the look on Donny's face was the same as when he had deliberately lied to her, as a little boy, "with the evidence plain as day all around him." They fired the tutor and enrolled Donny in a public school. The story ended with his running away from home. The mother wondered what she could have done to save him. It is a good question. Although the parents were unaware of their son's pathology, there were many hints that more astute and involved parents would have picked up.

Why, for instance, had neither one been aware of the poor quality of Donny's homework? Why is the father barely mentioned in the story? Why didn't he attend the first principal's meeting? Why did Daisy do nothing when she knew that Donny had lied to her as a little boy? Why did she so readily believe his lies as an adolescent? Why didn't Donny confide in his parents about his difficulties in school? Why did it come as a surprise when they were called into the principal's office? Why would Donny go along with any of his friends' suggestions, no matter how unscrupulous?

Cases such as Donny's are listed in DSM 111[4] under "Conduct Disorder" (p. 45–46), which it defines as "a repetitive and persistent pattern of conduct in which either the basic rights of others or major age-appropriate societal norms or rules are violated." If Donny continues his anti-social behavior and poor functioning into adult life, he could be diagnosed as an Antisocial Personality Disorder. And yet the psychologist may have been right. According to Anna Freud, nobody, no matter how experienced or skilled, is able to predict from the behavior of an adolescent how he or she will turn out. While unlikely, it is entirely within the realm of possibility that Donny will return home, "shape up," and become a well-functioning adult.

18

THE RIGHT THING

RICHARD YATES

W hen Michael Davenport's first book of poetry was about to be published, in the spring of 1955, he labored hard over the "autobiographical statement" that would be printed beneath his picture on the back of the book jacket. He secluded himself to try and get it right, knowing he was taking too long over it but knowing too how closely he had always read such statements by other new poets, knowing how subtly and infernally important these things could be. He brought the finished copy out for his wife's approval:

"Michael Davenport was born in Morristown, New Jersey, in 1923. He served in the Army Air Force during the war, attended Harvard, lost early in the Golden Gloves, and now lives in Larchmont, New York, with his wife and their daughter."

"I don't get the part about the Golden Gloves," she said.

"Oh, honey, there's nothing to 'get.' You know I did that. I did it in Boston, the year before I met you. I've told you about it a hundred times. And I did lose early. Shit, I never even got beyond the third—"

"I don't like it."

"Look," he said, "It's *good* if you can work a light, self-depreci-ating touch into something like this. Otherwise it's—"

"But this isn't light and it isn't self-depreciating," she told him. "It's painfully self-conscious, that's all it is. It's as though you're afraid 'Harvard' may sound sort of prissy, so you want to undercut it right away with this two-fisted nonsense about prizefighting."

Michael had been hurt by her reaction. It had been growing increasingly clear to him that she was coming to think of him as a fool. In the end, though, he decided she was probably right about the jacket copy. The world, or rather whatever infinitesimal frac-tion of the American reading public might bother to pick up and glance over his book, would never know that Michael Davenport had once lost early in the Golden Gloves.

In 1968, after years of swearing that an English teacher was the last thing he would ever want to be, Michael Davenport, now with three books of poetry published, finally felt he was ready for it. He prepared a resume and had it photocopied and mailed it out to the English departments of as many American colleges and uni-versities as he could find in the public library. He didn't care what part of the United States it might take him to, and his new wife said she didn't care either. The important thing, for both of them, was to start a new life.

Very few colleges replied to Michael's application, and the only job offer that seemed decent enough to consider was from a place called Billings State University, in Kansas.

"Well, Kansas does sound a little bleak," Sarah said. "Unnec-essarily bleak, I mean. What do you think?"

But neither of them could tell. He had grown up in New Jer-sey, and she in Pennsylvania, and they were almost total strangers to the rest of the country. He waited a little while to see if some-thing better would turn up; then he accepted the Kansas job for fear it might be given to someone else if he didn't.

The place they rented in Billings, Kansas, was the first mod-ern, efficient house Michael had ever known—and Sarah said it was the first of its kind in her life, too. It was built all in one story, a "ranch house," and didn't look like much from the road. You had to go inside to find how generously long and wide and high it was, with a bright hallway connecting its several spacious rooms. Each room held a window air conditioner against the late August heat, and there were thermostats to control the brand-new furnace that promised steady protection in the winter. Everything worked.

He would walk these solid floors despising the memory of the funny little houses he had lived in earlier, chagrined that he could ever have imposed such daily discomfort on his first wife for what now seemed no reason at all. Still, only fools consumed themselves with looking back; and whenever he looked ahead, thinking of Sarah, it surprised him all over again to know that the world was ready to give him a second chance.

Sarah had been right on one important point, though: there *was* something unnecessarily bleak about Kansas. The earth was too flat, the sky was too big, and if you had to be outdoors on a clear day there was no way to escape the punishing sun until it finally, splendidly, went down. Cattle stockyards and a slaughterhouse lay a mile or two beyond the university, and when the afternoon breeze came from that direction it carried a faint, nostril-puckering stench.

The house provided an excellent place to hide from all that for the first week or two—he even managed to complete a short poem called "Kansas" that seemed good enough to keep, though he would later throw it away—but then it was time for school.

And except for a brief series of lectures at a writers conference in New Hampshire, where the very exhilaration of lecturing had apparently been enough to carry him through, he felt unequipped for this kind of work. Writing copy for a trade magazine might have been a repugnant way to make a living all those years, but nothing about it had ever frightened him; now he was clammy with fear each time he walked into a classroom. He couldn't read the faces of these young strangers, couldn't tell whether they were bored or daydreaming or paying attention, and the allotted time for each period was always much too long.

But he survived the lecture classes and the "poetry workshop" classes without incurring cause for shame, and survived the easier hours of conference with individual students as well; then, at home, he would hunch with a pencil over their lame, flimsy poems or their earnest and point-missing "papers" on poetry, and so he was able to believe he was earning his salary.

"Well, but why do you spend so much time at it?" Sarah asked him once. "I thought the whole point of a job like this was that it would give you some freedom for your own work."

"Well, it will," he told her. "Once I get the hang of this I'll be doing it with my left hand. You'll see."

There were faculty parties several times a month in Billings, and the Davenports went to most of them until Michael began to complain that they were all alike.

The walls in most faculty homes displayed giant black-and-white photographs of old movie stars—W.C. Fields, Shirley Temple, Clark Gable—because this kind of decoration was said to be "camp"; in some houses too an entire wall would be given over to the spectacle of an American flag hung upside down, as proof of bitter and wholehearted opposition to the war in Vietnam. Once, finding his way to the bathroom in such a house, Michael came upon a mock recruiting poster:

JOIN THE ARMY
VISIT EXOTIC PLACES
AND KILL PEOPLE

"And I mean what kind of horseshit is that?" he asked Sarah as they drove home that night. "Since when has it made any sense to blame the war on the soldiers?"

"Well, it's not a very good poster," she said, "but I don't think that's what it was meant to suggest. I think the idea is more that everything about war is wrong."

"Then why isn't that what it said? Christ's sake, all the kids in the Army today are there because they were drafted, or because they couldn't find work anywhere else. Soldiers are the *victims* of wars; everybody knows that." Then after a few miles of silence, he said, "I don't think I'd mind these faculty parties so much if the people weren't all so busy being 'political.' You get the feeling that if it weren't for the Antiwar movement they wouldn't have anything in their lives at all. Or maybe all I'm trying to say is that I wouldn't mind them so much if I could ever count on getting a halfway decent drink. Jesus; wine. Wine on top of wine. And all of it warm as piss."

So they found ways to avoid most of the parties, until one day when the English department chairman stopped Michael in the corridor, gave him a friendly tug of the sleeve, and made a half-joking suggestion that it might soon be time for the Davenports to have a party of their own.

"Oh," Sarah said that night. "I didn't realize these things were sort of—obligatory."

"Well, I don't think they are necessarily," he told her. "But we have been acting a little aloof, dear, and that's probably not a very good idea in a town as small as this."

She seemed to be thinking it over. "Okay," she said at last. "But if we're going to do it, let's do it right. We'll have real whiskey, with a whole lot of ice, and we'll put real bread and meat on the table instead of all this crackers-and-dip nonsense."

On the afternoon before the party there was a phone call from a young man with a shy, hesitant voice. "Mike? I don't know if you'll remember me—Terry Ryan." And the voice did sound familiar, but the name might not have helped if he hadn't followed it quickly with "I used to be a waiter at the Blue Mill restaurant, in New York."

"Hell, of course I remember you, Terry," Michael said. "I'll be damned; how are you? Where are you calling from?"

"Well, the thing is I'm in Billings for a couple of days, and I—"

"Billings, *Kansas*?"

And Terry Ryan gave a brief, self-effacing laugh that brought him instantly alive in Michael's memory. "Sure," he said. "Why not? It's sort of my alma mater, after all—or at least it would have been, if I'd ever been able to pass the foreign language requirement. All that was before I went to New York, you see."

"So what are you up to now, Terry? What're you doing?"

"Well, that's the funny part. I got drafted; then I guess the Army managed to get me trained, more or less, and now I've gotta be in San Francisco tomorrow afternoon."

"Oh, Jesus; are they sending you to Vietnam?"

"That's what I hear, yeah."

"What branch are you in?"

"Oh, the infantry, is all. Nothing fancy."

"Well, Jesus, Terry, that's—that's really bad news. That's lousy."

"But I took this little detour, you see, to see some friends of mine here in Billings; then when I heard you were teaching here I thought I'd give you a call. Thought you might come out for a beer or something."

"Good," Michael said, "but I've got a better idea. We're having a party at my house tonight, and we'd be delighted if you can come over. Bring a girl."

"Well, I can't promise the girl," he said, "but the rest of it sounds fine. What time?"

And even before they'd finished talking, Michael had begun to feel privileged and kind.

Terry Ryan had been younger, smaller, and skinnier than any of the other Blue Mill waiters, and he'd clearly been the brightest of them, too. His quick, nervous face always let you know when he had something funny to say; then he'd say it, usually while putting dinner plates on your table, and he'd get away fast every time, heading back for the kitchen or the bar, before there could be any hint of an intrusion on your privacy. And on some nights, after his working shift was over, he and Michael would drink together at the bar until closing time. Terry's ambition was to be a comic actor—he alluded modestly to having been told he had the talent for it—but his greatest fear was of ending up as what he called a theater bum.

"You're a little young to be worried about ending up as anything, aren't you, Terry?"

"Well, I see what you mean. Still, everybody's gonna end up some way, sometime, right?"

Right.

"Sarah?" Michael said, ambling over to where she stood at work with the vacuum cleaner. "Listen. We'll be having a special guest tonight."

The department chairman and his wife, John and Grace Howard, were among the first to arrive. They were both in their fifties, and often said to be a lovely couple. He was tall and straight, with a closely trimmed moustache; she had retained her dimpled, "cute" good looks of a much younger woman, though her hair was white, and she usually wore full skirts cut short enough to empha-size her attractive legs. At another recent party they had waltzed together on a cleared floor for twenty minutes, Grace lying back in John's arms to gaze up at him in girlish rapture, and most of the people watching them agreed it was the prettiest thing they'd ever seen.

"You're to be congratulated, Michael," John Howard said. "It's about time somebody served an honest drink in this town."

And that opinion was echoed by a number of other guests—people who always showed up at these parties whether they liked one another or not because there was hardly anything else to do in Billings, Kansas. Most of them were teachers but there were gradu-ate students, too, with their wives or girls—some smiling as uncer-tainly as children at a gathering of grown-ups, others leaning against the walls and observing everything with thinly veiled expressions of disdain.

When Terry Ryan came in he looked even smaller than Michael had remembered—he must have been barely tall enough to qualify for the Army—and he'd chosen not to wear his uniform. He wore jeans and a gray pullover sweater that was too big for him.

"Come on, Terry," Michael said, "we'll get you a drink and then we'll find you a place to sit down. All the introductions can wait. Far as I'm concerned you're the guest of honor tonight. Hey, listen, though: you remember Sarah?"

"I don't think so."

"No, I guess I didn't start taking her to the Mill until after you'd quit working there. Anyway we're married now, and she wants to meet you. See the one over there by the window? With the dark hair?"

"Nice," Terry said. "Very nice. You've got good taste, Mike."

"Well, what the hell: why marry some plain girl when you can get a pretty girl instead?" From the tone of his own voice Michael could tell he had begun to drink too much, too fast, but he was sober enough to know he could still repair the damage by staying away from whiskey for the next hour.

"Wait right here," he told Terry, who was perched on a tall wooden stool brought from the kitchen and nursing a bourbon and water. "I'll go get her."

"Baby?" he said to his wife. "Would you like to come and meet the soldier?"

"I'd love to."

And from the moment he left them together he knew they would get along. He went to the kitchen and drank water. Then he busied himself at the sink, washing out glasses to kill as much as possible of the time before he could go to the liquor table again. When two or three students drifted into the kitchen he conversed with them in a quiet, humorous, good-host kind of way that seemed to prove he was getting better, though his watch said there was almost half an hour to wait. He strolled back into the living room to give other people the benefit of his presence, and he almost collided with John Howard, who looked tired and ill.

"Sorry," Howard said. "Damn good party, but I'm afraid I'm not used to the hard stuff—or maybe I'm too old for it. I think we'd better be on our way."

But Grace wasn't ready to leave. "Go then, John," she said from the sofa, where she sat among her friends. "Take the car and go, if you want to. I can always get a ride." And it occurred to Michael that this was undoubtedly true: all her life, Grace Howard must have been the kind of a girl who could always get a ride.

When the whole of his hour was mercifully over, he felt righteous as he fixed himself a good one at the liquor table. And that

oddly bracing sense of righteousness persisted after he'd turned
back to mingle with his guests; it seemed to enhance the joviality
of his drawing the more sullen students away from the walls, win-
ning their smiles and even their pleasing laughter. It *was* a damn
good party, and it was getting better all the time. Looking around
the room, he could see men he thought of every day as fools, or
bores, or worse, but now he felt a comradely affection for all of
them, and for their nicely dressed women. This was the old fucked-
up English Department; he was an old fucked-up English Department man—and if they had suddenly begun to raise their voices
in the opening verse of "Auld Lang Syne" it would have brought
tears to his eyes as he sang along.

Soon he lost count of how many times he'd replenished his
glass at the liquor table, but that no longer mattered because the
evening was well past the strain of its early stages. And his greatest
pleasure was in watching Sarah move gracefully from group to
group, the perfect young hostess. Nobody could have guessed how
reluctantly she had organized this thing.

Then he turned and saw Terry Ryan on the tall wooden stool
with no one to talk to. It was possible that Sarah had taken him
around to meet other guests and that he'd come back after running out of polite things to say, but it was possible too that he'd sat
here all this time, allowing his last night of freedom in the United
States to evaporate before his eyes.

"Can I get you something, Terry?"

"No thanks, Mike; I'm fine."

"You met any of these people?"

"Oh, sure; met quite a few."

"Well," Michael said. "I think we can do better than that." And
he stepped around to stand behind him, firmly clasping one thin
shoulder beneath the fabric of his sweater.

"This young man," he announced in a voice loud enough to
leave no doubt of his intention to address the party as a whole, and
most other talkers in the room fell silent. "This young man may
look like a student, and that's what he was at one time, but not

anymore. He's an infantry soldier on his way to Vietnam, where I imagine his personal problems will soon be a great deal worse than any of our own. So suppose we all forget about college for a minute, please, and let's have a hand for Terry Ryan."

There was some clapping, though nowhere near as much as he'd hoped for, and even before it was over Terry said, "Kind of wish you hadn't done that, Mike."

"Why?"

"I don't know; just because."

Then from across the room Michael saw Sarah looking at him in disappointment or disapproval.

"Well. Jesus, Terry, I didn't mean to embarrass you," he said. "I thought they ought to know who you are, that's all."

"Oh, I know; it's okay; forget it."

But it was a thing that wouldn't be forgotten.

Grace Howard was on her feet and making her way through the smoke, bearing down on Terry Ryan with one stiff index finger aimed at his chest.

"May I ask you something?" she inquired. "Why do you want to kill people?"

And he smiled bashfully. "Oh, come on, lady," he said. "I never killed anybody in my life."

"Well, but you'll have your chance now, won't you? With your automatic rifle and your hand grenades?"

"Hold it, Grace," Michael said, "you're way out of line here; this boy was drafted."

"And maybe they'll give you a little radio, too," she went on, "so you can call in the artillery and the bombs and the napalm on women and children. Well, listen—"

"Oh, *stop* this," Sarah called, hurrying to Terry's side as if to protect him.

"—Listen," Grace Howard said. "You're not fooling anybody for a minute. *I* know why you want to kill people. You want to kill people because you're so *small*."

Some of Grace's friends managed to take charge of her then:

they turned her around and walked her back across the room and out the front door, which closed with a little slam.

"Terry, I'm sorry as hell about that," Michael told him. "I knew she was drunk, but I didn't know she was crazy."

"Look, the hell with it, okay?" he said. "Fuck it. The more we talk about it, the worse it's going to get."

"Exactly," Sarah said quietly.

Later, when everyone else had gone at last, Sarah made up the bed in the spare room so that Terry could spend the night there. But there wasn't much left of the night: they had to get up early to drive Terry to his friends' place. There he changed into his Army uniform, which Sarah said was "very becoming," and picked up his duffel bag, and they drove him twenty miles to the airport. There was some mild and pleasant talk in the car—all three of them had reached the stage of easy good humor that sometimes follows a night of too little sleep—but none of them mentioned Grace Howard.

When it was time to say goodbye at the gate to Terry's flight, Michael shook hands with him in a little excess of old soldier's heartiness: "Well, stay loose, Terry. And keep a tight asshole."

Then Sarah opened her arms for him. She was taller than he was, but that didn't make it an awkward embrace. She held him, however briefly, in the way a man ought to be held before going to a war that nobody would ever understand.

They rode in silence for much of the drive home, until Michael said, "Well, hell, the whole damn thing was my fault; I know that. I never should've made that dumb little speech." Then he said, "But the point is, baby, when I was in the Army you wanted people to pay attention the night before you went overseas. It was nice to have civilians make a fuss over you—and they did, if you were lucky."

"Well, I know," Sarah said, "but that was another time. That was before I was born. Before Terry was born, too."

And when he glanced away from the road again he found she was quietly crying.

She went to sleep as soon as they were back at the house; that gave him a chance to drink two cold beers in the kitchen and try to get his brains together.

Then the phone rang. "Michael? John Howard here. Listen: Who was that kid you had in your house last night?"

"Friend of mine from New York, is all; he was just passing through. Why?"

"Well. I understand he was very rude and offensive to Grace after I left."

"Oh?" And Michael instantly knew there would be no point in trying to clear up this messy business. Terry Ryan was a thousand miles away in the sky now, rid of Billings, Kansas, forever; nobody's brave words could defend him any longer. "Well, I'm sorry there was any unpleasantness, John," he said with what he hoped was an edge of scorn, and he hung up the receiver before Howard could say anything more.

If Howard called back at once to persist in his false grievance there would be nothing to do but tell him the truth about what Grace had done; if not, not. And the phone didn't ring a second time.

Sarah was still asleep, which was probably all to the good; that way, there might be no need to talk it over, ever again. Still, he wished she were awake, so she could assure him he'd done the right thing.

The Right Thing, by Richard Yates, is an understated tragedy about Michael Davenport, a man with a conflict between his instincts and society. He just didn't see eye to eyes with other people, including his two wives. Yet he desperately wanted to do "the right thing," and be accepted by others. But because he had little idea of what the "right thing" was and a poor social sense, especially when he was drinking, he rarely knew what he had done wrong.

As an example of his poor judgement, Michael announced at a party that one of the guests, his former student Terry Ryan, was a soldier on his way to Vietnam. Many people felt and feel about the Vietnam war as Michael did, but few would say such a thing at a party of fellow faculty members who were vociferously against the struggle. After making the announcement, he felt righteous and good about himself, and ostensibly was the only person at the party who was surprised when his declaration didn't go over big with anyone else.

Michael was older than his wife and Terry, and at the time of the story was in the Midwest, which certainly exacerbated the fiasco. Yet he hadn't managed to agree with his first wife either, who was closer to his age, and like him, from the northeast. Such conflicts in values are operative from childhood on, when Michael's thinking almost certainly was different from that of his family. One of my patients with a similar type of personality was "jokingly" told by his parents that he had been left on the doorstep by gypsies.

Despite his Harvard education and the publication of his poetry book, Michael was an insecure man, who needed the approval of others to feel right about himself. He was "clammy with fear" every time he walked into a classroom to teach. He did not have any insight into his behavior nor grow during the time span of the story. It is unlikely that he ever will. At the end of the party, even though it is evident that his present wife is finished with him, he longs for her to tell him "he'd done the right thing."

As well as being a study of one man's character, the story is an indictment against the egocentricity of society, as well as the narrowness of university faculties, who often are unable to accept people different from themselves. But since this is the way most people are at this point in time, the misfortune of Michael Davenport is that he was a fish out of water with everyone he knew. What seemed perfectly "right" to him was not "all right" with them. Perhaps later in his life, he would be fortunate enough to find a wife and friends who shared his thinking and beliefs, or who would be big enough to allow Michael his own feelings and like him anyway.

19

MY APOLOGY

WOODY ALLEN

O f all the famous men who ever lived, the one I would most like to have been was Socrates. Not just because he was a great thinker, because I have been known to have some reasonably profound insights myself, although mine invariably revolve around a Swedish airline stewardess and some handcuffs. No, the great appeal for me of this wisest of all Greeks was his courage in the face of death. His decision was not to abandon his principles, but rather to give his life to prove a point. I personally am not quite as fearless about dying and will, after any untoward noise such as a car backfiring, leap directly into the arms of the person I am conversing with. In the end, Socrates' brave death gave his life authentic meaning; something my existence lacks totally, although it does possess a minimal relevance to the Internal Revenue Department. I must confess I have tried putting myself in this great philosopher's sandals many times and no matter how often I do, I immediately wind up dozing off and having the following dream:

(The scene is my prison cell. I am usually sitting alone, working out some deep problem of rational thought like: Can an object be called a work of art if it can also be used to clean the stove? Presently I am visited by Agathon and Simmias.)

AGATHON: Ah, my good friend and wise old sage. How go your days of confinement?

ALLEN: What can one say of confinement, Agathon? Only the body may be circumscribed. My mind roams freely, unfettered by the four walls and therefore in truth I ask, does confinement exist?

AGATHON: Well, what if you want to take a walk?

ALLEN: Good question. I can't.

(*The three of us sit in classical poses, not unlike a frieze. Finally Agathon speaks.*)

AGATHON: I'm afraid the word is bad. You have been condemned to death.

ALLEN: Ah, it saddens me that I should cause debate in the senate.

AGATHON: No debate. Unanimous.

ALLEN: Really?

AGATHON: First ballot.

ALLEN: Hmmm. I had counted on a little more support.

SIMMIAS: The senate is furious over your ideas for a Utopian state.

ALLEN: I guess I should never have suggested having a philosopher-king.

SIMMIAS: Especially when you kept pointing to yourself and clearing your throat.

ALLEN: And yet I do not regard my executioners as evil.

AGATHON: Nor do I.

ALLEN: Er, yeah, well...for what is evil but merely good in excess?

AGATHON: How so?

ALLEN: Look at it this way. If a man sings a lovely song it is beautiful. If he keeps singing, one begins to get a headache.

AGATHON: True.

ALLEN: And if he definitely won't stop singing, eventually you want to stuff socks down his throat.

AGATHON: Yes. Very true.

ALLEN: When is the sentence to be carried out?

AGATHON: What time is it now?

ALLEN: Today!?

AGATHON: They need the jail cell.

ALLEN: Then let it be! Let them take my life. Let it be recorded that I died rather than abandon the principles of truth and free inquiry. Weep not, Agathon.

AGATHON: I'm not weeping. This is an allergy.

ALLEN: For to the man of the mind, death is not an end but a beginning.

SIMMIAS: How so?

ALLEN: Well, now give me a minute.

SIMMIAS: Take your time.

ALLEN: It is true, Simmias, that man does not exist before he is born, is it not?

SIMMIAS: Very true.

ALLEN: Nor does he exist after his death.

SIMMIAS: Yes, I agree.

ALLEN: Hmmm.

SIMMIAS: So?

ALLEN: Now, wait a minute. I'm a little confused. You know they only feed me lamb and it's never well-cooked.

SIMMIAS: Most men regard death as the final end. Consequently they fear it.

ALLEN: Death is a state of non-being. That which is not, does not exist. Therefore death does not exist. Only truth exists. Truth and beauty. Each is interchangeable, but are aspects of themselves. Er, what specifically did they say they had in mind for me?

AGATHON: Hemlock.

ALLEN: (puzzled) Hemlock?

AGATHON: You remember that black liquid that ate through your marble table?

ALLEN: Really?

AGATHON: Just one cupful. Though they do have a back-up chalice should you spill anything.

ALLEN: I wonder if it's painful?

AGATHON: They asked if you would try not to make a scene. It disturbs the other prisoners.

ALLEN: Hmmm...

AGATHON: I told everyone you would die bravely rather than renounce your principles.

ALLEN: Right, right...er, did the concept of "exile" ever come up?

AGATHON: They stopped exiling last year. Too much red tape.

ALLEN: Right...yeah...(*Troubled and distracted but trying to remain self-possessed*) I er...so er...so—what else is new?

AGATHON: Oh, I ran into Isosceles. He has a great idea for a new triangle.

ALLEN: Right...right...(*Suddenly dropping all pretense of courage*) Look, I'm going to level with you—I don't want to go! I'm too young!

AGATHON: But this is your chance to die for truth!

ALLEN: Don't misunderstand me. I'm all for truth. On the other hand I have a lunch date in Sparta next week and I'd hate to miss it. It's my turn to buy. You know these Spartans, they fight so easily.

SIMMIAS: Is our wisest philosopher a coward?

ALLEN: I'm not a coward, and I'm not a hero. I'm somewhere in the middle.

SIMMIAS: A cringing vermin.

ALLEN: That's approximately the spot.

AGATHON: But it was you who proved that death doesn't exist.

ALLEN: Hey, listen—I've proved a lot of things. That's how I pay my rent. Theories and little observations. A puckish remark now and then. Occasional maxims. It beats picking olives, but let's not get carried away.

AGATHON: But you have proved many times that the soul is immortal.

ALLEN: And it is! On paper. See, that's the thing about philosophy—it's not all that functional once you get out of class.

SIMMIAS: And the external "forms"? You said each thing always did exist and always will exist.

ALLEN: I was talking mostly about heavy objects. A statue or something. With people it's a lot different.

AGATHON: But all that talk about death being the same as sleep.

ALLEN: Yes, but the difference is that when you're dead and somebody yells, "Everybody up, it's morning," it's very hard to find your slippers.

(*The executioner arrives with a cup of hemlock. He bears a close facial resemblance to the Irish comedian Spike Milligan.*)

EXECUTIONER: Ah—here we are. Who gets the poison?

AGATHON: (*Pointing to me*) He does.

ALLEN: Gee, it's a big cup. Should it be smoking like that?

EXECUTIONER: Yes. And drink it all because a lot of times, the poison's at the bottom.

ALLEN: (*Usually here my behavior is totally different from Socrates' and I am told I scream in my sleep.*) No—I won't! I don't want to die! Help! No! Please!

(*He hands me the bubbling brew amidst my disgusting pleading and all seems lost. Then because of some innate survival instinct the dream always takes an upturn and a messenger arrives.*)

MESSENGER: Hold everything! The senate has revoted! The charges are dropped. Your value has been reassessed and it is decided you should be honored instead.

ALLEN: At last! At last! They came to their senses! I'm a free man! Free! And to be honored yet! Quick, Agathon and Simmias, get my bags. I must be going. Praxiteles will want to get an early start on my bust. But before I leave, I give a little parable.

SIMMIAS: Gee, that was really a sharp reversal. I wonder if they know what they're doing?

ALLEN: A group of men live in a dark cave. They are unaware that outside the sun shines. The only light they know is the flickering flame of a few small candles which they use to move around.

AGATHON: Where'd they get the candles?

ALLEN: Well, let's just say they have them.

AGATHON: They live in a cave and have candles? It doesn't ring true.

ALLEN: Can't you just buy it for now?

AGATHON: O.K., O.K., but get to the point.

ALLEN: And then one day, one of the cave dwellers wanders out of the cave and sees the outside world.

SIMMIAS: In all its clarity.

ALLEN: Precisely. In all its clarity.

AGATHON: When he tries to tell the others they don't believe him.

ALLEN: Well, no. He doesn't tell the others.

AGATHON: He doesn't?

ALLEN: No, he opens a meat market, he marries a dancer and dies of a cerebral hemorrhage at forty-two.

(They grab me and force the hemlock down. Here I usually wake up in a sweat and only some eggs and smoked salmon calm me down.)

❧

Who would ever have thought of Woody Allen as a great philosopher? I have spent years looking for insights about death, reading great tomes on the subject by philosophers, like Kirkegard and Ernest Becker, theologists like the great archbishop of Chicago, Cardinal Joseph Bernadin, and psychologists, such as Freud and Jung, but I don't know any more about death now than when I started the research.

When I heard that Montiverdi's opera, *The Coronation of Poppea*, contained the death scene of the philosopher Seneca, I eagerly looked forward to seeing it, anticipating that at last I would hear some great thinking on the subject. But I'm afraid Seneca was not much wiser than the rest of us, when it comes to leaving this vale of tears.

Seneca: (*to messenger who brings the news that Emperor Nero, Seneca's former pupil, has ordered him to kill himself for conspiring to have Poppea murdered*) "If you bring me death you need not ask for forgiveness. I laugh when you bring me such a fine present. Friend, the hour has come when I am to practice the virtue I praise. Death is a brief agony, a wandering sigh that leaves the heart where for many years it has stayed as a guest. Like a wanderer it flees to Olympus, the true dwelling of happiness."

No, Seneca is no help. So who ever would have thought I would find the truth in Woody Allen's short story, *My Apology*?

Allen dreams he is in Socrates' sandals. He is told by Agathon that he has been sentenced to death.

Allen: "Then let it be! Let them take my life. Let it be recorded that I died rather than abandon the principles of truth and free inquiry....Er, what specifically did they say they had in mind for me?

Agathon: "Hemlock."

Allen: "I wonder if it's painful."

Agathon: "I told everyone you would die bravely rather than renounce your principles...!"

Allen: "Right....right....Look, I'm going to level with you—I don't want to go! I'm too young!"

Agathon: "But this is your chance to die for truth!"

Allen: "No—I won't! I don't want to die! Help! No! Please!"

Then, as if Allen can bear it no more, the plot changes and the dream takes an upward turn. A messenger arrives and says that the senate has dropped the charges and has decided to honor Allen instead of killing him.

Ah, Woody, you alone know the truth about death. Death is not noble, it is not a fine present, it is not the "true dwelling of happiness." It is an unbearable horror, and only you have the courage to say so.

NOTES

1. See Bond, Alma H., "The Masochist is the Leader," *The American Academy of Psychoanalysis,* vol. 9, no. 3 (1981): 375–389.

2. Paul's diagnosis, as listed in DSM111, is "Schizoid Disorder of Childhood or Adolescence (p. 60)."

3. Deutsch, Helene: "Some forms of emotional disturbances and their relationship to schizophrenia." *Psychoanalytic Quarterly,* vol. 9, 1942.

4. Diagnostic and Statistical Manuel of Mental Disorders (3rd Edition), American Psychiatric Association, Washington, D.C., 1980.